The Power of Grace

By Sharon Turner

Copyright © August 18, 2016
Sharon Turner
All Rights Reserved

No part of the publication may be reproduced,
stored in a retrieval system,
or transmitted in any form, or by any means,
without the prior, written
permission of the publisher.

ISBN-13: 978-1537174440
ISBN-10: 1537174444

DEDICATION

This book is dedicated
to all the wonderful people,
living, or dead, who have resided
in Calhoun County,
West Virginia, and my Emmaus Family
who are shining examples of the love and
service of the Body of Christ.
They are some of the finest people
you will ever find on this earth.
This book has been an attempt
to convey what life is like when living
in a Christian community where God's
Grace is extended to all, as a matter
of daily practice.

Psalm: 121
King James Version (KJV)

¹ I will lift up mine eyes unto the hills, from whence cometh my help.

² My help cometh from the LORD, which made heaven and earth.

³ He will not suffer thy foot to be moved: he that keepeth thee will not slumber.

⁴ Behold, he that keepeth Israel shall neither slumber nor sleep.

⁵ The LORD is thy keeper: the LORD is thy shade upon thy right hand.

⁶ The sun shall not smite thee by day, nor the moon by night.

⁷ The LORD shall preserve thee from all evil: he shall preserve thy soul.

⁸ The LORD shall preserve thy going out and thy coming in from this time forth, and even for evermore.

(The scripture was chosen by my 91 year old Mother. Thank you, Mom)

Table of Contents

Chapter One 1
Chapter Two 11
Chapter Three 26
Chapter Four 29
Chapter Five 35
Chapter Six 37
Chapter Seven 44
Chapter Eight 53
Chapter Nine 58
Chapter Ten 63
Chapter Eleven 79
Chapter Twelve 89
Chapter Thirteen 99
Chapter Fourteen 106
Chapter Fifteen 116
Chapter Sixteen 118
Chapter Seventeen 135
Chapter Eighteen 153
Chapter Nineteen 161
Chapter Twenty 168
Chapter Twenty-One 181
Chapter Twenty-Two 190
Chapter Twenty-Three 193
Chapter Twenty-Four 202

Chapter Twenty-Five 217

Chapter Twenty-Six 223

Chapter Twenty-Seven 231

Chapter Twenty-Eight 237

Chapter Twenty-Nine 244

Chapter Thirty 257

Chapter Thirty-One 264

Chapter Thirty-Two 271

Chapter Thirty-Three 286

Chapter Thirty-Four 302

Chapter Thirty-Five 310

Chapter Thirty-Six 313

Chapter Thirty-Seven 315

Chapter Thirty-Eight 320

Chapter Thirty-Nine 323

Chapter Forty 328

Chapter Forty-One 332

Chapter One

December 25, 1862

It was Christmas night, 1862, and the rich memories of the day filled the hearts and minds of all within that beloved little cabin. Little Ben and Granny had long been asleep, cuddled together in Granny's room, while Ben, Sarah and Kevin sat talking at the table.

Grace listened to her family's low voices and occasional laughter as she lay watching the candle glow and flicker on the ceiling above her bed. *Her bed*. The words warmed her heart. One year ago today, she would never have believed she would have her own room, in her own home, with her own parents, friends, and neighbors.

As she held the doll her new mother had given her for Christmas, her mind wandered back in time to her birth mother. She remembered clearly seeing her mother kneeling in front of her, gripping both of her arms, and saying, "I am so sorry I have to leave you here. But you are going to be fine. You are a strong girl. Now take care of your brother. I am counting on you."

Each phrase, each sentence, held its own significance to her at different times in her life. In the days that followed her mother's departure she kept hearing over and over that her mother was sorry she had to leave them there. So why did she not come back for them? She had spent days silently pleading with her mother to come back, and hoped against hope that she would. But as the months passed, those feelings calloused over and her mother's reminder that she was a strong girl got her through the horrible nights when Mr. Dunge, the man who ran the orphanage came to her bed. She relied on her mother's words about how strong she was, and gritted her teeth as she arose from her bed every morning, and faced the day burdened with the emotions of an abused child.

Occasionally in that first year, her mind would wander to her mother's announcement that she was now responsible for her brother, and that her mother was counting on her. At the time, it seemed such a reasonable request. All she had to do was remind him not to take the Lord's name in vain, and possibly attend to him if he had a cold or was injured.

But now that she was older, she realized just how unreasonable it was to place that burden on a child of ten. The anger and resentment growing in her heart was alarming and caught her by surprise. It was an unfair weight to place on the shoulders of a child, and that child, buried inside the young lady lying there, finally gave into tears.

"I am counting on you." Those were the words that both encouraged her, and trapped her into not giving up when she and her little brother, Benji, were homeless and she was stealing food to keep them alive. She had never wanted that much responsibility, nor did she want the responsibility of the baby she had just months after escaping the orphanage. But this was her duty. The role she had to play in what was left of her family. Or perhaps the last ditch effort to keep up the pretense that she even had a family at all.

Her thoughts wandered to the day she met Ben and Sarah, and she smiled as she remembered the way this new little make-shift family had come together, and how hard she had worked at not accepting her new parent's authority. But the results were above and beyond anything she could have dreamed on her own. Not only in the view of the community they had found themselves living in, but in their hearts as well, they had become a family in the truest sense. Regardless of their secret pasts, they had found a way to work together to heal and learn to trust again.

For a brief moment, she felt guilty as if she had betrayed the woman who had given birth to them, and began speaking to her mother as she never had. *I love you, Mama, but I love them, too. I did everything you asked of me, and now I want to move on with my life. I hope you understand and better than that, I hope it is what you wanted for us.*

A calm came over her and she was surrounded with complete peace. She became aware that this was a moment in her life, a plain where she had landed after a long tiresome climb. She felt she had just walked through a long passage, stepped through a doorway into a different world, and was breathless from the view. All anxiety was gone. All her fears had been lain to rest. She had the sensation that today was the beginning of her new life: the one she was born to live.

The gratitude in her heart spilled over into prayer. *I thank you my Father, my God, and my King.* As her mind sailed from one happy moment to the next, her gratitude sailed with it and grew into an awareness of just how blessed she was.

She took a deep breath and her face broke into a broad smile as she thought about the walk she had taken with her Papa right before dinner. It was beginning to get dark when he had asked her if she would like to take a walk with him. The glint in his eyes when he looked at her Mama told her something was up as she took her coat off the hook and followed him out into the snow.

"Do you remember," he asked, "last Christmas when we had only known each other for twenty-four hours, and we found the cabin we live in now, just as it started snowing?"

"Yes, but it certainly wasn't a house then! I thought it was the poorest excuse for a building I had ever seen." They both walked along in the snow, remembering how happy they were to find that old shed with the jar of dried beans in it.

"It was definitely better than the cave the five of us slept in the night before!" Ben said as Grace nodded her head in agreement.

Suddenly, Grace was flooded with embarrassment as she remembered the hard time she had given Ben and Sarah that first day in the cabin, and as she felt her face fill with color, she stopped walking and said, "Papa, have I ever told you how sorry I am for being so difficult that first few months?"

Ben stopped in the snow and said, "Come on now. I do not remember those things. In fact, I have *completely* forgotten about your running away and taking the bean pot with you!"

Both enjoyed a hearty laugh and just as it was subsiding, Ben added, "What were you thinking?" And the two of them laughed so hard they had to wipe away the tears.

Finally, Ben looked back at the house and smiled. "Grace," Ben began as she turned to face him, "one of the most heartbreaking things I ever heard was said by you, on that first day we were here in this cabin. We were all sitting around the fire telling each other what our perfect Christmas would be like. Do you remember? It was Christmas day."

"Oh, I do remember!" she said. "None of us had ever had much of a life before, and few special Christmases. None of us felt like we even deserved a wish, but we all had daydreams about what we would have loved to have had in our lives. And today, one year later, I have every single thing I ever hoped for, and more."

"Well, not everything, yet." Ben told her to close her eyes, then turned her toward the cabin. As she slowly opened her eyes, she saw the tiny little house with the most beautiful Christmas tree in the entire world, lit by candles that sparkled in the window. It had just become dark and the lights twinkled like brilliant stars. The pine wreath on the door, with the deep red ribbon, and the crisp white snow surrounding their little home was the most beautiful sight she had ever seen.

Ben said, "Do you remember what you said that first Christmas day?"

Grace clearly remembered the envy she had felt when she had spoken of the girls who had dolls and rooms of their own. And… she gasped… her desire to walk by a house, see a Christmas tree in the window, and know she was welcome there.

"Oh, Papa," she said as she turned and ran into his arms. "How did you remember that? How did you…?" Her voice trailed off as she was overwhelmed by the love she felt for her Papa. She dissolved in tears, and Ben handed her his handkerchief. When she managed control over her crying, she said, "I am speechless that you would not only remember that, but also love me enough to see to it that I got every single thing I mentioned so long ago." She looked up at Ben and searched his eyes, "How did you remember that? Even I had forgotten it."

Ben was clearly overcome with emotions, and paused before saying, "Because it broke my heart. And you do not soon forget something like that." He tipped his head back and looked up at the stars to compose himself, then continued, "At the time, we were all running from something. I had no idea what the next day would bring. But I did know that if I ever got a chance to give you children a better life, I would do it. I guess I loved you even then and just didn't know it yet," he said with a laugh.

"No, Papa," Grace said, "I believe it was God tugging at your heart. He had a plan for all of us misfits, and He was calling you to be my Papa, to love me, and protect me. **God** was preparing you to listen to my heart and make all my dreams come true." She looked down at her gloved hands and said, "I wish I had something to give you in return for all you have done for us; for Rebecca, Little Ben, and me. But I know of no way to ever repay you for your patience with me. And for the security you have given me."

Ben's emotions were about to get the better of him, so he looked at the absolute darkness surrounding them now, and said, "Well, I think we had better head back to the house. It is getting bitter cold out here."

Grace knew him well enough to know he was touched by her words, but not yet ready to speak, so she waited patiently as they walked home, their boots making crunching sounds as they broke through the frozen snow.

When they got to the door, Ben stopped and said, "Someday when you are married to a good, good, man," he said and then paused and thought how to word what he wanted to say. Although she had no interest in being Rebecca's mother now, some day, as a grown woman she might enjoy having children with someone she loved and trusted.

But how to word that without shaming her for her feelings about the baby she had had when she was yet a child? "Well, I just wanted to say that then, you might choose to have children together. Only then will you know what you have already given me, Grace. Only then will you know what a joy you make every single day of my life."

He looked like he was about to say more, but the door flew open and Granny yanked at their jackets to pull them back into the house. "What are you two trying to do? Freeze to death? Now get those coats off and come sit by the fire. I am makin' you hot chocolate!" The dish rag she had used to swat them with in the pretext of ridding them of snow, now was balled up in her fist as she hurried to the stove, while mumbling about youngin's today not knowing enough to come in out of the cold.

As Grace lay in her warm, toasty, bed, the memory of that moment with her Papa again warmed her spirit, and she knew she would remember that walk as long as she lived.

December 26, 1862

The minute Ben awakened, he sat straight up in bed, awaking Sarah in the process. "It is Grace's birthday," he said, knowing he need say no more. Last year the day came and went without either of them remembering it and the regret they had carried all year was about to be atoned for. They immediately threw the covers back and began the morning of celebration of their daughter's birthday.

Under Granny's watchful eye, Sarah had made her first ever cinnamon rolls, complete with the Granny's special icing to pour thickly over them. With Ben's help, Little Ben had made a miniature cradle for Grace's new doll, and Sarah had made a lovely dress for the doll out of an old lace handkerchief. Granny had made a tiny little quilt out of the same materials she had used to make the large one she had given the family for Christmas. The gifts were hidden carefully in Granny's room until it was time for the surprise.

Little Ben awakened next and came rushing down the ladder from the loft, completely skipping the last few rungs and jumping to the floor. The loud boom shook the entire cabin and awakened Baby Rebecca. Sarah pulled the hot cinnamon rolls from the oven, and rolled her eyes at Ben as she sat them on the table. "Just for that, young man," she said sternly, "you will be icing the cinnamon rolls!"

She smiled as Ben began jumping up and down, because she knew he loved to ice the cinnamon rolls. Somehow he always managed to wind up with more icing on his shoes, shirt, and fingers than he did on the cinnamon rolls, but he loved watching the spoon full of icing drip and roll across the hot buns. "That one is MINE!" he stated. He need not point. Sarah only had to look for the one buried in icing to know which one he meant.

"You are going to need a bowl for that one!" she added with a smile.

"Granny, can I lick the bowl?" Ben asked.

"May I lick the bowl," Sarah corrected over her shoulder as she hurried toward the table.

Little Ben's shoulder's slumped as he turned to Granny and said, "May I lick the bowl, Granny?"

Granny looked at him and said, "Yes, you may, young Benjamin. But this time use a spoon and don't stick your head down in the bowl. It took us a month of Sunday's to get that sticky icing out of your hair!"

"Oooooh! Cinnamon rolls!" Grace said as she walked out of her room. She ran her finger through the icing, licked her finger and asked, "Where are the men?"

"Oh, they had an errand to run, but they will be back soon," Sarah said as casually as she could manage. But her eyes went nervously to the door, hoping they would return before the surprise was spoiled.

"Grace, would you please wash your hands and tend to the baby for me?" Sarah asked. She was quite proud of how well her stalling tactic worked as Grace went over to the sink and washed her hands in the hot soapy water.

Suddenly, the door opened with a bang and in with the wind and snow came two completely snow covered men. They looked like identical snow men standing in the door.

"Whew!" Ben said as he knocked the snow off his hat and on to the floor! "It is a blizzard out there!"

Kevin was unwrapping the large scarf tied around his neck when Granny tore into them like an old Banty rooster! Smacking them with the broom she shouted, "Git back out there and knock that snow off on something besides my clean floor!"

"But Mama!" Kevin protested, "you can't dry yourself underwater! The snow will cover us up again as soon as we step outside!"

"Well, you can take this broom and knock off what is caked on the both of you! Here! Take this and don't come back in here until you get rid of them snowballs!"

The door slammed with a thunk, and Ben and Kevin looked at each other in puzzlement. "How can that tiny little sprite of a thing toss two grown men out of their own house?" Ben asked.

Kevin only smiled and said, "I have no idea. But I do know that even though she is five feet nothing, I have no intentions of going back in there until I am completely cleared of the snow." He lifted the broom and swept the snow off his feet, then handed it to Ben and said, "Will you please do the honors?"

Ben took the broom and began sweeping the snow off Kevin's shoulders, coat, and pants, and then it was Kevin's turn. "I must admit, Benjamin, there was more snow on us than I first thought." They looked down at their feet and saw almost a foot of 'snowballs' as Granny called them, piled up around their boots. With a stomping and brisk rubbing of their arms, the two men cautiously opened the door.

At that, Sarah lit the small candle on the table and shouted, "Happy birthday, Grace!

The look on Grace's face as she sat holding the baby, looking at each and every one of her family members as they clapped and shouted happy birthday, was priceless.

Tears flowed down her cheeks as she stood and walked into her Mama's arms. Granny motioned for Little Ben to run into her room and retrieve the small cradle, new doll dress, and tiny quilt.

Just as he placed them on the table, Grace stepped back, and saw the beautiful gifts. "No! No! I was blessed with gifts yesterday! This is too much!" As she approached the small cradle, she ran her fingers over the quilt, and noticed it was an exact replica of the one Granny had given the entire family.

"This is the most beautiful thing I have ever seen," she said. "I have never in my life had a birthday like this. Thank you, Mama," she said as she hugged her Mama. Next was Granny, who stood teary eyed as Grace bent down to hug her. "Thank you, Granny. You made the quilt didn't you?" Granny wiped her nose and nodded her head quickly before shushing Grace away.

Little Ben said, "I made the cradle! Well, me and Papa made it." Sarah opened her mouth to correct him, but before she had drawn a full breath, Little Ben said, "I know, Papa and I."

Sarah smiled when she looked at his little freckled face.

Sarah picked up the little dress made from a lace trimmed hanky, and said, "Mama, did you make this?" Sarah smiled and nodded. "This is just beautiful, Mama. I will cherish all of these as long as I live."

Ben and Kevin had finally shucked off all their outer clothes and had not only hung them up, they had swept the extra snow out onto the front porch, which pleased Granny immensely.

Kevin licked his lips and said, "If we are going to eat those cinnamon rolls while they are hot, we had better get on it! We are burnin' daylight!" They chuckled at the saying Kevin had picked up from one of the neighbors, as they noisily brought the chairs up to the table and sat down together.

As they all held hands, Sarah looked at Kevin and said, "Kevin, would you bring the blessing?"

"Certainly," Kevin replied. As a hush fell over the room, Kevin prayed, "Father, we humbly bow before you, overwhelmed by the love that fills this room. It is with awe that I am reminded of your all-consuming love for us. As I look out at these faces I have come to know and love as family, I am taken aback by my lack of understanding of the gifts you have to shower over those who simply trust and obey. I praise you, Father, for the gifts you have given: this family you have given to each and every one of us, and the food on this table, Lord, which was provided by you, Jehovah Jireh, our provider. And now by your Grace may you bless this food to your use, so that we may better serve you in the days to come. Amen."

Little Ben was the first to jump up to get his cinnamon roll, and on his Mama's advice, he had brought a bowl.

Chapter Two

By the time they had eaten their cinnamon rolls, tidied up the cabin, and gotten Rebecca down for a nap, the blizzard had stopped. Benjamin walked by the window for the eighth time, and finally smiled as he saw the sunshine peering out through the thick grey clouds of the threatening snow sky.

"Oh!" he said as he hurried over to place his coffee cup onto the table! "Miss Grace, did I forget to tell you that the men of the family also have a couple of birthday surprises for you?"

Grace's eyes brightened and as she tried to figure out where the surprises were hidden, both men donned their coats and went to the door to leave. "Get your warmest clothes on children. Our surprise is outside!"

The house erupted into the sounds of running feet, chairs scraping on the floor, and joyous giggles. Grace wanted desperately to be a composed young lady, but the little girl inside her took over and she giggled as she ran and lifted her coat from the peg. Just as she stood on one foot to step into her boot, Little Ben ran past her to open the door, and knocked her against the wall. She intended to only smack his arm as he ran by, but hit him at an angle that made him trip over his own feet and go flying out into the snow face first. When he got up, his feelings were clearly hurt, so Benjamin approached him, and whispered softly for him to go around back and get the horse that was to be Grace's surprise.

Proud of his new responsibility, Little Ben dried his tears and headed around to the back of the cabin. In a moment, his head appeared from around the side, and he said, "Which one, Papa?"

Ben motioned for the boy to come to him, and when he got there, said, "What do you mean which one? The horse is tied in the back, and I want you to bring her up here."

"But there are two of them, Papa!" Little Ben said with wide eyes.

The two of them turned and made their way to the back where Kevin had tethered the horse and given her hay, but when they got there, Ben was surprised when he did indeed see Grace's new horse with a smaller one beside it!

"Kevin," Ben shouted. "Were you aware that there are two surprises back here?"

Since he was aware of how sound carried, and did not want to spoil the surprise for Grace, Kevin did not shout that there was the horse from Ben, and the saddle Kevin had gotten for her. But when he turned the corner he, too, was surprised by the fact that there were two animals eating the hay. "Where did that come from?" he asked.

"I have no idea," Ben said. "Do you think she had a baby horse that followed her here?"

Kevin looked at his feet to hide his smile, then patiently said, "Just so you know, Ben, *baby horses* are actually called foals. Male foals are called colts, and female foals are called fillies, just for future reference, and no. I do not think your mare had a *foal* that followed her here, in fact that would be very unlikely, because *that* is a *mule*."

Ben was so pleased that it was Kevin that heard him call them *baby horses* instead of Denzel or Abram!

Kevin briefly looked puzzled and then said, "Unless the Bensons have a donkey that might somehow have…"

"The Bensons don't have a donkey, Uncle Kevin." Little Ben said innocently.

"What does a donkey have to do with it?" Ben said. There was no use pretending he knew everything, because obviously, he did not.

So Kevin proceeded to inform them that mules were not a species of their own. They were a product of a male donkey and a female horse.

The looks on the two Ben's faces made Kevin double over in laughter. Ben lowered his head and shook it back and forth slowly. "There is so much I don't know," he said as he looked shame faced at Kevin.

"That's ok, Papa! Me and you can learn together!" It was meant to ease Ben's suffering, but just added to it.

Oh, great! I have the mind of a child, Ben thought to himself. But Little Ben's face told him he wanted to help so badly, that Ben finally said, "Thank you, Son. That was a grace filled thing to say."

Kevin smiled and winked at Ben then said, "You are welcome to my knowledge as I learn from the five of you, how to be a member of a family!"

There was no pretense of airs. They were all friends as well as family now, so there was no need to pretend to be something you weren't. They loved each other, short comings and all.

They left the mule to eat the hay while they walked Grace's new horse to the edge of the house. "Go get your sister, Ben," Benjamin said.

When the door opened, out stepped Little Ben with his sister in tow. He had made her close her eyes, because that was the way surprises were done, and she stood on the porch waiting patiently.

The men walked the horse around to the front of the house, and Ben said, "Ok. Open your eyes!"

Grace slowly opened her eyes, then let out a high pitched squeal and threw her arms in the air, which sent the horse rearing its head and stepping backwards. "Whoa!" Ben said as he had seen Denzel do with his own horses. Strangely, it seemed to calm the mare, and before long, all the children had taken a turn riding the horse. Rebecca rode in front of Grace and giggled the entire time.

The sky was darkening as the snow clouds gathered, and Sarah was getting nervous that everyone had been out too long. Granny said she had made hot chocolate for the children, and coffee for the men, and wanted them to come in right now, "before they kitch their death of cold!"

They all sat down around the table and began telling the story of the famous snow ball fight. They were laughing and interrupting each other, arguing over the facts and embellishing the defeat of the other team, which elicited much protestation.

Kevin watched, thoroughly entertained as the snow began pounding down outside the cabin! This was his family. He wasn't sure how it happened, but he knew in his heart that he loved them, and they loved him. His solitary life as a Priest had seemed adequate until he met this very strange and unusual group of people. They had opened their arms to him and had never looked back. He loved them, almost immediately.

And by love, he did not mean he respected and admired them, although he did respect and admire them very much. It meant far more than that. It meant that if any one of them needed comfort, he would give it. If they needed somewhere to live, he would open his home to them. And unbelievably, he knew that they felt the same way about him. It meant they were connected at some basic level for life. So being a member of this family meant they could depend on each other for those things always. That in some way, he was theirs and they are his. And it did not matter if they lived close or far away, or if they saw each other often or seldom.

Kevin's thoughts were interrupted when he heard a loud 'Boom!' Ben's feet hit the floor as he jumped up, knocking over his chair. "What's wrong, Ben!" Sarah shouted. Ben stood there in total shock, sending dread into the heart of Sarah. "What is it, Ben? Are you sick?"

"I know that mule!" he said while he ran to the door. "That is Jeb's mule, Doc! He is out there somewhere in this blizzard!"

Kevin looked puzzled, but without a second's hesitation he followed Ben and began dressing to go outside.

Little Ben began pulling on his boots, and Ben said, "Stay here with your Mother, Ben."

The boy started to argue, but the door opened and the men stepped out into the blinding snow, slamming the door behind them.

"Who is Jeb, Sarah?" Granny asked with a look of horror on her face.

"Oh, Mama, when we first got here, we got off the boat late one evening," Sarah began distractedly. "We had nowhere to go, and one of the soldiers took us to a house where he thought we would be able to lodge with the children. His name was Jeb, and he had a contrary old mule named Doc."

Grace gleefully continued the story by telling about how Doc had gotten his name from the time he cured Jeb's back by kicking him through the shed door, but her face could not betray her feelings. She was in a panic as well. Not only because she knew Jeb was out there lying in the snow somewhere, but because now her beloved Papa and Uncle Kevin were out there, too, and it was getting dark.

Rebecca had started to cry, so Sarah announced that Grace was to take her in and put her to bed, while Little Ben was to help her clear the table.

Little Ben carried one load of dishes to the sink, then stood there drawing in the soapsuds mindlessly. With a swat on the butt from a dishrag, Granny said, "What are you doing standing there, boy? Your Mama gave you a job to do!"

After a long sigh, Little Ben said softly, "But I am worried about Papa and Uncle Kevin. What if they get lost, or the winter gets them?"

Granny turned him toward her and said, "You listen to me, boy, 'cos this is important. Draggin' your feet and worryin' don't go together. Them worries pile in on you, and if you don't do somethin' about it, they will bury you like ole Hank's mule!"

"I thought it was Jeb's mule, Granny," Little Ben said curiously.

"Oh, no, Little Ben," she said as she drew him over to the table and gave him the last of the morning's cinnamon rolls. "God made more than one mule that year you know. Now you sit right there and I will get you some hot milk."

Little Ben took the fork and absentmindedly dipped it into the icing. He had the fork in his mouth, licking all the flavor off of it when Granny returned.

"Now Hank's mule was an ornery cuss," she said as she set the hot milk in front of him. She placed her own cup of coffee on the table and sat down with him. "One day, Hank could not find that mule anywhere, so he got on his horse and went to look for him. Well, don't you know he could hear that mule a brayin', and a brayin'! But he couldn't see him nowhere!"

She motioned for Little Ben to get on with eating, then resumed, "Well, as he was riding along, he looked down, and sure enough, there was his mule! He had fallen into a hole that was deeper than the mule hisself!"

Granny was pleased when Little Ben's eyes opened wide in wonder, so she continued, "Well, Hank was so fed up with that mule, he reckoned he wasn't worth diggin' out of there, so he just decided to throw some dirt in on him and bury him alive right where he was!"

Little Ben was appalled. "What happened next, Granny? They wouldn't really bury him alive would they?"

"Well, he tried!" Granny said.

He threw dirt in on that mule, and that mule just shook hisself like he'd been stung by a swarm of mud daubers! He was stompin' his feet, and shakin' his head like he had gone mad, but that farmer just kept throwing in dirt. Hank wouldn't give up and neither would that stubborn ole mule."

"Which one of them won, Granny? Was the mule ok?" Little Ben's heart was about to explode with worry over Hank's mule, his Papa, Uncle Kevin and Jeb. Granny, an experienced story teller, knew it was time to relieve that stress.

"Well," Granny said with a smile on her face, and a twinkle in her eye, "after a time, the old farmer, Hank, had plumb filled that hole with dirt, and that ole mule just walked right out of there! That mule would have been buried alive if he woulda done what you're adoin'! But instead, he just kept on moving; and kept on fighting."

Little Ben grinned broadly at his Granny, and she at him. But then she remembered the point of her story, and rose to her feet and said, "Now get up, shake off them worries, and do what your Mama told you to do, boy! She got enough on her plate without you worryin' her." Little Ben had jumped up and was picking up the cups when Granny turned toward him and said, "Now you remember this day and the story I told you. Worry and laziness don't mix. You gotta keep movin' and shakin' those troubles off your shoulders. Especially when you don't feel like it. When you don't feel like it is when you got to fight the most! Ok?"

"Ok, Granny," he said as he gave her a big hug. With his arms around her he looked up into her face and said, "I love you, Granny."

Granny's eyes began to water, and she barely choked out the words, "I love you, too, boy. And I am right proud of the man you are becoming." She then broke the moment, turned quickly and said, "Didn't I teach you nothin'? Get movin' and do what your Mama told you to do. Right now!" She punctuated that statement with a swat to the behind with the dishrag.

Little Ben knew she meant business, so he said, "Yes, Ma'am," and finished the dishes as instructed.

Grace was having trouble getting Rebecca to bed. She was fourteen months old now and had been weaned from the breast for only a few weeks. She had hardly missed it, unless she got too tired, or was upset as she was now. With the events of the day, no one had put her down for a nap, so now she was exhausted and inconsolable.

"Grace, why don't you help Granny with the dishes. I think your being in here just reinforces Rebecca's desire to nurse. I will put her down," Sarah said.

Grace had almost forgotten that she was the mother of Rebecca instead of Sarah. They had pretended to the world that it was the other way around, and since Rebecca was weaned, Grace's responsibility for the child was finally over. She briefly chided herself for feeling that way, but remembered what Sarah had said. Grace was barely a child herself when she had had this baby, and since Rebecca was in good hands, it was alright for her to let go. It was not the life she had wanted for herself, but it was her life, and she would deal with it as best she could. Just as she began to let her mind wander to the man who had taken advantage of her as a child, she stopped herself. She decided instead to use that energy to do something that could help Jed, Uncle Kevin, and her beloved Papa. She began to pray.

"Our Heavenly Father, you are so full of grace, and love. Your kindness is felt by me every waking hour. I am so privileged to have your love and protection, your guidance and your patience. My Father, I come to you now to bring you a new worry. Jeb is lost in the snow, and although I am proud of my Papa and Uncle Kevin, I am worried about them as well. I give them to you, this very moment, because I can do nothing to help them. I am at my weakest, God. I am asking you to be my strength. And I am asking you, in the name of your son, Jesus Christ. Amen"

The dishes were done, the coffee pot was on in the hopes that the men would soon enter, and the ladies were exhausted. Little Ben had fallen asleep on the floor in front of the fireplace with his new Christmas puppy, Dusty, as his pillow. The little dog had spent this entire day running, sniffing, wiggling, and exploring, and now he was as exhausted as only a puppy can be. Sarah smiled as she looked at her little boy with his dog, and wished the children could always be this age.

"Well, I'm goin' in for the night," Granny said with a sigh. "There's nothin' my getting' wore out can fix." She stood slowly and turned to go into her room just as Little Ben awakened and saw her.

"Granny, can I sleep with you tonight?" he asked.

Sarah thought he was a little big to sleep with Granny, but tonight was not the night to deal with that. "Can I Mama?" Sarah was even too tired to correct his grammar, so she just said, "Whatever your Granny says is fine with me."

Granny just smiled and winked at Little Ben, and the two of them disappeared into her room, with Dusty on their heels. Within minutes, Little Ben returned to the front room, retrieved his coat from the hook, opened the door, and said, "Come on, Dusty. Granny says she's not having you pee in her room again!"

Sarah and Grace talked into the night, and finally fell asleep, their heads cradled on their arms on the table.

December 27, 1862

The morning announced itself with a bright stream of sunshine that flooded the room. Sarah was the first to awaken, and sat up slowly to work the "cricks" out of her back, as Granny put it.

She went straight to the chamber pot, then built up the fire. A glance up at the loft told her the men hadn't come back and she sighed as the memories from last night settled on her with a steady, great weight.

She was standing with her back to the fire, her skirt gathered up in her hands so that her backside could get warm, when she thought she heard the sound of horses.

Grace awakened as Sarah hurried to the window to look out. "Grace!" Sarah shouted, "the men are home!"

They waited until the men climbed down off the horses and thanked Abram, Elias, and Denzel for their help. But as soon as the men left with Jeb's mule in tow, they opened the door and rushed out into the morning's crisp, cold air.

They ran into the arms of Ben and Kevin before they realized just how cold it was outside! Encouraged by the smiles on the men's faces, Sarah said, "Come on into the house and tell us all about it."

The house was buzzing with the activities of making coffee, frying bacon, eggs and potatoes, slicing home-made bread, setting the table, and telling tales of what had happened the night before.

Apparently, Jeb and two other men had been sent to scout out upper Leafbank. There had been complaints about three Confederate soldiers who had gotten lost from their unit, and were stealing chickens from a homestead up that holler, and they were sent to settle the matter.

On the way back, not far from the Benson's home, Jeb had stopped briefly to 'wet his shoes' as they often called relieving one's self, and the other men deemed it safe to continue without him. Apparently, the Rebels had jumped him, left him for dead, stole Doc and headed down the holler. That was where Ben and the other men had found Jeb. Lying face down in the dark red snow circling his head, so near death that the snow on top of him had not melted.

They had taken him to the Benson's because it was the nearest house. Bessie and Cali were tending to Jeb's injuries, while Midgie started making a strong broth to warm his 'inards.'

The Confederates were starving and had planned to eat the mule as soon as night fell so they could build a fire far in a valley, far from sight of the houses. The plan went well they thought, until they realized that Doc had no intentions of being anyone's meal. There was no sign of the Rebels, but there was plenty of blood, two teeth, and a Confederate hat to indicate that Doc had made his opinion of the situation clear to all of them.

Their laughter woke up Little Ben who came running into the room, landing in his Papa's arms.

"Hey, Little Ben! What is going on here? You are wet!"

Little Ben looked down at his pants and a red color crept up his neck and into his face.

Grace was so happy to find that everything was ok, she forgot herself and pointed at Little Ben and said in a mocking tone, "Ben! Aren't you a little big to pee the bed?"

Ben was humiliated. "I did NOT pee the bed! I have not done that in years and you know it!"

"Hey, hey!" Benjamin said, "Ben, go change your clothes and don't worry about it, son."

"But I didn't pee the bed, Papa!"

"I wasn't saying you did. Just go change your clothes, right now. It is too cold to be running around in your bed clothes anyway, so go on."

Ben turned to say something to Grace, but Sarah beat him to it. "Grace! What on earth came over you?" Grace looked at the floor, thoroughly ashamed of herself.

"I'm sorry, Mama. I just… well, he is still my brother, and sometimes I just like to tease him." She looked up with a smile, because she thought it was funny, but one look at Sarah told her it was not.

"I think you owe your brother an apology," said Benjamin.

"I'm sorry, Papa." Grace said, looking at her hands.

"Don't tell me! Tell your brother!"

At that moment, Little Ben came out of the bedroom, wiping his tears on his sleeve. "Little Ben, I am sorry I teased you."

"Yea, right." Little Ben said.

"I would like to say something if I may." Kevin said.

"Certainly," said Sarah.

Ben added, "You need not ask, Kevin. After all you are a part of this family, a treasured part I might add, and any words of wisdom you might want to share, are more than welcome. Even if it is about foals!"

The men erupted into laughter which lightened the mood.

"Little Ben, would you join me at the table, please?" Kevin asked.

Little Ben pulled out the chair next to where Kevin was sitting and sat down with a dejected plop.

"I want to ask you a question, Little Ben, and I want you to think carefully before you answer." Little Ben nodded.

"If I confided in you…"

"What does that mean?" Little Ben asked as he looked at Sarah.

Sarah said, "It means, to share a secret with you with the expectation that you will not tell that secret to others."

"Oh," Little Ben said as he returned his attention to Kevin.

"So," Kevin continued, "if I confided in you that after my parents were killed suddenly, and I had to decide whether I wanted to go to an orphanage or a monastery, that I started wetting the bed again, would you love me any less?"

Little Ben was reeling from the reminder that his Uncle Kevin might have had to have gone to an orphanage just like he and Grace had had to do. The horrors had filled his mind, and then he heard the question. He had mixed feelings because on one hand, his heart was broken for Uncle Kevin, but on the other hand, Kevin obviously thought he had wet the bed; which he had not.

"Little Ben, Uncle Kevin is waiting for an answer," Sarah said.

His eyes shot up to Kevin's and realized that his uncle was 'confiding' in him that he had been a bed wetter, and it deserved a kind answer.

"No, Uncle Kevin, I could never stop loving you." He stood and hugged Kevin's neck, and Kevin pulled him onto his knee.

Kevin was touched. He said, "I wet the bed even after I went to the monastery, Ben. Lots of things can trigger that. Being upset, being tired. I know that you did *not* wet the bed. But, if ever you meet someone who does, please be very compassionate and understanding. It is not something to be ashamed of."

"I understand, Uncle Kevin. Thanks." Little Ben said. As he stood up from Kevin's knee, he caught Grace's eye, and stuck his tongue out at her.

Grace threw him a mean look, which Kevin saw, and said with great authority, "Alright! The two of you, right here!" He pointed at the floor in front of him and sat upright in the chair. The children obeyed instantly.

"Now, Grace, I believe you made fun of Ben, here, for allegedly wetting the bed." Grace's eyes went to the floor. "And Ben, when Grace apologized, I believe you said, 'yea, right.' Did I report that fairly? Both children hung their heads and nodded in agreement.

"Well," Kevin continued, "I believe there is a far better way to handle this. After all, we all make mistakes. But the best way to learn when you make an honest mistake, is to then do your best to fix it. Are you willing to try?"

Both Grace and Little Ben looked up with hope in their eyes. Sarah's and Ben's eyes met and a small smile appeared on their lips.

"Well, here is what I want you to do. I want you to tell me your side of the story. Grace, why don't you go first."

"I guess I was just feeling a little giddy because everything was alright from last night. I had felt so bad for so long, that I was like a rabbit set free, and I just wanted to laugh about something, and… that something was Ben when he came in with his pants wet. I know now that it hurt you, and worse, embarrassed you, and I really am very sorry, Benji." She had used her pet name for him in the hopes that his heart would be softened to her apology, and this uncomfortable situation would be over.

They hugged, but Kevin was not finished. "Now, Ben, why don't you tell us your side of the story."

Little Ben stood up straight as an arrow and said, "I do not lie. And I did not wet the bed. But nobody would believe me, not even you Uncle Kevin. Had I wet the bed, I would have called Mama, or Grace into Granny's room to help me. I would have owned up to it. I would have!" he said as he looked around the room defensively, before continuing, "But when the time came to trust my word, nobody did. And it was worse when my own sister made fun of me and pointed at my wet pants."

Sarah realized that Little Ben was telling the truth, rolled her eyes at the thought of the puppy, and went into Granny's room as they continued.

"Well, now, Ben. Your sister has apologized, and I believe she meant it. Now it is your turn to extend a Christian hand and say, *I forgive you*."

"But I don't!" Little Ben said emphatically! Kevin almost laughed, but managed to continue with his lesson.

"Well, that was certainly honest, and admire that as I do, it is still your turn to say something. And that something should be, I forgive you. Apologizing and forgiving are two very difficult things to do. But Christ requires it of us. He says we must forgive over and over and over. I know you love your sister, Ben. So say it." He hesitated briefly, then added, "Please."

Little Ben turned to his sister, and said, "I forgive you."

Kevin was about to say something when they heard the growl or scream of an animal caught in a trap coming from what sounded to be behind the cabin. No one was sure where the sound was coming from until they saw Benjamin heading for Granny's room.

Ben entered to find Sarah rocking her precious Mama back and forth like a baby. Granny's arms swung lifelessly and her head fell back as Sarah screamed for her Mama not to go, but it was too late.

Apparently, she had passed away during the night, and had released her urine the moment she died.

The children appeared at the door, but Kevin took them back into the front room, wishing he had somewhere to take them away from the mournful sounds of a daughter longing for her Mama. But death was a part of living, and as much as he wanted to shield them from it, he could not.

Ben's heart was breaking and he found himself being consumed by anger at his loss. He had just started being happy with his life and now his Mama was taken from him just as he was learning to love her so deeply. But the look on Sarah's face brought him back from his own personal needs, he realized she was falling apart and knelt to hold her in his arms.

"You have to let go of her, Sarah," he whispered softly.

"I can't! I cannot let her go!" Sarah screamed.

Ben's arms surrounded both Sarah and his beloved Mama and he held them tightly as they wept.

Chapter Three

The next few hours were a blur. The preacher came and went as did the rest of the community. "The hands and feet of Christ," as the preacher had often said in his instructions to the congregation. "You must be the hands and feet of Christ in this world," he would remind them as they departed on Sunday mornings to go out into the world to make a difference in people's lives.

And that is exactly what they did for the Waters family. They fed the horse, mucked out the shelter Ben had made for the animal, made their meals, brought in fire wood, cared for the baby, and helped with the funeral arrangements. All while the Waters' family mourned and sat stunned as they were reminded to 'eat a bite of something,' or given something to drink.

It was customary to have the body in the home for a few days before the funeral, so the women arrived to pick out the dress Granny would wear, and prepare her for her burial.

Grace heard the gentle knock at the door and saw the door open, but the light outside was so bright she could not see who was entering at first. Suddenly she realized it was Eileen Rogers, the woman Grace had gone to rescue from her grief when her son, Seth, had been killed in the war.

The look on Eileen's face told Grace that she keenly knew her grief and that great compassion was Grace's undoing. The two women embraced and cried for all the lost boys and mothers in this world, while the other women crept in quietly, began placing more baskets of food and supplies around, sweeping out the snow, and checking to be sure Little Ben had been fed and was alright.

Finally, Eileen stepped back, holding Grace's hands gently, and looked Grace in the eye. Their faces spoke volumes without one single word being said. The things Grace had said to Eileen when she was mourning her son, Seth, came back to her clearly: words of acknowledgement of her grief, words of both sorrow and encouragement, even the unspoken threat of dumping water over her head if she gave up, gleamed in Eileen's eyes, and the moment cheered Grace immensely.

Bun Morrison, the preacher's wife, placed one hand on Grace's shoulder and said, "Grace, there is no easy way to bring this up, but if you would get Sarah for us, we came to prepare your Granny for the wake and the funeral."

Grace glanced at Sarah's bedroom door and knew instinctively that Sarah could not handle this part of the preparations. Sarah had already been overwhelmed at her Mama's death and almost unable to function at such an unexpected personal loss. But at noon, the men had come to explain that the ground was so frozen her Mama could not be buried until spring. Their explanation that she would be placed in a building used for that purpose until the ground thawed enough for her burial, however, took the last of Sarah's energy to cope, and she had gone to her room to escape the world, the people, the decisions, and the reality of her loss. And so it was Grace who took control.

She led them into Granny's room where Granny's little bird house and a partially drunk glass of water sat on the table beside her bed. Granny was covered with the quilt she had lovingly made for the family as her Christmas gift to them. The familiarity of the room and the realization that Granny was gone was too much for Grace to bear. She collapsed onto the foot of the bed and dissolved into tears.

Eileen Rogers knelt beside Grace, holding her hand and whispering prayers for strength for the family and healing over the loss, while Bun found Granny's dresses. After a time, Bun asked Grace which dress was her Granny's favorite.

Grace smiled and said, "Oh, the purple one. Mama made it for her out of a bolt of cloth she bought in Parkersburg, and Granny called it her Sunday go to meetin' dress. She *only* wore it when she went to church." The thought brought a smile to Grace's face as she remembered her Granny alive and full of spice, but then reality returned like a heavy shroud of suffocating darkness, and the tears threatened to return.

But Grace looked down at her hands, and remembered who she was. She was the one her mother had trusted, and she had met the challenge, growing stronger in the process. Christmas night she had lain in her bed, enjoying her childhood, holding her doll and thanking God for her own room and family. Today, she stepped into adulthood and took her place as the strong woman God had intended her to be. She took in a long slow breath, exhaled with a sigh and looking up at Eileen, said, "What else to do we need to do?"

As Grace stood, she accepted that everything that had happened to her in this life had made her the woman she was. She pictured her Granny sleeping in the cold on the streets of Parkersburg, inside that tent they had found her in, and decided that she was most like her Granny, and found a new pride in what they had survived. Her chin set with resolve, she helped the women make the final arrangements, then bathe and dress her Granny.

Chapter Four

Ben was doing his best to manage the guests and look after Little Ben and Rebecca while Sarah rested and Grace cared for his Mama, but truth be known, he was just going through the motions, unsure of where his feet were taking him.

A knock at the door brought one more guest, one more person to try to smile at, thank, and invite in. But this time as the door opened, Ira Benson bounced in and asked if he could see Little Ben's new puppy. The joy in the little boy's enthusiasm was like a breath of fresh air to Benjamin, giving him the energy to look up at Abram who was standing in the doorway.

Abram removed his hat, and said, "I thought you might want to take a walk and get out for a spell."

Ben turned and looked at the tiny house, bursting with well-meaning friends, and grabbed his coat and hat. He had no idea how badly he needed to get out until he and Abram reached the top of the hill in front of the cabin, and all the activity was far behind him.

They stopped for a moment, and Abram waited patiently when Ben took a few more steps and fell to his knees in the middle of Granny's snow covered garden. Without a word, Abram turned and looked at the magnificent view from that hilltop, while Ben sobbed and cried like a child, collapsed in the snow, far from the cabin.

When Ben had recovered, he stood and looked at Abram, wiping his nose on his handkerchief, and said, "I feel like a fool, crying and all."

Abram said, "You loved her, Ben. Don't ever feel foolish for responding to love and its needs. Besides, it is just us up here. Honesty between friends is a good thing."

They walked for a while, talked about hunting, and the weather, and about anything else they could think of, except Granny. They even laughed a little about the antics of the twins, Wheat and Paul.

"Wheat?" Ben asked.

"Yep," Abram answered, "them boys heard that her name was Ouita Nancy, and started calling her Wheat right off. I guess it stuck. They've got us all callin' her Wheat now."

They walked in silence for a while, and then Ben stopped and said, "I don't know how to help her, Abram."

Abram was silent for a minute, and then said, "Women folk take things to heart more than we do, Ben. As hard as it is on you, it is almost unbearable for a woman to lose her Mama."

Ben couldn't explain that Granny was just as much his Mama as Sarah's, because no one knew Sarah and Grace had just found her on the street in Parkersburg and brought her home. Nor could he explain the strong attachment they had to her, having known her for such a short time. So he just looked up at Abram and said, "You are right. Sarah is broken hearted and I can't seem to find the strength to help her. Or even figure out *how* to help for that matter."

"You just need to be together. You're a family and can help each other through this. Just don't hide your feelings, Ben. There may be times when you need to be strong for them, but that doesn't mean you can't share your sorrow with Sarah when you are alone. Just let your family's love lift you and carry you over the heartbreak."

Abram looked at the sky and realized it was darker than it should be in late afternoon. It was about to snow again so he had to say what needed to be said. He put his massive hand on Ben's shoulder and broached the subject, "Your cabin is too small for the funeral, and even for the wake, Ben. So they will be taking Granny to the church here in a few minutes. The snow is comin' and folks will be needin' to get home soon, so it has to be now."

Ben's face showed his shock at the prospect of having to let her go. "No," he said. "No, it's too soon. We can't do that to Sarah and the children!"

"Ben," Abram said, "there's a mighty snow storm coming, and it might be days before we can get back here to take the body." Ben flinched at the reference to his beloved Mama, as 'the body.'

Abram winced and wished he had used different words, but said, "Ben, look down there, they are ready to take her. We need to get back down. For the next little while, you need to set your feelings aside, and be strong for your family."

Ben turned and looked down the hill at the site of the men pulling up the wagon, and realized he needed to be with Sarah and the children when they took his Mama out. He dried his eyes and began to walk briskly toward the cabin.

In Ben's absence, Kevin had been overseeing the process of greeting, making room for more pies and baskets, and just watching the entire process unfold. How often had he, as a priest, been called to go to a home where a death had occurred? How many times had he reassured people that someday they would see their loved one again, or read scriptures meant to comfort? But what he was feeling now ripped through his heart like a knife, and no words of comfort seemed to help.

When he had lost his parents in that tragic accident as a child, his mourning was diluted with the overwhelming fear and knowledge that their lives would never be the same. He and his brother had to choose between going to an orphanage or joining a monastery, with the question always looming as to whether they would be together or separated for life.

But now, as a grown man, completely aware of his surroundings and totally in control of his own life, he was losing something so precious to him, words could not express. His dear family was enduring the loss of the one who gave them direction, the Matriarch of the family. The homeless woman he, as a Priest, had cared for and protected all those years, had become his Mama within a day's journey.

His thoughts wandered to the days when he, as the priest of a large parish, would take food and clothing to the old lady who lived in a tent behind the church. Anna, whom he now called, Mama, had lost her mind when her only daughter, and loving husband were killed in a buggy accident. He remembered the cold nights when he would pack her up, complete with her little bird house, bundle of sticks, and a stack of neatly torn rags she insisted on keeping with her, and take her into the church for shelter and a bowl of hot soup. She would only eat a small portion of her meal, and insist he take it back out to the tent for the cat she had become attached to. Kevin had never seen the cat personally, but *she* believed she had one, so he would wrap himself in his coat and scarf, and go out to leave the hot soup for the cat she called Rascal.

His heart was warming at those memories when he saw Benjamin and Abram reenter the front door.

"They are ready to take Mama," Kevin said to Ben.

"I know," Ben said as he grabbed Kevin's forearm and looked him in the eye. "Can we do this?"

Kevin's eyes filled with tears, and then he straightened and said, "We will, because we must." The two men looked at each other for strength and called for Little Ben and Grace to come to them.

Their guests put the finishing touches on the evening meal, and began collecting their coats and preparing to leave when they saw that Kevin and Ben were gathering the children.

Abram called Ira to him, and the boys pleaded for just five more minutes to play. But Abram snapped his finger once, and Ira grabbed his coat, ran to the door, turned and said, "Bye, Ben. See you tomorrow," and darted out the door.

The house was so quiet it hurt their ears as the last person left and the door closed behind them. Ben started to speak, but instead just scooped Little Ben and Grace up in his arms and gave them a long hug.

With a single knock, the door opened and Rev. Morrison stepped into the room. One nod told them it was time.

"Now I want you to listen to me," Ben began. "I am asking you to be strong for Mama right now." Both children nodded their heads in agreement before they were even told what was going to happen. "It is time for them to take Granny to the church where she will be until the funeral, and I need to go get your Mama and tell her."

Both of the children were appalled at the thought that they were taking Granny away from their home, but Ben reasoned with them and told them of the pending storm, and the necessity to get people back their homes before the blizzard hit. "It is going to be hard enough on your Mama when they take her. I am asking you to accept what is, and support your Mama. Can you do that?"

Grace took a deep breath as a reminder of who she was, and said, "Yes, Papa. I will look after Little Ben, and you take care of Mama. Where is Rebecca?"

"She is with Midgie, and will be for a day or so. She will be fine. We need to take care of ourselves right now. Is that ok with you, Grace?"

"Yes, Papa. Ben and I will be fine," she said as she put her arm around her little brother.

As Ben stood to go in to Sarah, Little Ben turned and sobbed into his sister's dress. Kevin watched as Grace bent down and said, "Now you listen to me. I know you are feeling alone and hurt right now. But what you are not thinking about at this moment, is that you are a part of a family now, a family that loves you very much. It isn't just the two of us anymore. We have Mama and Papa, and Uncle Kevin to love us, and they miss Granny just as much as we do. Now we all have to support each other, and we will get through this together, won't we Uncle Kevin."

In an instant, Grace had changed Kevin's status from bystander, to participant in a family tragedy, and Kevin rushed in to take his part.

He swooped Little Ben up in his arms and hugged him tightly, whispering in his ear that he loved him, and always would.

"But when you go back to Parkersburg, Uncle Kevin, it will be only the five of us. And what if something happens to Papa or Mama?" Little Ben asked.

Kevin retrieved a chair, and sat with Little Ben on his knee. "You know, Ben, when a tragedy like this one occurs, we begin to feel shaken, like there is nothing we can count on. All the fears we never noticed before, rear their ugly heads and threaten to rob us of the security we normally feel. But it is not healthy to pile all that sorrow on top of ourselves. Let us just deal with the loss of Granny right now, and enjoy the comfort of being with those we love."

Grace noticed the bedroom door open and went to assist her Mama as she exited the room. "Mama, I was thinking," Grace said. "Why don't we give Granny one of Jeb's warm blankets to take with her."

Sarah looked up wistfully, and said, "Yes! Yes! Please, Grace, go get one for her. I just cannot bear the thought of her lying there so cold!" Sarah sobbed and turned into Ben's arms as Grace ran to retrieve the blanket. Then the heartbroken family huddled together as the men carried Granny's body out on a homemade stretcher, covered safely in Jeb's warmest blanket.

Chapter Five

Rebecca was still with the Bensons, and Little Ben had wanted to sleep with Grace that night. Kevin had long been asleep, but as exhausted as Ben and Sarah were, they just could not seem to make it to bed. They stared at the walls, stunned by the events of the day and sipped the last of the coffee.

Sarah looked over at the abundance of food filling the room, and smiled at the thoughtfulness of their church family. "I don't know what we would have done without them today," she said.

With a deep sigh, Ben stood and held his hand out for Sarah to take.

"I need to do up the dishes," she said.

"No. Leave them right here. We can do them together in the morning."

They blew out all the candles, except the one they were carrying, and went into their room. As they lay there, face to face, they began to remember all they had done in the short year they had been together. Sarah was grateful for the window Ben had installed that was letting the bright moon send streams of soft light in and bathe the bedroom with a soft glow. They laughed about the night Grace ran away, and reminisced about the first night they spent in the cave.

Ben finally rolled over onto his back and said, "Come over here."

Sarah scooted over and laid her head on his shoulder, cuddling close to him for the very first time. Her tears flowed freely in the safety of his arms, and Ben felt helpless to lift her out of her sorrow. He had no idea what to do, other than to give her the grace Abram had given him when he cried. He just waited for the tears to subside, and then looked down at her. Something about seeing her cradled in his arm made him ache to kiss her, hold her, and be close to her.

Their lips touched and suddenly the pressures of the day seemed to be pressing them toward each other. For the first time since they had met, they clung to each other with such a need that all barriers disappeared. In him only could she find the joy that had been snatched away that very morning. And only Sarah made him feel life was worth living.

The silent conversation continued between them. Unspoken requests, with silent movements that granted permission gave them a rush of freedom in a world where they had only known captivity and restraint. The world as they knew it disappeared and they joyfully entered a realm where only the two of them existed in spiritual joy and physical pleasure. They looked at each other in the soft moonlight and felt no pain, no sorrow. Like two people alone on an island, they experienced a world filled with nothing but pleasure, joy, and timeless, eternal, love.

The warmth of their embrace, and the joy they both felt in knowing that this was right and good, carried them to a place they had never even dreamed of. The satisfaction of giving what the other needed and getting more than they ever expected, bonded them in a way they previously had no knowledge of. In the past, they had thought they were as close as they could possibly be, and now they knew better.

They smiled at each other and kissed again and again. They had become one person, drinking from the same pool of intense and powerful love, and life in the Waters' household would never be the same.

Chapter Six

Although the burial had to wait until spring thaw, they had the funeral service anyway, in order to allow people to pay their respects and to show support of the Waters' family.

The Bensons came by with their sleigh to pick up the Waters, but Kevin had decided to walk to the church. He was processing all that had happened to him since Mama's death, and trying to come to a decision about something that was life changing for him.

As much has he had loved being a priest, he found that he was now rather homesick when he was away from this family. When perfectly honest with himself, he realized that now his heart was here, with the people he loved and wanted to be with.

Before, when he thought about retiring, he felt lost, and could not imagine what he would do with his days. He had been old enough to retire for several years, but just could not for the life of him, figure out where he would go, or what he would do with himself.

When he was here he found himself wishing he could help plant the garden and harvest when the time came, yet he was torn by the responsibility he had as the priest of the largest Catholic church in Parkersburg.

He had pondered this conundrum several times over the last few months as he came and went from the Waters' home, but when Little Ben sat on his lap and cried about his leaving, it seemed his heart finally took a stand. He wanted to come home.

What was it about the loss of a loved one that strangely brought things into perspective? He had a certain clarity about his life he had never experienced and he was enjoying it. Yes, he would speak to Sarah and

Ben about moving home, he decided as he approached the church. *Home*, he thought. Such a lovely word.

~~~~~~~~

As Kevin opened the door to the church, he realized he was late and had already missed the first hymn. He took off his hat and gloves and started to sit down quietly in the back, but Little Ben's head bobbed up from the front seats, and he quickly motioned for Kevin to join them.

"We saved you a seat," Little Ben whispered so loudly the whole church heard him, and a murmur of laughter arose as Kevin took his place with the family.

Preacher stood and said, "I am reading from the book of Daniel today, chapter 3, for those of you who want to follow along in your Bibles." There was a rustling of pages turning then Preacher continued. "I am not going to keep you long today. We are gathered here to mourn the loss of our beloved Granny," he smiled at the congregation as their heads nodded.

"For she indeed was everybody's Granny," he continued. "She never hesitated to speak her mind about anything she felt needed correcting, did she?" Laughter arose in the room and folks wiped tears as they remembered the antics of the old woman who had stolen their hearts. When first introduced to the congregation, she had insisted they all call her Granny, which thrilled young and old alike. Everyone loves to have a Granny, and she enjoyed playing the part.

Preacher continued, "She mothered, scolded, demanded, adjusted, praised, and fixed anything she deemed a problem. She loved on the babies, always had candy for the youngin's, and somehow knew before even the Mama did, that a baby was on the way. She was magical, and will be missed, greatly."

The children had loved her so. The only time the children were allowed to get up in church without permission, was when they would quietly get up, go to Granny, who always sat in the back row of the middle aisle, in the far right corner, hold out their hand and receive a piece of candy without a word. But much was said in the smiles of gratitude from the children, and loving hugs from Granny. All of them loved her deeply, and Preacher could see the toll this service was taking on them.

"So why would such a sweet and loving person be taken from us without warning? Why do things like this happen to God's faithful? Shouldn't a God of love protect us from this kind of thing happening to us?" The congregation was stirring now as Preacher began to echo their thoughts over the last few days. Now he was stepping on toes, as they called it, and though it was a relief to know they were going to hear the answers, it was still uncomfortable to know he understood their thoughts so clearly.

"And this brings me to the book of Daniel. Daniel and his friends, Shadrach, Meshach, and Abednego, were far from their homeland. They were captives in a country that did not observe their customs, and as so, they had to change many things about their lives. They were the smartest and finest of their homeland, and that is why they were taken to be raised in the court of King Nebuchadnezzar, far from their families and the countryside they called home."

Preacher could have spoken for days on this subject, but chose to get to the point. "The King had the power of life and death over Shadrach, Meshach, and Abednego as well as everyone else who lived in his land. So one day he decreed that a golden image would be made, and everyone would fall on their faces and worship his God every time they heard the sounds of the trumpets, the cornet, flute and harp!"

"Can you imagine that? What do you think you would do if you were told to do that or die? Well, I can tell you what these three young men did. They did not dance around the King and try to fool him. They said very bluntly that they simply would NOT," Preacher shouted as he pounded the pulpit. "They would NOT BOW DOWN TO ANY GOD BUT THEIR OWN!"

Then softly he added, "Because their God was and is the one true God." He waited until the nods and words of agreement died down, then continued. "Even though they KNEW THEY WOULD BE BURNED IN A FIRE," Preacher shouted, "They simply stood for what they believed in, much as we do on a daily basis, don't we? Do we not forgive when we would rather hold a grudge or get revenge? Do we not support our fellowman in times of trouble? Share what we have to give? Go when we are needed?"

After a moment of reflection, Preacher continued, "So why then do bad things happen to us? Why would someone as beloved as Granny be taken from us so soon, and so abruptly?" Tears came again while people silently waited to hear what they had come for.

"Well, you might notice in Daniel 3: 20-25 that Shadrach, Meshach, and Abednego, WERE thrown into the fire! God did not keep troubles from happening then, and He does not keep troubles from happening now! According to verse 20, 'And he, meaning King Nebuchadnezzar, commanded the mightiest men that were in his army to BIND Shadrach, Meshach, and Abednego, and to CAST THEM INTO THE BURNING, FIREY, FURNACE!' Isn't that where we find ourselves right now? We are hurting, confused, and longing for the one we love." Sarah sobbed loudly and Ben placed his arm around her so she could lay her head on his shoulder.

"But God did not LEAVE them in that fire! God did not turn his back on them, and HE. WILL. NOT. TURN. HIS. BACK. ON. US!" Preacher said, emphasizing each word powerfully.

"No," Rev. Morrison continued, "Even though the fire had been SEVEN TIMES HOTTER than they usually built..." Preacher paused for effect. "Even though the fire was so hot that the men who THREW THEM INTO THE FIRE PERRISHED FROM THE HEAT OF THE FLAMES..." Again, he paused. "Even though their HANDS WERE BOUND WITH ROPES OF LEATHER!" He paused and began again, "THESE MEN WERE NOT CONSUMED! THEY WOULD NOT BOW DOWN TO ANOTHER GOD! THEY WOULD NOT BEND AT THE SOUND OF THE TRUMPETS! AND THEY

WOULD NOT BURN!" He stopped for a moment before finishing his sermon.

"And this brings us to the point of my message today," he concluded. Now listen carefully to what happened in verses 24 and 25." He stopped, placed the open Bible in his left hand and walked to the side of the pulpit. "Then Nebuchadnezzar the King was astonished, and rose up in haste, and spake, and said unto his counsellors, 'Did not we cast three men BOUND into the midst of the fire?' They answered and said unto the king, 'True, O king.'" He closed the Bible with his right hand, finger holding the page and walked closer to the people. "Did not we cast three men BOUND! Into the midst of the fire?"

"Now right here is God's blessing for us. God does not want to take away our troubles in this world. We are here to learn to trust HIM in times of trouble… as well as in good times. Listen to what happened next."

He resumed his position behind the pulpit, opened his Bible and began to read verse 25, "Remember the King had asked, 'Did not we cast three men BOUND into the midst of the fire?' His men agreed that it was true. Then the king answered and said, 'Lo, I see four men LOOSE! Walking in the fire and they have no hurt; and the form of the fourth is like the Son of God."

He left his Bible on the pulpit and walked closer to the family. "Have you seen our God walking with you? Have you been fed and cared for by the children of God since the tragedy?" The family nodded yes as the tears flowed.

"Yes, God is here with us in our joys and in our sorrows. He lifts us and gives us support through those who follow Christ's example, but He does FAR MORE THAN THAT during these times of sadness and tragedy. FAR more!"

"What is important to notice in this scripture, is that they went into the trial by fire BOUND UP! Just like have been BOUND by our own misunderstandings of life, BOUND by our own stubbornness, BOUND by our selfish desire to satisfy our own needs, BOUND by our fears, and BOUND by our belief that WE ARE IN CHARGE OF OUR OWN LIVES!"

"But when we walk with God... when we trust in God's word, His power, and His grace... we are FREED from our bondage! Just like Shadrach, Meshack, and Abednego, we will walk through this fire together, and come out with not one HAIR ON OUR HEADS, scorched. Missing ONLY, the bonds that hold us back. When we walk through life's storms with God, we, like these young men, will come out, with NOTHING LOST, but the CHAINS THAT HELD us from the abundant LIFE God has to offer." Sarah and Ben looked at each other with a private and intimate secret in their eyes, and a deeper understanding of the scriptures. They were now experiencing the love God had wanted for them, free from their fears, unfettered and alive.

"We are sad at the passing of our Granny. But we must know that because Christ died for our sins, to overcome death, that death is not the end of life. It is just *a part* of living. Life changes, sometimes for the better, and sometimes for the worse. But we should have no fear, for God is with us wherever we go and whatever stages we pass through."

Grace understood what Preacher was saying. She realized that had God not intervened in her life, and sent Sarah and Ben to rescue her, her life could have turned out to be very different. The thought of what she may have had to do to feed her brother and her daughter made her shudder. But the family she had been given enabled her to grow into a woman her Granny and Mama would be proud of. She remembered sitting in the room with Eileen Rogers, and Bun Morrison, when she decided what she had to do. She pledged right then and there, to dedicate her life to giving to others the grace she had found in this community of faith, and in her family.

She turned and looked up at Kevin who was sitting on her right, and her Mama who was sitting on her left, and without a thought, placed her hands in their's.

Kevin looked down the bench at the family who had won his heart, and decided that whatever it was that had held him to his position in the church, had been removed. It was time to retire, and he felt satisfied with his decision. It was true, his bonds had been removed. He understood why he had such clarity now. They would all see Granny again someday; he was certain of that. But life on earth must continue, and now he was free to live it.

Chapter Seven

Sarah had been deep in her own thoughts throughout the service and numbly greeted those who offered their condolences afterwards. But a deep, nagging, issue kept troubling her soul. She could not quite put her finger on it until she stopped and took an accounting of the family she had all but forgotten in her sorrow. She first looked at Benjamin and smiled with a deep warmth of love in her heart. Her eyes then went to Grace, who was holding the baby and trying to get her to talk to Bernie and Dorothy, a wonderful older couple who had just had their first grandchild, a precious little girl named Emma Grace.

Little Ben. Where was Little Ben? She glanced outside and saw a group of boys playing chase among the tall ancient trees, but try as she may, she could not find Little Ben.

Benjamin retrieved her coat from the small room right inside the church door, but when he handed it to her, she shoved it aside and went back into the church to look for her son.

She was half way down the aisle when she saw him sitting in the pew, hat in hand, staring down at the floor. All this time she had been lost in her own sorrow; her own thoughts. Little Ben had been so quiet and undemanding that she had completely overlooked his needs, and now, here he sat, lost in his own sorrow and grief.

"Ben," she began. When he didn't say anything, she just sat back in the seat and took hold of his hand. Out of the corner of her eye, she saw Benjamin approach, and then pause just off to one side. She realized that she had Benjamin to comfort her over the last few days, and both she and Grace had the verbal skills to define what they were feeling, and spoke often. But, she had assumed Little Ben was just being a little boy, playing with his new puppy and the neighbor boys who had come by, or staying at the Benson's in a house full of children to play with. It was only now she realized how injured he was, and that she had completely neglected him.

"My sweet boy," Sarah began as her thumb ran back and forth over his tiny hand, but he just sat there staring at the floor.

She had no idea what to say to him so she looked up at Benjamin who nodded, and said, "Let's get you home, boy." At that, Little Ben stood, turned, and walked toward his father.

Ben and Sarah followed the lost little boy out of the church, and Sarah leaned over to Ben and whispered, "I want him with me on the way home."

As they piled into the Benson's sleigh, Ben lifted Little Ben onto the back, and into the waiting arms of his Mama. Sarah had wrapped a blanket around her shoulders and opened it to welcome Little Ben into the warmth of her blanket and her arms.

"Grace, everyone else is ready to go," Ben shouted to her. What was she doing anyway? He looked up to see her engaged in conversation with Eileen Rogers' son Caleb, whom Sarah had locked out of his own home when she was caring for Eileen after the death of her beloved son, Seth. Grace turned and looked at Caleb unhappily, threw both hands in the air, and stomped toward the sleigh.

"Is everything alright?" Ben said to her as she climbed briskly into the sleigh.

"Yes!" Grace said as she took her seat and yanked on her clothing to create order and regain control over her emotions. Ben looked from Grace to Sarah with a question in his eyes. Sarah shrugged and shook her head no as an indicator that she had no idea what was going on.

The Bensons and the Waters rode along silently for a few minutes, and then Grace said through clenched teeth, "That Caleb Rogers is the most infuriating human being I have ever met!"

Ben and Sarah's eyes met in confusion, but they didn't have to wait long until Grace continued, "First of all, he wanted to know if I needed a ride home! He could clearly see that I was with my family; that we were all getting into the sleigh together! But 'no' was not enough for him! He asked if he could ride home with us because he wanted to check out my horse! CHECK OUT MY HORSE? Why would HE need to check out my horse?" Again she grabbed the waist of her dress and tugged it down into place, completely unaware of the smiles of understanding that passed between her parents. Sarah looked at what a beautiful woman Grace was becoming and realized that soon she would have a family of her own.

Sarah sighed deeply, and looked down at Little Ben. She cradled his cold cheek in her hand in an attempt to warm him, smoothed his hair back out of his eyes, and held his hand all the way home, but still, there was no response. He was completely lost in his sorrow, and Sarah had no idea how to reach him.

Finally, their little cabin came into view and they found themselves home. They thanked Abram and Midgie for all they had done, said their goodbyes, and entered the cabin as a family, alone for the first time in days. Kevin realized the situation with Little Ben, so after Grace had placed the sleeping Rebecca into her bed, he asked her to help him warm up some of the food the neighbors had left, so Ben and Sarah could be with Little Ben.

"Come here, boy," Benjamin said as he picked his son up and sat down in the rocking chair he had made, and just held Ben against his chest and rocked him back and forth. Sarah knelt beside the boy and said, "Is there anything I can get you, Little Ben?"

The boy just looked at the floor and sighed heavily. For the first time since they had found the cabin, Sarah saw the same little boy that had crawled out of those bushes so long ago. The same emptiness in his eyes; the same look of resignation; and the same acceptance of what life had handed him; completely devoid of any hope.

Sarah went in to help Kevin and Grace prepare the meal, but her assistance proved to be little more than pretense. She gathered the plates in order to set the table, but placed them on the edge of the wash sink. She took the last cup of coffee, and did not think to make more, and had to be asked more than once to step aside so they could finish preparing the meal.

Finally, Kevin took her by the hand and led her over to her spot at the table, insisting she sit down and rest. Her eyes went over to the rocker with that man whom she loved more than life itself, rocking a sleeping boy in his arms.

Tears welled up in her eyes and Kevin stooped down so he could look into her face. His years of experience comforting those who had lost loved ones, told him there was nothing he could say. Instead he just handed her his handkerchief, and as he expected, the tears and the words began to flow.

"I do not know how to help him," she whispered as she looked over at the sleeping boy. "I have been so self-absorbed that I totally overlooked Little Ben and his feelings. I sent Rebecca and him off to the Bensons and just assumed he was playing and having a good time. What kind of a mother am I that I completely missed how much he was hurting?"

"You are a marvelous Mama, Sarah," Kevin said earnestly. "You have survived a tragic event, and there is much to be said for that. As for Little Ben, well, you cannot keep life from happening to your children, Sarah. He is grieving, as are we all. And his grief has called his Mama's heart to his aid," he said smiling. "You noticed! Because that is what a Mama does. Punishing yourself will do no good. Give yourself the grace you would extend to your children."

The afternoon passed quietly with many bouts of sorrow and tears. A darkness hung over the little cabin as they noticed Granny's little coat hanging from the hook by the door, and her tiny apron hanging from a nail in the kitchen, and found themselves setting a place for her at the table. With all the company gone the quiet seemed like a tomb, and nothing they did could be done without thinking of Granny and how much they missed her.

A knock sounded at the door, so softly they were not sure if it had happened or not. They waited and listened intently as another knock sounded. Sarah got up and walked to the door, cracking it a bit so as to see if it was human or animal, and was delighted to see Bernie and Dorothy standing there with their guitars!

"Welcome," Sarah said as she swung the door wide open. They had brought their dog with them, and the effect on Little Ben was amazing. The larger dog, King, was terrified of Dusty, and the antics of that huge dog trying to escape the exuberance of the puppy's energetic interest and playfulness was a great source of amusement for them all.

"I hope you don't mind our bringing our dog," Bernie said. "He is really old, and when the fire dies down in the house when we are gone, his bones begin to hurt him."

Dorothy smiled and said, "Besides, he keeps me warm in the buggy. I wrap him up beside me and we both are warm in the worst of weather." At this, Grace took a good look at Dorothy and noticed how frail she looked. She had not noticed this before, but now as she looked at her, she saw a sorrow in her eyes, much like she had seen in Little Ben's eyes so many times before.

As the adults chatted, Ben wrestled on the floor with Dusty and King and was a happy child again, until his mind forgot she was gone, and he rose from the floor to show Granny the dogs. A darkness fell on him, and sorrow flooded his very soul. Instead of crying, he simply stared at the floor with absolutely no expression on his face.

This time, Sarah noticed immediately. "Little Ben, come over here and look at these wonderful musical instruments Mr. and Mrs. Siers brought." She held out her hand for him to come sit with her, and he did what was expected of him.

Bernie showed the children how the sound changed on the guitar when he placed his fingers on each string, lengthening it, or shortening it to change the pitch. "Little short strings make high pitched sounds, just like little animals do," he said as he ran his fingers down the neck of the guitar. "But the longer, larger strings make lower sounds, just like larger animals do." He had thought the comparison to the animals might catch the young boy's eye, however, he saw nothing in the child's eyes at all. "How about we play a joyful tune called, Goin' Up to Cripple Creek?"

The instant he began stomping his foot on the ground to establish the rhythm, Sarah picked up the pounding rhythm and began clapping her hands and tapping her foot, bouncing Little Ben who leaned quietly against her leg. She watched Little Ben in the hopes that he would find joy in the moment, but his expression never changed.

Bernie and Dorothy were certainly making a joyful noise with the two guitars playing expertly as they sang, "Goin' up to Cripple Creek! Goin' on the run! Goin' up to Cripple Creek to have a little fun!" Dorothy was a bit more reserved than Bernie who was stomping his foot and occasionally hitting his guitar to accent the rhythm that was pounding through the walls of the little cabin.

Kevin and Ben found themselves caught up in the moment, clapping and laughing as the singers sang faster and faster. When the song was finished the Waters family had their first big, hearty laugh since Christmas day, and it felt sublime.

Sarah looked down at Little Ben with certainty that he was by now caught up in the celebration of music, but instead he turned and looked at her and said, "Mama, can I go on up to the loft now. I am really tired."

Sarah's heart dropped. She had no idea how to reach this child: *this* child she did not know. She knew how to comfort and tease the little boy she had lived with day after day for over a year, but this little guy was an enigma to her, and she felt helpless to reach him, because wherever he had gone was beyond her, and she felt at a disadvantage, unfairly, because she had never been a *real* mother.

Her face must have dropped, she thought because at that, Bernie and Dorothy stood to leave. "We did not mean to impose," Dorothy said. "We just hoped we could lift your spirits a little. We know how quiet it is after everyone leaves, and we just hoped we could…"

Kevin stepped up and said, "And you certainly did! I was afraid I had forgotten how to laugh, and your kindness brought us a badly needed reprieve from all the sorrow."

Grace had watched Mrs. Siers' entire demeanor change when she was playing the guitar and singing. She had not seemed fragile, nor sickly as her fingers played the guitar and she watched her husband as she sang. "Mrs. Siers," Grace said, "I was wondering if you thought I could learn to play a guitar as you do!"

Dorothy's eyes widened and her face filled with joy as she reassured Grace that she certainly could learn to play.

"Could I come by sometime then? Maybe you could show me a little about it, just to see if it was possible for me to learn?"

Grace was amazed at the transformation in Mrs. Siers at the thought. She stood taller, seemed stronger, and walked with purpose as she left the house.

By the time the goodbyes were said, and the couple had left for the evening, Little Ben was already in his bed far beyond the well-meaning words Sarah had intended to say to him.

Kevin and Benjamin went outside to make sure the horse was fed and cared for, as Sarah and Grace began taking up supper and washing the dishes.

They worked side by side for several moments, then Sarah swallowed her pride, turned to Grace and said, "I was wondering if you could shed some light on how to help Little Ben through all this. He seems so quiet and lost within himself that I just…" She burst into tears and Grace quickly dried her hands and put her arms around her Mama.

"Oh, Mama! Come. Let us sit down and have a cup of coffee and talk. You must be exhausted."

"I did not know you drank coffee," Sarah said.

"I don't," Grace said. "I just thought it was the right thing to say," she said with a giggle.

Sarah looked up, grateful for the comfort and acceptance she always found in her daughter. "I love you, Grace Waters." Sarah said as she placed her hand on top of Grace's.

"I love you, too, Mama. And I am so sorry. I had not even noticed how upset you were about Little Ben until just now. I have been so wrapped up in my own sorrow that I have been careless with the feelings of others I suppose."

At this Sarah's tears and laughter flowed freely. "Oh, my dear Grace. I fear there is a lot of that going on. It is exactly how I feel about Little Ben. I was so immersed in my own self-pity about losing Mama, that I didn't know what a hard time Little Ben was having with it. He seems to have gone somewhere I cannot follow, not even to comfort him."

Grace said thoughtfully, "To be perfectly honest, I had not noticed the difference in him." She examined her life with him carefully, and said, "I guess when it was just the two of us, I had so much to deal with, finding food, a dry place to sleep, the baby when it came, that I just never had time to coddle him. He just had to take life as it came." She was thoughtful for a minute and then said, "I fear that I am to blame for this, Mama. When Benji would cry or whine for food, I would just tell him to keep it to himself. I was doing the best I could, and he would just have to live with it."

The shame on her face prompted Sarah to come to her aid, "Grace, you did a marvelous thing just keeping the three of you alive. You did the best you could, with what you had at the time. Please do not blame yourself."

"But I do. I did not take time to even consider his feelings. I was just worried about what I was going through."

"Alright, enough of that. You will not realize until you are much older, what an extraordinary thing you managed to do at such an early age. So I want you to put that away for now, and think of it only when you are much older, and have a better perspective. Meanwhile, life is for learning, and if Little Ben learned how to hide his feelings, he will just have to learn how to express them." And with that, Sarah patted Grace on her knee, stood and said, "Now, would you like some more coffee?"

Grace smiled as she remembered her shock when she first attempted to drink coffee, and said, "Milk please, Mama."

Chapter Eight

The next few days drug by as they mourned the tiny, little woman who had made such an impact, and brought such joy into their lives.

They cleaned, they made meals and ate, but the spark had gone out of their lives. Everyone had carefully avoided going into Granny's room and Little Ben was still quiet and withdrawn.

"Family, if we could gather around the table," Kevin started, "I have something I would like to discuss with you."

It was the first event that had actually captured their interest since the funeral, and they all rose to the occasion by bringing chairs to the table.

"Coffee anyone?" Kevin asked as he poured himself a cup and approached his place at the table.

"Yes, I would like a cup," Benjamin said.

"I would also," Sarah said as she rose to assist him. "Let me help, Kevin."

"No, no! I am fine," Kevin said as he used the time to gather his courage to actually present what he had been thinking. It had never occurred to him until that very moment that they may not like the idea, or what he would do if they turned him down.

Little Ben got a cup of milk and sat by his father, and sipped it like coffee whenever Benjamin took a drink.

"Well, I would like to discuss something with you that has been on my mind for some time," Kevin began. "As you know I should be leaving soon to go back to my parish in Parkersburg."

Little Ben did not say a word, or move in any way, but huge fat tears rolled down his cheeks and dripped onto the table. He still had that haunting stare which showed no feelings at all, but his tears made it clear to everyone there that he could not bear one more loss.

"Now wait a minute, Little Man," a nickname Kevin had started using for Little Ben. "Come over here and sit on my lap for a minute." He pulled the boy onto his lap, noticing the unchanged expression on the boy's face.

"I have been old enough to retire now for quite some time, but I never had any reason to," Kevin looked around the table at the faces he had come to know and love, and continued, "until now."

The realization of what he had said occurred to Little Ben first. "You mean it, Uncle Kevin?" His face lit up as he turned to hug the bear of a man upon whose lap he sat.

"Well, there are several things that must be settled first," Kevin warned. He was pleased that Little Ben had just assumed he would be living with them, yet there were others to consider as well. "I would indeed love to retire and come home…" He was going to say "if that is alright with the four of you, and if all the arrangements could possibly be worked out," but the table erupted with squeals of joy and they began hugging him with such an unexpected celebration that he was taken aback.

"Oh, Kevin, you can have Mama's room!" Sarah exclaimed as Benjamin pounded him on the back in agreement with Sarah.

"Now, please, I must ask you to return to your seats, I want you to hear my entire proposition." Kevin was overwhelmed and yet aware that he was not really a part of the family, and wanted to offer what he could. "I must say, I was pleasantly surprised at your response," he wiped his eyes and nose on his handkerchief, and then continued, "and I thought that I might indeed rent Granny's room from you until I could purchase a place of my own, or perhaps build something appropriate."

He was met by confused stares from every single person at the table.

"Rent?" Sarah's eyes were as round as saucers. "Rent a room from your family?"

Next Benjamin found his voice and said, "Kevin, you are as much a part of this family as we are!" Benjamin did not realize just how revealing that statement was to Kevin, and continued, "This is your home! We want you to come home and live here with us. There will be no rent, or time limit. You can stay here the rest of your life if you want. And in case you did not notice, we are pleased you want to!"

The shock and surprise that registered on Kevin's face melted into smiles and tears as he realized they were being completely truthful with what they were saying, and the entire family erupted in to making plans, and how Little Ben could show his Uncle Kevin when and how to tap Maple trees. They were lifted from mourning for this short period of time and the relief was welcomed beyond belief.

"So here is how I imagined it," Kevin began. "I, thought I might take the children with me to Parkersburg. I would resign my position, and the children could help me go through my things and pack up my belongings. It is totally up to you, though," he said as he nodded at Ben and Sarah.

"You said, the children." Sarah stated. "Do you also want to take Rebecca?"

"Well, I was looking forward to showing all the children off at the rectory, but if you are not comfortable with that…" Kevin said.

The Little Ben and Grace broke out into a cacophony of irrefutable reasons why this would be the best solution, and why they should be allowed to go.

Ben and Sarah looked at each other with the same worry on their minds. They could not share with Kevin that they were worried about somebody recognizing the children, but they needed to think that through.

"Do you think it would be safe?" Ben asked as he looked at Sarah and the children. A hush fell over the table as the four of them weighed the dangers against the opportunity.

Kevin was aware there was something going on he was not privy to, and watched as they disappeared into a time and place he had never been a part of. Sensing the uncomfortableness of the moment, he said, "We would go directly from the sleigh to the church, and then the children would be inside the rectory until we are ready to leave." Seeing the relief on their faces, he added, "They will even be taking their meals with the rest of the priests who live there, so the risks will be minimal."

They each looked at the others to weigh what they were thinking and Kevin thought he saw an opportunity that might bring the results he hoped for. He continued, "I can assure you that the children will be kept quite safe under the continuous eyes of the priests and nuns who reside there."

He realized this was exactly what they needed to hear, but did not want to take them against their better judgement, so he added, "Of course, if you think there is any chance they might not be safe, I do not want to take them. I could not bear being the one who caused any harm to happen to them."

"I think it will be fine," Grace began. She wondered how to convey her message without exposing her secret and continued, "We have grown quite a bit since we were there before. I think we are quite healthy enough to endure the journey without becoming as sickly as we were at the end of the last trip."

Sarah and Ben both processed the fact that the children were hardly recognizable as those two malnourished waifs who appeared out of the trees and shrubs the first time they saw them. Their eyes locked and a silent agreement passed between them.

"I think you are right, Grace," Sarah said, "You have grown quite a bit, but you would have to be careful. We would not want anything to happen to you."

Grace nodded knowingly.

Ben said, "If you think it is safe for Little Ben, Grace, then I would trust that. But you both must stay close to Uncle Kevin, do not wander around on your own, keep Rebecca with you at all times, and wear your hats and scarves when you are outside."

The children realized it was more for a disguise that Ben suggested that, but for Kevin, it was meant to be against the cold weather's chill. Both children nodded in understanding.

"When will you leave?" Sarah asked. She was nervous, of course, but reminded herself that she could not keep her children by her side forever, and sighed deeply as she waited for the answer.

"I thought we could leave day after tomorrow, if that is alright with you." Kevin watched for their reaction and was pleased when it was decided that day after tomorrow would be the day.

Grace said, "Tomorrow we should clean Granny's room so when we get back, Uncle Kevin can move right in."

Ben and Sarah nodded in agreement, but Little Ben just sniffed as the tears rolled down his cheeks again. Kevin suggested that he just take the bed by the door, but the boy had already climbed the steps to the loft where he lay silently, crying for his beloved Granny.

Sarah rose to go to him, but Ben put his hand on hers and said softly, "This is the first real cry he has had. Let him be."

It broke Sarah's heart when she realized Ben was right, but she managed to control her instinct to go to him, and sat back down in the chair.

Little Ben finally cried himself to sleep and truly rested for the first time since the day Granny died.

Chapter Nine

The next day dawned with a purpose. Grace brought in snow to melt for cleaning and washing, and Sarah retrieved rags from the rag box. Kevin followed the women into the room where he finally announced, "Please, I am used to caring for myself. I would like very much to help, if I might be so bold."

Sarah had just heard Rebecca awaken with a cry and turned to Kevin, handing him her wash rag and the bucket of soapy water intended for cleaning the window. "Here, you may certainly take over the window washing while I tend to Miss Rebecca!" Her smile brightened the entire room as she left, thankful for the activity of once again cleaning and caring for the happy baby.

Grace had stripped the bed and piled the sheets up in the middle of the floor, knocking Granny's little bird house off the end table. She knelt to pick it up just as Kevin's big hand covered the little bird house. The look in his eyes was wistful as he stood and examined the little house he had retrieved so many times for the homeless lady when he brought her in for soup on those cold winter nights. His eyes filled with tears, and without thinking he said, "She had had this for years, you know."

Grace was taken aback by his words, but just stared at him without making a sound. He looked up into her eyes and realized he had almost given away that he had known Granny, or Anna, for many years before she and Sarah had pulled her off the streets and brought her home.

They stared at each other for an awkward moment, then both resumed their missions. Grace was not quite sure what to make of his words, but she realized her family was not the only one with secrets. She turned and looked at Kevin with new eyes, but returned to her work quickly when Kevin looked back at her.

Then at that moment, Kevin heard a noise at the door and turned to see Little Ben leaned against the doorway, watching them tear apart his Granny's room. "Little Man, would you mind helping me for a moment. There is a place I cannot reach on my own."

Ben rose to the challenge and ran to Kevin's side. "See? The top of those windows are just too far for me to reach. I thought I would lift you into the air. Why, you could sit on my shoulder and wash the tops of those windows for me if you would."

Little Ben was thrilled with the fear of sitting way up in the air on Uncle Kevin's shoulder, and also elated that he was the only one in the household who could!

Just as the last corner of the window sparkled, Grace said, "Look at this!"

Kevin lowered the boy to the ground and they both turned to see Grace sitting down onto the edge of the bed with a stack of papers in her hands.

"What are those?" Kevin asked as he joined her, seated on the bed.

She passed the papers to him, one at a time as she first showed them to her brother, and then on to Kevin. "They are Granny's drawings," Grace said. "These are beautiful!"

Kevin asked what they were of in particular, and Grace replied, "Just everyday things! Papa sitting at the table drinking coffee. Mama rocking Rebecca. Just odds and ends of things. Oh, look! Here is Little Ben in the garden!"

Little Ben took the picture from her hands and smiled at the likeness of him in his bibbed overalls he had already outgrown since last summer.

"What is this one?" Grace asked. "It isn't of us, or our garden. And that is not Papa. I don't understand."

Little Ben took the paper out of her hand and stared down at it for only a moment. Then his face broke into an ear to ear smile, and he said, "Oh, yea! That is Hank!" Without explanation, he ran into the big room and shouted, "Look, Mama! This is Hank!" He placed it on the table so everyone could see, and was proud that he, and only he, knew what this picture was about. He looked up into the faces of Ben, Sarah, Grace, and Uncle Kevin, and retold the story as told to him by Granny, of the old mule whose owner tried to bury him alive.

His baby face was covered with tears as he remembered Granny's warning that, "Worry and laziness don't mix. You gotta keep movin' and shakin' those troubles off your shoulders. Especially when you don't feel like it. When you don't feel like it is when you got to fight the most! Ok?" Granny's words resounded in his head as if she had just said them today.

His breathing became deeper and deeper, and he threw himself into his Mama's arms and said, "I miss her, Mama! I miss her and I want her back. It isn't fair! It isn't fair!"

Sarah looked up at Kevin as he nodded and closed his eyes slowly. This was what the Little Man needed to do, to let it go and share his grief with his family. Kevin motioned with a nod of his head, for Grace to return with him into Granny's room so Ben and Sara could have some time with Little Ben.

As they worked and cleaned, Ben worked out his fears and anger with his parents who loved him more than life itself. They knew it was not over, but at least Little Ben was talking with them, sharing with them, and hopefully, letting them help carry his burdens.

An exhausted family sat down at the evening table, held hands and prayed. Little Ben had insisted they set a place for Granny, and after the prayer, he scooted into her chair.

Ben glanced at Sarah while passing the mashed potatoes and with a wink, said, "Little Ben. Tell me how you intend to honor Granny's memory?" The boy looked confused, so Ben continued, "Well, your Mama and I were just wondering how you intend to 'shake your troubles off your shoulders?' You know your Granny was very wise about that, and we think it would be a great way to honor her by taking her advice and finding something to do that will keep you busy."

"Well," Little Ben said after a thoughtful moment, "I am going to work really hard to help Uncle Kevin get packed up. I will carry boxes, and if he needs me to, I will sit on his shoulders and clean every window in the rectory!" He beamed for a minute because he remembered the word, 'rectory,' because for some unknown reason, he liked that word. It sounded like a good name for a dog, and made a mental note to name his next dog that.

Kevin said, "I would greatly appreciate that, Little Man!"

Knowing looks passed between the adults at the table. Kevin knew without asking they wanted him to keep the boy busy, and remind him of Granny's words. She was a wise woman to have prepared him for this moment.

The children retired early as did Kevin. He had worked harder, physically, than he had in years, and wondered how long it would take his body to adjust to being a farmer after all those years of being rather sedentary. But before he had time to process any answers, he fell into a deep and restful sleep.

Ben and Sarah were wrapped in each other's arms as the moon shone into the room, lighting their faces.

"So... three or four days completely alone," Ben said with a knowing smile.

"Ben Waters!" Sarah said with a blush. "Here I was worried about missing the children, and you..." her voice trailed off as she hid her face in his nightshirt.

"Well, we never did have a proper honeymoon!" Ben laughed and rolled toward her, tickling her ribs and listening to that golden giggle that only she could make.

"Stop!" She whispered loudly, "the children will hear us!"

"Well, there are worse things than children hearing their parents laugh when they are together!"

At that Sarah relaxed and laughed softly. "I love you, Ben Waters."

"I love you, too, Sarah Waters," he said with a depth of feeling he did not know was possible. They looked deeply into each other's eyes and kissed passionately.

But Sarah remembered Granny, and moved closer into his arms and said, "How will we ever live without her, Ben?"

Ben sighed deeply, hugged her against him and said, "We will all grieve together, cry together, support each other, and then heal together. We have no choice but to learn to live with the fact that she is gone, but we can keep her memory alive, and someday I hope we have more happy memories of her than we have grief. That is what I hope at least. It is hard to imagine, but it is my hope."

Chapter Ten

Little Ben was up with the chickens, excited about the day's adventure. He had stoked up all the fires, and had potatoes and bacon frying on the stove before any of the adults had awakened.

Grace was the first one out and smiled at her brother's enthusiasm. She had regretted the way she had treated him when he had brought his troubles to her when they were smaller, and was relieved to see it had not permanently damaged him. To Little Ben's surprise, Grace was overcome with how much she really did love her brother, crossed the room and engulfed him in a huge bear hug.

"What was that for?" Little Ben asked indignantly.

"Oh, I just do not think I tell you enough how much I love you, Benji." She took up a pan and began cracking eggs into it. "I think I am going to do that more often!" She giggled at his look of horror and began whipping the eggs with great fervor.

"You seem happy this morning," Ben said to Grace.

"I guess I am excited about going to Parkersburg with Uncle Kevin," Grace said realizing for the first time just how excited she was.

"Yea, me, too," Ben said. "You don't think Granny would mind do you? I mean, would she think I wasn't sad long enough if she saw how excited I am?"

"No, Ben. She would want you to get up and get on with life. If she were here right now, she would swat you with a dish rag and tell you to stop moping around and git goin'! Now you know she would!"

Suddenly the memories of Granny were not as hurtful as they had been. It made them feel like they had had a visit with her, and that made the chores go more quickly.

Before they knew it they were on the sleigh with their Uncle Kevin, who had Rebecca safely covered with his coat and a blanket, scooting along on the frozen river, packages in hand, and tucked securely under a heavy wool blanket.

Sarah had packed a lunch for them, complete with baked potatoes to keep their hands warm until they finally ate them. Kevin was thrilling them with stories about the rectory and his friends who lived there with him. He warned them of Sister Sistine, whom everyone lovingly called Sis in the privacy of the kitchen and dining room. "She will pinch your cheeks off if you don't stop her! She loves children and will feed you so much you will not be able to fit into the sleigh on the way home!"

The children were quite amused, so he continued, "But watch out for Father Ed. He does NOT like children, or anything else that might make a mess or interfere with his meticulous keeping of his fine stock of wines and spirits."

"Really?" Ben asked with astonishment on his face. "I didn't think priests and Nuns did things normal people do."

Kevin laughed heartily at that, and said, "Well, wait until you meet Sister Mary Margret. She has the mouth of a sailor. I could not believe it myself until I heard her after her bucket of dirty water somehow got kicked over onto her clean floor." He looked at Little Ben's face and amended his statement somewhat. "But I do believe she was very stressed at that moment, so we could forgive her for that, right?"

Little Ben nodded and smiled, then was quiet as could be for a minute. "I can sleep with Sissy, right?"

Kevin hesitated briefly. He had never heard Ben call her Sissy for one thing, and for another, the look of fear and dread on Little Ben's face was quite frightening.

"Yes, of course, Little Man," he said reassuringly. "Of course you can sleep with Grace if you want. Is everything alright?"

Little Ben looked up with a peaceful look and said, "Sure! I just wanted to be certain."

Kevin noticed the look of compassion and something like gratitude on Grace's face as she and Little Ben looked at each other, but knew not to ask.

By the time they arrived at the rectory it was dark. The children were cold and exhausted, so Kevin asked Sis to fix them a quick meal which they ate hungrily. He then showed them to their room, built up the fire, and said goodnight.

As they cuddled in the massive bed, Grace said to her brother, "Benji, I appreciate that you asked to sleep with me. I must admit I was a little worried, too."

"Nobody is ever going to hurt you again, Sissy. I am not very big, but I am wiry, and I am short enough to get a good punch in between their legs if I have to. And you could run!"

Grace was touched by his forethought and said so. "You are becoming a fine man, Ben." She looked down at him and cradled his face in the palm of her hand. "Mama would be so proud of you," she said as a tear slid down her face.

"She would be proud of both of us," Ben said. "I never thanked you for all you did for me, did I, Sissy?"

"You do not have to thank me," she said, "It was what Mama asked me to do. And I am glad I got to."

"But I do need to thank you, Sissy. When I was a little kid, I didn't think much about it. But I am becoming a man now, and a man thinks about those things."

Grace managed a thoughtful and sincere face, and said, "Oh, I see." She tugged the covers over her shoulders and said, "Well, then. I accept your thanks, and appreciate it."

"Really? You aren't making fun of me are you?"

"She sat up onto one elbow and said, "No! I am not making fun of you. It pleases me to see the man you are becoming, and I take your appreciation to heart. Now go to sleep! We have a lot of work to do tomorrow."

The next two or three days flew by. Kevin had them sorting and boxing up the many, many, many, possessions he had collected over the years. In fact, there were *so* many, he found it difficult to believe how much there was. Some of what he had collected had particular emotional attachments to him, like the small white Bible he had been given by one of his mother's friends when he entered the monastery. There were letters from his brother stored in a small wooden box, some toys he had taken from his home when he left, and then surprisingly few artifacts he had been given, or had purchased during his life as a priest.

But his books were his family. Try as he may, he could not bear giving his beloved books away. How many nights had they kept him company? How many times had he used them to distract him from his grief over the family he had lost? He knew each one well enough to find within seconds, a particular message he needed, or story that would be appropriate for an individual who needed counseling. No, his books were his treasures, and although he would have to take several crates with him, he felt it was well worth the effort.

The day arrived when it was time to travel home. The children had seen quite enough of the city of Parkersburg, and were getting really homesick, just as Kevin was becoming overwhelmed regarding how much he would miss his own quarters where he had lived for what seemed like a lifetime.

"Children," he said, "why don't the two of you go down and be sure we have everything we packed. Count the boxes of books, be certain my three pieces of luggage are there, and scoot that box of New Testaments away from the other boxes. I want to leave those with Father Ed."

"Are you not coming with us, Uncle Kevin?" Little Ben asked with a trembling chin. Kevin was touched by the child's attachment to him, and gently said, "Yes, of course, Little Man. I just need a moment to say goodbye to my friends and take a look around to be certain I have not forgotten anything. Go on, now. I will bring Rebecca with me when I come."

Little Ben looked confused and was about to comment on how they had already looked the apartment over several times, when Grace knowingly turned him around by the shoulders and led him out the door. As she turned to wave at her Uncle Kevin, he smiled at her and whispered, "Thank you."

As they stepped into the sunlight, Grace looked up at the birds sitting on top of the surrounding buildings. Having lived most of her life in cities, she was both pleased and surprised to find that her heart was now in the country where birds landed in trees, and sang into her open windows in the spring. She breathed deeply and realized that even the air smelled differently in the city than it did at home, and homesickness overcame her, bringing tears to her eyes. She shook her head in order to clear her thoughts and regain her composure, and began looking around for Little Ben.

"Benji! Beeeeen-ji! Where are you?" She shouted as loudly as she could, but he was nowhere in sight. She felt her body go numb as she looked up and down the street and saw no sign of Ben.

"I'm right here, Sissy!" he shouted while running toward her. He was holding up the fat red apple he had charmed a merchant into giving him.

"You scared me to death, Benjamin! Don't run off like that without telling me!"

"Well, well," a deep voice said.

Grace turned to find a huge silhouette standing before her blocking the sun. "If it isn't Miss Oddy and her little runt of a brother, Benji."

The sound of his voice, and the smell of his breath were all Grace needed in order to recognize him. She need not see his face clearly to know it was Mr. Dunge, the man who ran the orphanage she and Benji had escaped. She should have thought about the fact that the Orphan Train would be coming through, but now it was too late.

"RUN, BENJI!" Grace shouted at her brother. She hoped he would obey, but she knew in her heart he would not leave her.

"You know I'll hurt your sister if you do!" Dunge shouted at the boy, knowing him well enough to know he would never leave Oddy behind.

Little Ben stood frozen in place and looked helplessly into his sister's eyes, chin quivering.

"Now, according to my paperwork, I own the two of you." He was enjoying the looks of fear on their faces so he allowed that to hang in the air for a few seconds, just for the sake of drama and torture. Then he added, "Now, you can come peacefully, or I can have the police escort you to the jail where you and your brother would be separated, for… well, hopefully, only a few months."

Grace's breath caught in her chest. Separated? Just like that, she had fallen back into the world of terror she thought they had finally escaped.

He was enjoying the horror on their faces and thought of it as his reward for all the heartache they had given him. After all, he had almost lost his position as Headmaster of the orphanage after those two had disappeared, and they well deserved a great deal of punishment. Yes, he had earned his pound of flesh, and he was going to get it.

His demeanor changed as did his wicked smile. Lust filled his face as he stared down at the beautiful young woman who once was the skinny, little urchin he had known. He looked at her slowly from head to toe and then back again, and said, "Perhaps I have been hasty. A jail is no place for a young lady like you. Perhaps I could find a hotel room close to mine, for you to stay in until all this is settled." He licked his lips sickeningly and smiled at the horrified young woman who was feeling as helpless as the child he had hurt so many times before.

At that moment, Little Ben took measure, bent low and with full force, ran forward and buried his little head square between Dunge's legs. The man grabbed himself with both hands, blew out all the air in his lungs and bent over double.

As if they had rehearsed it, Grace stepped forward, balled up her right fist and with a swift uppercut, hit him square in the eye, by way of his now broken nose. By the time her left fist hit him in the ear, Little Ben had regained his balance and in an instant was on top of the man who now lay writhing on his right side in the dirt, his hands still between his legs. Grace added her weight to their victim by straddling his shoulder and then proceeded to pound the left side of his face with her fists until her arms were completely worn out. But that did not stop her, she continued her beating by kicking him with her right foot repeatedly, peeling the hide off his left ear. All the years of frustration poured out of her in a rage she had never realized she could experience. She screamed, cried, and pounded on her tormenter until she was exhausted physically, mentally, and emotionally.

Little Ben was doing his best to continue his attack on the man's most delicate parts, by kicking him repeatedly from the backside as Dunge lay in a fetal position, completely defenseless to the attack.

Suddenly, Little Ben was lifted into the air by one of the passersby, as Grace was unceremoniously dragged off to one side by another. The commotion had caused such a stir it had caught the attention of those on the main floor of the church. Sis, Father Ed and others poured out onto the street to see what was happening.

Kevin came running from the rectory, handed Rebecca to Sis, and ran over to investigate why Grace and Little Ben were being man handled by these total strangers.

To the onlookers, the man had just been having a pleasant conversation with the children, when suddenly the "two little monsters," as one man put it, attacked the fine gentleman, with absolutely no provocation!

A heavy set man with a white apron on, came running down the street with an officer of the law he had found two blocks away. "There they are," the stranger announced as he pointed to the three dirty and badly disheveled people before him.

The crowd had helped Dunge to his feet and dusted him off, found his hat and returned it to him, and were all talking at once about the very unusual brawl they had witnessed.

"All right! All right!" the officer said to the crowd that had gathered. "The party is over, go on about your business! I will handle this, go on now! Off with you!" Only Kevin stood nearby, staring at the man the children had attacked, trying to place whether or not he knew who he was. He decided he did not, but somehow his looks reminded him of someone.

The officer turned and looked in amazement at the two children who were clearly from a good home and wearing fine clothing that was now ripped to shreds and covered with dirt and blood.

Grace was rubbing her right fist and arm to ease the pain she was feeling after the pounding she had given Dunge. Her right shoe was covered with blood from her attempt to dislodge the gentleman's left ear from where it sat, annoyingly, on the side of his head, and she was panting from all the exertion.

Little Ben, however, was looking quite pleased with himself as his plan of attacking a full grown man had worked quite nicely! Completely oblivious of any pain or discomfort from his own wounds, the boy was not finished with the man who had hurt his sister, and was hoping the policeman would turn his head for a moment, so he could deliver just one more blow.

Dunge, however, did not look as though he had weathered the storm nearly as well as the children. He was limping for one thing, and kept turning his body away from the boy, while his head was turned in a way so as to keep his eye on the girl. The entire right side of his face was bleeding profusely, and his left ear was nearly torn off: a sight that made Grace smile sardonically.

"Let's get you some medical help first, then we will all discuss this later," the officer said with great compassion. "Come with me, children!"

"No! Absolutely not!" Dunge said emphatically. "I am the head of the New York City Shelter and Home for Orphaned Children. I *own* these children, by the authority of the state of New York! They are the runaways I have been looking for, for over a year. I am certain you have seen the fliers, Officer!"

The policeman looked at the children and recognized them immediately. "Yes, yes, I do recognize these children from the fliers," he said as the pieces fell into place in his mind. "I am afraid you children are going to have to come with me. Although I do not appreciate the word, *own*, when speaking of children," he said as he looked disgustedly at Dunge, "I believe he does have custody of you two. You will be returned to New York on the next train, and they can sort it out." At least the officer had the compassion to look at the children with understanding and empathy.

Kevin's head was swimming. He thought these were the children of Benjamin Waters. He had married Ben and Sarah so if anything happened to Ben, Sarah could have custody. He was confused. He had to think. He had to say something to stop what was happening, but what? "There must be some mistake!" he said frantically. "These are my sister's children!"

"So you must be the one who has been aiding and abetting these runaways! Officer, arrest this criminal!" Dunge said.

It was now Dunge's turn to be caught off guard. The officer smiled thoughtfully at Kevin and nodded. "Father Kevin," finally acknowledging his presence.

"Morris," Kevin returned the greeting with a nod.

The two men smiled at each other, then the officer turned and said, "I am afraid that if Father Kevin says these children are his niece and nephew that I would be inclined to believe him, sir. After all, I have known him for more than thirty years. And he *is* a Priest."

Dunge looked defeated, but only briefly. "You cannot deny that you recognize these children from their pictures! You said so yourself!"

The officer looked at Father Kevin and said, "I am afraid he is right, Father. The pictures make the children younger and not as well fed, but they are the boy and girl in the picture. Can you explain that, Father?"

At once Grace knew that he could not. And the last thing she wanted to do was to have her Uncle Kevin suggest they contact Ben and Sarah and bring them in for questioning. Before Kevin could speak, Grace said, "Yes, we are the children who escaped from the train last year."

Little Ben stared up at his sister in complete incredulity. "What are you doing, Sissy! We can't go back with him! You know he will…"

"Hush!" Grace said without looking at her brother. Immediately Little Ben fell silent, but he looked at Dunge with a threat in his eyes that made the horrible man step behind Officer Morris for protection.

Kevin had no idea how to help, what to say, or how to clear the confusion. He stood helplessly as he watched Grace continue.

"I took my brother and ran away from that horrid place because I thought I was going to die, and I didn't want Benji to be left alone there. I thought I could find him a good home somehow, but we just…"

She needed time to think. She did not want to mention Ben and Sarah, so she had to think where to go next with the story.

"There you have it," Dunge said. She admitted they are the ones, they belong to me!" Dunge saw the officer's eyes narrow and revised his statement reluctantly. "They are wards of the state of New York, and therefore are to be returned to me immediately!"

"Alright, I have heard your side of the story, now I want to hear what Father Kevin has to say. Father?" the officer said as he turned to look at the priest.

Kevin was at a loss. He had lied about his relationship to the children, and his head was still reeling from the news that these children were, only a year ago, in an orphanage in New York. He suddenly realized why the children looked so sorrowful when he mentioned his decision to go to an orphanage or a Monastery. His hesitation was quite suspicious to the law man, and a clear indication to Dunge that the good Father was lying.

Grace remembered who she was. She was the Granddaughter of a Granny who was tough as nails. A survivor, and better than that, she was a victor. Grace took a deep breath, lifted her chin and said, "When I left New York, as I said, I thought I was going to die. But I wasn't sick. I was with child."

Both Father Kevin and Officer Morris gasped. Dunge thought he was going to vomit, and all three men stood in complete shock, staring at Grace with their undivided attention. Little Ben just stared at his shoes as she continued, "I was with child because this sorry excuse for a human being, raped me night after night." The tears returned and her anger got the better of her. She stepped forward and landed a hearty kick right on the ridge of his shin. As the officer pulled her away from him, she screamed, "And I am not the only girl there he raped."

Dunge shouted, "You are a lying, little, b...," and raised his fist to hit her but was stopped by one of the largest and angriest priests anyone has ever encountered. It was all Kevin could do not to break the wrist of the man whose hand he had caught in mid-air. His other hand went around the man's throat, and he trembled with rage as the Godly man warred with the human being inside his heart and soul. He wanted to kill the man standing in front of him with every cell of his being. He wanted to murder this man who had done such a despicable thing to this beloved child. He had never experienced such rage, and such a desire to take the life of another human being, and the feelings terrified him.

He finally came to his senses as Dunge fell to his knees, red faced, and nearly unconscious. Only then did he become aware that both children were pulling on him, shouting, "Uncle Kevin," and begging him to let go. Morris, too, was calling his name and trying to pull him off Dunge, to no avail.

Suddenly, Kevin felt weak and completely spent. The news that Grace had been assaulted, and with child was too much for the peace loving man to begin to fathom. How she had remained so sweet and compassionate after all that was a conundrum too mysterious for him to solve in that moment, so he turned slowly and looked at the young woman he would have given his life to save, knelt and held out his arms to the children who ran into his embrace.

Dunge finally recovered enough to say, "Well, are you going to do your duty or not, Officer?"

Morris looked at the children, then Dunge, then back to the children. When Kevin stood, Grace and Little Ben turned and stood with Kevin's hands on their shoulders protectively.

Officer Morris said, "You said you were with child."

Grace nodded.

"What happened to the baby?" he continued. "Did it live?"

All eyes were on Grace. Kevin wished he could help her, but he knew nothing about her situation, so he watched as Grace stood and looked at the officer for a brief moment. Finally, she turned and looked at Rebecca. "She is right there."

Kevin's knees buckled. This was too much. He could not breathe and his heart pounded in his chest when he realized she was talking about Rebecca. He stared mindlessly as Sis, who had taken the nod as a request for the baby, walked forward and placed Rebecca in Grace's arms.

"Look at her," Grace said. "She looks exactly like him." There it was. The reason she could not love that baby as a mother should. Every time she looked at the child, she saw *his* face, *his* hair, *his* eyes, *his* hands, and *his* ears.

Kevin looked at Dunge and realized why he had looked so familiar. He looked *exactly* like Rebecca, and Officer Morris saw it, too. The red hair and blue eyes of the child were exactly those of her father. Even the shape of her face and mouth were those of the man now hated by everyone present.

"Now wait a minute," Dunge started as he began backing away from them, "you aren't going to take the word of a little whore are you?"

This time it was Kevin who had a cool head. He simply grabbed Dunge and roughly placed his hands behind his back where they were secured by Morris, who said, "I will take him to the local jail for now. I am sure there will be an investigation by the state of New York. Meanwhile," he said clearly so that Dunge would certainly hear, "I sure do hope the other inmates don't get word of what he did. There are a lot of fathers and brothers in there who will not take kindly to the likes of him." Dunge looked appropriately frightened at that, which pleased both Kevin and Morris.

"Father," Morris stopped and looked back at the priest, "I have my hands full at the moment with my prisoner." Morris said giving Dunge a shove. "Could I impose on you to return your niece and nephew to their family?"

The relief in Kevin's face was quite evident, "Yes. I can do that. Thank you, Morris."

"Take good care of them," Morris continued. "They certainly deserve all the good the Lord can give them."

"I will," Kevin said, and hugged the children to him protectively.

Morris stopped again and said, "I may need you to bring the child in again for the inquiry. I am sure they will take my word for it, but if not... Well, I know where to find you!"

No, you won't. You will have no idea where to find me after this day, Kevin thought as he made a mental note to not leave any information with the church as to his whereabouts.

"Could you wait just a minute?" Grace shouted to Officer Morris. She handed the baby to Kevin, turned and ran back toward the church. When she came back, she passed them and walked right up to Dunge.

She handed something to the police officer, then stepped back and looked up at Dunge boldly. "That is the New Testament," she said breaking eye contact. "You are going to have some time in there to think about your life. I hope you read this and find God's grace the way I have." She was looking at her shoes because what she was saying was difficult for her. She knew in her heart she did NOT mean it right now, but that she would someday, with God's help.

"God loves you," she said, then made eye contact with her rapist and continued, "even though you are a despicable person." She looked at the ground, took a deep breath, looked him boldly in the eye and continued, "This is your chance to find God. He has a plan for your life, even though..." Her voice trailed off and she looked at the ground to gather her thoughts and her composure. Finally, she said, "Well, I found God's Grace, and you can, too. It says it in there better than I can, so I suggest you read it while you are sitting in there with all the time in the world to think." She was relieved to have said what she wanted to say and turned to walk away.

She stopped, faced him again and said, "And I want to say one more thing. Uncle Kevin has taught us to say we are sorry when we are wrong, so I want to say I am sorry for trying to tear your ear off. That was wicked of me."

Kevin and Morris were caught off guard by her words, and could not help but laugh out loud. But they quickly regained their composure as she continued, "I just wanted to hurt you as badly as you had hurt me, but I know now that isn't possible. And," she stopped and took a deep breath, "I forgive you for what you did to me. Because that is what my God and my King expects of me." She stood there for a moment and looked at him as if she were going to say something else, but instead turned and walked back to her brother and Uncle Kevin.

Dunge looked completely baffled and stared at the back of the girl's head as she walked away. What had just happened? He had been forgiven? But he was the one who had control over her! How dare she act as if it was her right to release *him* from *her* grip. He was the one with the power over her! Morris tugged at his sleeve as the bewildered Dunge turned to go with the officer to the jail.

The sound of a wagon approaching interrupted their thoughts, and just as they turned to see what was happening, a boy jumped down off the wagon seat and began loading the boxes of books and other belongings. Kevin looked at his pocket watch and realized they were going to have to hurry if they wanted to make the sleigh home.

Grace grabbed her grip off the wagon and said, "I need to change Rebecca before we go. I will hurry," she promised as she disappeared into the rectory. When she returned, her hair was straightened and she was wearing a clean dress. She seemed to have gotten control of her feelings and was a happy child again.

"Ok. We are ready to go, now!" She shouted with a smile and joined Little Ben in the back of the wagon.

Kevin wished desperately that they could talk about what had happened, but the presence of the driver allowed no privacy. They drove along in silence until they reached the river with Kevin's head spinning at all the strange information he had received that day. He had been aware that the Water's family had secrets, and yet the ones that unfolded in his presence today had been far more drastic than he had imagined. He was disappointed he could not discuss the day's events with Grace on the way to the boat.

The sleigh held all of Kevin's boxes, their luggage, and with Rebecca sitting on someone's lap, one more passenger, a tall man who was quiet and stayed to himself. The crowded situation was not conducive to a private conversation, so again, Kevin sat with thousands of questions pounding in his head, but no answers.

Grace and Little Ben appeared to be not at all shaken. Grace played peek-a-boo with Rebecca and chatted light heartedly with Little Ben as if nothing at all had occurred, which only deepened the mystery for Kevin. When they left on the trip, Grace had been a delightful young, innocent, girl whom he loved with all his heart. Now, she was the mother of a child who was going on two years old, a priest in her own right, and a short, but mighty, prize fighter, as well. He would never see Grace the same way, ever. She was a woman to be respected, and he discovered he loved her even more.

Little Ben had always appeared to be just an innocent boy who was delightfully unaware of life and its troubles. But now that Kevin thought about it, he remembered the look of relief on both children's faces when Kevin had given permission for Little Ben to sleep with Grace. He could not help but wonder if that was Ben's way of protecting his sister, and if so Little Ben was not as innocent as he had believed. He was impressed with the children in his care, and grateful to God that he would walk through life with them.

Upon occasion, Kevin's and Grace's eyes would meet but then Ben would ask a question, or Rebecca would tug on Grace's hair and she would look away. There were so many questions left unanswered.

Chapter Eleven

Before they knew it, they were home. Ben and Sarah stood on the bank of the Little Kanawha River waving and encouraging the boat to dock so they could hug their loved ones. It was a glorious scene as they handed Rebecca to her 'mother,' and Sarah cooed and insisted that she had grown an inch while they were gone.

Kevin handed Little Ben to Benjamin, then held Grace's hand as she carefully stepped out of the boat onto land.

Ben had wanted to borrow Abram's sleigh to come get them, but Denzel had insisted on coming with them. He said the sleigh could be contrary sometimes, but Ben was not fooled. He knew he wanted to see Grace, and he was fine with that. As long as he was there with them, that is.

He was grateful he had both the sleigh and Denzel when he saw the amount of boxes Kevin had brought with him.

Kevin saw Ben looking at the boxes and said, "Yes. And they are all quite heavy, I must admit. They are full of books I am sorry to say."

Ben smiled and said, "Well, Sarah is going to love that. She loves to read and has a very limited supply I fear."

Before long the boxes, luggage, and family were packed tightly onto the sleigh for the long trip home. Denzel wanted Grace to sit beside him, but she insisted on sitting in the back with the rest of the family, making Kevin wonder if she would ever have a normal relationship with a man. His heart physically hurt for the lovely young woman who had been so badly mistreated, and then realized that only God could have changed all that pain into the wonderful woman she was becoming.

"There is a great deal of news to share with you," Sarah shared. First of all, the sad news. Reverend Morrison has been called back to his home. His father has passed away, and he has chosen to take a church near his mother so he can help with the farm and be there for her.

Little Ben took the news very hard. "NO! NO! He can't leave!" He burst into tears and was inconsolable. Sarah and Ben knew Little Ben would take it hard, but they were quite taken aback at how grief-stricken the boy was.

Kevin and Grace passed a knowing look between them. They understood the pressure he had been under, not only from that day, but from the passing of Granny, and now the loss of someone else in the community that he loved.

Sarah held him as he wept, and after a time, Grace asked loudly, "What other news is there, Mama?"

"Well, there's to be a Liar's Contest!" Sarah announced and then looked at Kevin and the children for their response.

"A Liar's Contest?" Grace asked with a smile on her face. "Do you mean, like, who told the biggest lie this year?"

Kevin thought that if the Waters family, including himself, entered it, no one else would have a chance. Why, he had told bold faced lies this very day!

But then Sarah spoke again. "No, you have to make up the biggest lie possible, and then they judge who the Biggest Liar is. It is something usually done in the summer, around campfires at coon hunts, but this year has been a hard one, and everyone thought it would be a great distraction for all of us... you know, an excuse to get together, eat, and laugh together."

"You said it is usually done in summer around a campfire. Surely you don't mean it will be held outside in the cold?" Kevin asked.

"No, it will be held in the church Sunday afternoon," Ben said. "The women are fixing a meal for right after church, then the contest will be held right there around the potbellied stove. It will be Rev. Morrison's last Sunday there, so he wanted there to be a nice get-together before he leaves."

Little Ben was sad again at the thought of losing another person he loved from his community, but the idea of seeing people compete for the Biggest Liar title made the news a bit more palatable.

For days, he tried to come up with a great lie. He tried them out on first, Sarah, then Grace, then Ben, then Kevin. He figured that Granny would have had a bunch of lies that he could have told and he missed her so much he burst into tears again. Finally, he decided to enlist the help of his best friend, Ira Benson.

"Mama, can I go down to the Bensons' today. Me and Ira are going to think up a good tale to tell at the Liar's Contest!" Ben was so excited about the prospect of going to Ira's and thinking up a good lie that he thought of nothing else.

Mama, on the other hand stood looking at him with one eyebrow raised.

"What?" Little Ben asked, but received no explanation.

"Let's see. I did all my chores." He said staring up into the face of a woman who obviously was still not pleased. "What?"

"Ask again," Mama said.

"Can I go down to Benson's today. "Cos me and... Oh. I get it. Ira and I are going to..."

"Yes. Ira and I are going to. Never put yourself first." Mama said. "You know, you are too old to have to be reminded every time you speak, young man."

"I know. I'll do better, I promise. Now can I go?"

"MAY I go, Benjamin Waters, Jr.! MAY I go?" she said with intention.

"If you want to! I'm riding Shank's Mare though. So if you don't mind walking."

Sarah burst into laughter, bent down and swooped Ben up in her arms, and kissed him all over his little freckled face. "I love you, Little Ben. Do I tell you that often enough?"

"You must, because I sure do know it! And I love you, too, Mama. But…"

"YES! Yes. You may go, but watch for the cave and do not go near the top of it. You know you cannot see it from above, so do not go running wildly through the woods."

"Ok, Mama! Thanks!"

Little Ben walked out into the field with a new found freedom. Last fall he had been too little to go on his own, but apparently they thought of him as an older boy now, and he was pleased about that. He was fairly certain he knew where the correct trail was, but just in case he came down on top of the cave, he would walk very slowly and be careful with each step.

He was so sure he had taken the right path that he was a little shocked when he actually came down on the other side of the cave. He saw the water trickling down as the creek that ran in front of the cave was beginning to thaw, and measured whether or not it was a good idea to climb back up and try to cross over the top of the cave in the snow, or whether he should go in front of it and risk falling into the water.

His decision was made for him when he heard a sound and froze in place. It had sounded like someone's foot sliding in the loose gravel. Then the thought occurred to him that perhaps it was a bear, and if so, he had no way to run from it. But then he heard a loud sniff. Did bears sniff?

He had no choice but to step around the corner and look in, being a little boy who was just a little too curious. But what he saw first frightened, and then intrigued him. It was another little boy, just his age, staring back at him, but this little boy had skin as dark as night.

"What are you doing here?" Ben asked.

The boy just shook his head, no, and kept looking over Ben's head at something on the bank.

Ben turned quickly to see what the boy was looking at, but whatever it was had disappeared. His eyes then went to the inside of the cave the Waters family had spent their first night together, and what he saw was evidence that they boy had been living there. A small fire, a stack of fire wood, and some bones of an animal that had certainly been his dinner.

"You look cold," Ben said, "why don't you come to my house. My Mama will fix you something good to eat and you can sleep in the loft."

The boy's eyes widened and he shook his head more vehemently and said, "You better git!"

Ben did not know if it was a warning or a threat, so he backed off and decided to go up and around the cave, just in case there was someone else in there that might grab him.

By the time he made it to the Bensons, he had worked it out in his head that he should tell no one about the boy. There was no real reason why, except he knew that it was something out of the ordinary and he just wanted to think up a good lie with Ira.

He climbed up onto the porch at the Benson's and knocked before entering. "Mrs. Benson, may I come in?" he asked before fully entering.

Midge came out of the kitchen wiping her hands on a dish towel and said, "Why of course you may come in, boy! You are always welcome in our home. Land sakes you have good manners and schooling! Where did you get that, Little Ben?"

"My Mama teaches us, Mrs. Benson. A LOT!" He rolled his eyes which brought laughter from Midge.

"Well, Ira is upstairs if you are wanting him," Midge said, then added with a smile, "And Maxine is in the kitchen helping me, if that is who you came to see."

Ben's face reddened and burned hot as fire. "No Ma'am! I came to see Ira. Me and hi… He and I are going to think up a lie to tell on Sunday at the Liar's Contest."

He turned to run up the steps and Midgie smiled at his back as he took the steps by twos in his attempt to get away from the embarrassment that threatened to burn him to a crisp if he didn't escape.

Before long, Benjamin came on horseback to take Little Ben home and the boys said their fair wells. On the way back, Little Ben had to stop twice to wet his shoes, which Benjamin thought was a little curious. When questioned, Little Ben explained that for some reason, he was extremely thirsty today and had to go to the kitchen several times for a drink of water.

"Did you see Maxine today," Ben asked his son.

"Well, yea! She was helping her Mama bake cookies, but that isn't why I went in there."

"It wasn't, huh? Well, did she offer you a cookie?"

"Yep, and I ate it, too. She said she had made it all by herself, but, I don't think so. She is younger than me. I bet her Mama helped her some."

Benjamin rode along with his son in his arms, smiling as he wondered if he and Maxine might someday get married. He remembered that first time they rode to church with the Benson's and Little Ben was showing off by holding the baked potatoes the Benson's had brought to keep their hands warm, on his ears to make Maxine laugh.

By the time they got home, Little Ben was sound asleep and it was almost completely dark.

The next day was Saturday, and it was Ira's turn to come up to the Waters' house, but the boys had decided instead to meet half way. They spent some time trying to catch a rabbit with their bare hands, and tried once, to catch a fish the same way.

Suddenly they heard something in the woods, and Little Ben thought briefly it might be the boy in the cave, but they were too far south for that. They crept closer and closer to the sound of the high pitched crying until they could hear what an old woman was saying.

"Oh, God! I am cold and hungry! Please God, just send me a pot of coffee and a loaf of bread and I will praise you Lord for your goodness! Please, God! If I could just have a pot of coffee and a loaf of bread, I would be so blessed, Sweet Jesus, please, please, hear my prayers!"

The boys giggled as they decided to play a prank on her, and ran to the nearest house, which was the Benson's, sneaked into the kitchen and poured the pot of coffee into an old coffee can and covered it with a wash rag. Little Ben held it in his arms with his sleeves so as to not get burned, while Ira grabbed a loaf of bread and put it under his coat. The boys carefully ran through the woods to their hiding place to watch for the woman to go inside.

Before long she got up off her knees and went back into the house, so they quietly climbed the hill to her house, and approached the porch. Ira went first and placed his bread in the center off the porch, and then Little Ben carefully set the coffee can down beside the bread. They threw a rock at the door and took off running and tumbling down the hill.

The boys scrambled to crawl under the pine thickets that would hide them from view, just as the door opened and the woman stepped out to see what the single knock at the door had been. She stepped on the rock they had thrown and as she looked down at her feet, she saw the loaf of bread and the can of coffee. She fell to her knees in prayer, thanking God for his wondrous works! "Oh, God! I asked for just a loaf of bread and a pot of coffee, and you gave it to me. Praise the Lord for His goodness!"

The boys were laughing so hard they were afraid she would hear them, so they scooted on down the hill, using the trees to block her view and ran as fast as they could to the creek! They fell into the snow laughing at how the woman thought God had put the coffee and bread there until they heard Midgie ringing the dinner bell, which meant it was time for Little Ben to go home.

Perhaps to make themselves feel older, they had taken to shaking hands when they met and when they parted, so after a good solid hand shake, Little Ben began climbing the hill to his house.

When he got there, he saw his Papa outside chopping wood for the fire. He stepped up onto the porch and smelled homemade bread baking, stood looking up into the clear blue sky, watched the billowing white clouds floating by, and thought to himself that he was a lucky boy.

Benjamin stopped chopping, lifted his axe high in the air and brought it down mightily so as to stick it soundly in the stump he was using for a chopping block, and said, "Are your arms broken?"

"No, sir," Little Ben answered. He knew his father was telling him to help bring the wood in and he was a little embarrassed that he had to be told, so he thought he would lighten the mood a little by telling his Papa just what he and Ira had done with the coffee and bread.

"I know it wasn't right to take the bread and coffee from Mrs. Benson, but you have to admit it was funny!"

"What was funny, Son?" Benjamin asked as he piled up logs on his arm.

"That she thought it was from God!" Little Ben said innocently.

"Well, let me ask you this," Ben said. "Just why do you think you were there at that very moment, to hear her prayers?"

Little Ben stopped in his tracks. It had never occurred to him that God may have used the two boys to answer her prayers, and the thought was profound.

"Now you know God has used people in our lives to help us, to answer our prayers at times," Ben continued. "You know, Jesus died and left this earth. He isn't here anymore to take coffee and bread to a hungry woman. That is our job. To help one another. To feed one another. If you have given yourself to God, you can expect to answer a lot of prayers in your time on this earth. But don't ever forget who made it happen. And don't ever take the glory for yourself. To God goes all the Glory. You had no idea at the time that it was an opportunity to help her. But God used two little boys' desire to play a prank, to actually feed that hungry woman."

Little Ben was very thoughtful about what Papa had said. In fact, he didn't say a word all through dinner. That he could be used on earth to do God's will, was an amazing revelation to Little Ben. One that would ultimately be life changing.

That evening, Little Ben spoke to his Mama about it. He told her the entire story and then told her what Papa had said. Sarah could not help but think of his Granny, and how she had been living on the street. At Grace's request, they had allowed Little Ben to believe that she was indeed Sarah's mother when they brought her home, but they had actually bundled her up, and kidnapped her off the street. Sarah hadn't thought about her Mama's time in that little, cold, lean-to on the streets of Parkersburg for some time.

"Little Ben," Sarah started, "what if that were your Granny in that house all alone?"

Little Ben's face showed what he was thinking; that that would be an awful thing, and that his heart would break.

Mama continued, "I bet she could use some fresh meat from time to time. Or a loaf or two of homemade bread. Why don't you think about making friends with her? You two boys could be a great comfort to an old lady who is alone in this world."

Little Ben smiled at this. It would not be the same as having Granny, but it would be fun to have someone to hunt squirrels for, and to tell stories to. "I will talk to Ira about it at church tomorrow," he said. "Thanks, Mama! That is a great idea!"

Chapter Twelve

There was no coaxing Little Ben out of bed that next morning for church. He could hardly wait for the Liar's Contest. People were coming from all over the county, and there was going to be a dinner right after church! Maxine had promised to bring her cookies to the celebration and Ben was looking forward to seeing her again, although he would have to find a way to do it without her Mama or his Papa seeing them. He didn't know what all the fuss was about. He only wanted to get hold of a few more of her delicious Ammonia Cookies!

Sarah and Grace had been cooking for two days in order to have enough food prepared, not only for the usual group of people who come to church, but for the ones coming from town, and on out the ridge. But it had been joyous service, and the two women, though exhausted at night, had enjoyed each other's company thoroughly.

However, the joy of the day was tainted by the realization that this was the last day for Preacher and Bunny. Everyone was sad to see them go, and had no idea what church would be like without him, but they understood clearly his obligation to his mother and could not fault him for going.

When the Benson's pulled up in their sleigh to pick the Waters up for church, Sarah was the first one out. She held in her hands a very large pan of fried chicken, and was pleased with herself for the good show of food she was bringing. Next came Grace with several loaves of bread, and a bucket filled with cooked fodder beans.

However, they were stunned when they saw the back of the sleigh filled and overflowing with foods of all kinds! Both women bent at the waist laughing at how tiny their little offerings looked compared to the massive amount of food Midgie had fixed. How did she do that with all the children to watch and clothes to wash?

"You did fine!" Midgie said as they made good natured jokes about their small amount of food. Both Bens carried out jars of preserves, pickles, pickled beets, apple butter, butter, and a big pot of sauerkraut, which helped a little.

Kevin was the last one out, after having banked the fire to keep until they got home. As he stepped off the porch, Grace took Rebecca from Sarah, and Grace's eyes met Kevin's quickly as they passed each other and climbed onto the sleigh.

Kevin's years as a priest had rendered him quite patient. There were many secrets he had not been privy to, and many he had known far too much about, but had no say in. There were many mysteries he had heard only part of from a confession from someone involved, and he was used to not being able to ask questions. But this was his family. He had accepted them as they were, but now that they were his life, he felt a need to know and understand them, if for no reason other than to be of help in situations like the one they had barely survived in Parkersburg. But it was more than that, really. He wanted to be of help to Grace. He could counsel her, and help her deal with the trauma. He thought about that for a moment, and then realized, he just wanted to be trusted, and needed. He wanted to be more than an outsider.

Deep in his thoughts, Kevin was surprised when the sleigh stopped suddenly, and the busyness began. Boys ran up to greet Little Ben and the Benson boys, and were recruited to help carry in the food.

Grace was just gathering her skirts to step down from the sleigh when a hand appeared to her side. She looked down into the smiling face of Caleb Rogers. She had despised him when she was caring for his mother, Eileen, and she despised him now. Why would he be so bold as to try to help her down from the sleigh?

Just as she opened her mouth to say that, another hand appeared and Denzel Benson said, "I have it, Caleb. But thanks, anyway."

Grace stood and looked at the men who were now posturing like two roosters, and said, "I am perfectly capable of getting down from a sleigh by myself!" And with both men standing with their hands offered in mid-air, she grabbed the corner of the wooden sleigh and swung herself to the ground.

She said, "Now if you will excuse me," and walked between them as they turned to watch her walk away.

Sarah was waiting for her at the church door, smiling at the sight of Grace holding her skirts up in front of her and stomping toward the church in a tizzy.

"Why do men always think we are helpless? I swear, they would have carried me in had I given them the option." She tugged on her hat to straighten it as she began ascending the steps in a huff, and Sarah giggled softly to herself as she followed her up.

The service was a sad one. They counted the many memories they made while there at that little log cabin. The congregation took turns standing and testifying as to what the Rev. had done for them, or telling funny stories about times spent with him as sleighs and wagons began arriving outside the church. After a time, Rev. Morrison called for a prayer, and, holding his hands out over the people, he asked for a blessing to pour down over them, angels to guard them, and another man of God to lead and encourage them. His 'Amen' set into motion a bustle of activity. The women hurried to prepare the dinner, while the men moved to speak with Preacher about who he thought might be brought in to replace him. The children ran outside, partly to play, and partly because their parents wanted them out of the way while the meal was prepared.

Then after a while groups began forming to sing gospel songs in harmony off by the side. Since the community only sang shaped notes, the first round of verse and chorus were sung without the words, and with the shapes. "Mi fa sol sol sol sol sol, la sol mi mi mi mi mi. Sol me re re re mi fa fa sol fa mi." And so on.

The second time was with the words, an oh, what a blessing those words brought. The Yoak family led the singing and the four-part harmony raised the roof as everyone joined in.

"There will be a singing band, over in the glory land. There will be a mighty chorus over there! Singing of redeeming love, how He came from Heaven above. To this singing nothing earthly can compare! When the Great Celestial Choir begins to sing! To sing! To sing! How the melodies and harmonies will ring! Will ring! Will ring! Angels will be singing in that chorus! Angels with their folded wings will stand before us. And we'll SING! SING! Sing of our redeemer, Savior, Lord and King!"

By the time that song was finished, the meal was prepared and the children were called into the church. Reverend Morrison had a beautiful blessing, and Granny Yoak, who was the matriarch of the Yoak family stood, raised her hands and said, "Gentlemen first!" and the men entered the line for food. The children were not far behind, and most of the women ate while standing and being certain there was plenty of food and spoons available to serve it with. Everyone had to take their turn holding the Benson twins. They were both so sweet, such good babies, never minding who was holding them, sleeping in the arms of whomever had them at the moment. If anyone noticed the fact that Wheat was growing well, with a happy, round, chubby face, while Paul was much smaller and rarely interacted with anyone, at least no one commented on it.

Eileen Rogers and Midgie had provided homemade bread, causing quite a stir. Everyone knew they made the best bread around. Children jumped the line in order to get it slabs of the bread, covered with butter and apple butter.

Sarah felt valued indeed when several people told her that her leather britches, or fodder beans as many called them, were the best they had ever eaten. Sarah was quite proud of that, as she had soaked them for almost two days, washed them clean, and then cooked them all day Saturday to get them soft enough to absorb the bacon grease she had put into them for flavor.

She became melancholy as she remembered Granny patiently teaching them to take the green beans, string them on a thread, then hang them to dry as a way of preserving them. She became so lost in the memory that she laughed out loud as she remembered Little Ben's face when he had tried to string too many on one string, and it broke, sending green beans skidding across the floor. She must thank Granny for teaching them that, but... oh, no! The memory that Granny was gone flooded over her like a tub of hot wax. She found it difficult to breathe and burst into tears in spite of herself.

It was Little Ben who came to her knee. "I miss her, too, Mama," was all he said, and was all he needed to say. He stood there beside her, with his arm up around her shoulders like he had seen his father do when comforting her. The thought of what a sweet young man he was becoming touched her heart as she looked up at him, then gave into the temptation to kiss him on the cheek.

Little Ben jumped as if he had been shot. He looked around the room for the older boys to see if they had seen what she had done, and then darted off to hide somewhere, hopefully somewhere with boys who had not witnessed his deeply humiliating experience.

Sarah's face was one of confusion, and then laughter as she realized he was no longer a boy who could tolerate a mother's affections in public. She made a mental note to treat him more like a man, at least in front of his friends.

As Ben ran out, the first person he saw was Maxine Benson, sitting on the bench in the coat room. Having been nowhere near the source of his humiliation, he felt it was a safe place to stop.

"Oh, Hi!" Little Ben said nervously as he looked over his shoulder to see if Papa or Mrs. Benson could see him. He had taken enough teasing about Maxine as it was, and did not want to give them more fodder for the gossip mill.

"Hi," Maxine said, glancing up at him and then back down at the floor.

"What's wrong?" he asked as he forgot himself and sat down beside her on the bench.

"Mama won't let me help serve," she said dejectedly.

"Why not?" he asked, "isn't that what girls do?"

Her head shot up and looked him in the eye, "Oh sure! *Big* girls. Bessie and Cali are helping serve and they aren't that much older than I am, but Mama says I'm just in the way. Isn't that a mean thing to say?"

"Well, nothing against your Mama, but, well, it *was* a mean thing to say."

"I guess I am just not good at cooking," Maxine continued.

"Oh! Yes, you are good at cooking, Maxine! I LOVE your Ammonia cookies! See? I have one in my pocket!" He stood up to show her, but only produced a pocket full of crumbs. He looked at her with his bottom lip out and his eyebrows up, creating a look on his face that made her laugh. Then he said, "Maybe keeping them in my pocket wasn't such a good idea." Both children giggled as Ben sat back down on the bench beside Maxine, who was now in a much lighter mood as she watched him eat all the crumbs.

"I wish your Mama and Papa would adopt me. There are too many kids in my house, and nobody even knows I am there. I don't think *anyone* there loves me."

"Well," Ben said thoughtfully. He knew none of the adults involved would ever allow that, but he wanted so to cheer up Maxine. For some reason, seeing her upset, upset him more than he wanted to admit. "Someday, you can marry me. I will love you forever, and be kind to you, and treat you like a lady, always. You will never be in my way. I promise." He gave one nod as if to punctuate the statement.

"You will? Truly?" she smiled, showing missing front teeth, and then looked at her hands briefly while she considered his offer. "Then I will love you forever, too. And I will be kind to you, and treat you like a gentleman, always, too."

"Ok, then. It is settled." Just as he finished the statement, a bunch of boys came running in and said, "Come on, the Liar's Contest is starting!"

The children were on the front row, still as mice. They could not wait to hear all the lies, and see if it were true that nobody would get in trouble for lying, either! After some young boys made their first attempts at lying, in the hopes of winning the contest, the Master Liars stood up, and began to compete. The boys were in awe.

There were the typical lies about the size of the fish the men had caught. And stories about how one man shot a bear out of a tree, that fell on a stag that dropped dead, trapping a fourteen-pound rabbit in its rack. But the one that took the prize was about the famed Hoop Snake.

Finally, a big man stepped up onto the soap box, and started slowly. "As you know," Ivy Yoak began, "Hoop Snakes are everywhere here in Western Virginia. From here to the great Ohio River, a man must watch his step so as to not anger a Hoop Snake, and therefore experience its wrath."

"Well, now, as many of you know, when my great, great, great, great, great, great, great, Granddaddy came here, there were no trees anywhere." He delighted in dragging out the story by slowly saying "great, great, great," and counting off on his fingers each and every one! "Well, Western Virginia was just one big pile of dirt after another," he continued. "Lots of rocks! But not tree for hundreds of miles."

"Well, the only wood in these mountains was the handle on the hoe my great, great, great, great, great, great, great, Grandaddy brought with him to dig a garden and, of course, that wasn't big enough to do anything with. So he decided to make himself a house out of mud bricks. Well, one day, he was working away at making bricks, and digging up dirt with that hoe of his'n, when he heard a high pitched buzzing sort of sound that can only be described as a really high pitched whine."

His eyebrows drew down as if he were telling a horrible secret. "Now, if you have not heard the sound a Hoop Snake makes, I cannot explain it to you. But once you have, you will never forget it." He said these last words slowly, in a soft and low voice, indicating the fear that the very sound brings to the human heart.

"Well, of course, my great, great, great, great, great, great, great, Granddaddy knew that sound, and he also recognized that it was a male Hoop Snake, and everyone knows the males have the strongest venom! Not only that, he knew that it was so close, that it was too late to escape." He paused to allow that to sink in before he proceeded. "And not only was it CLOSE!" He had been speaking so softly the entire audience jumped as he shouted the last word! "It was MAD!" The old man shook his head from side to side with his eyebrows drawn down as he said this, making the boys wonder why they had been so careless in the woods, and why no one had ever warned them of this creature that lay in wait among the trees.

"Well, my great, great, great, great, great, great, great, Granddaddy knew exactly what to do. He put that hoe end on the ground beside him and held the handle up close to his ear. That old Hoop Snake put his tail in his mouth, like Hoop Snakes do, and made a large hoop out of himself, and began roooooollling down the hill toward my Granddaddy! But he just stood there!" He paused, "He never moved!"

Ivy shifted his feet on the soap box he was standing on, and continued, "Well, that snake was coming faster and faster. It was coming straight at him faster than one of them big trains you see in Parkersburg. But my Granddaddy Ira did not flinch. He stood there still as an owl, just staring right at that big, old, bull of a Hoop Snake, and just as it let go of its tail and started to fly through the air and strike! He stepped aside and let that snake hit the hoe handle instead!" Ivy stood silently for a moment, then said, "And that smart move saved my Granddaddy's life!"

The audience was pleased with the story, but not overwhelmed. It was an average story for the Yoak story tellers, but nothing that would win the prize. They were surprised and pleased when Ivy began again.

"Well, what happened next was the thing stories are told about! It was an amazing sight that never happened before nor after! That old, bull snake was so full of poison, that hoe handle began swelling up, bigger, and bigger, and bigger, until it was so big!" He waited and looked around the room, then began slowly counting off the "greats" on his fingers as he said, "that my great, great, great, great, great, great, great, Granddaddy decided to build himself a saw mill and cut it up for lumber!" The audience was smiling and nodding to each other, knowing the biggest lie was in the making.

"Now this is the truth! I am telling you the truth about this area when it was homesteaded. I know because my Pappy told me! And his Pappy told him! So listen now, and learn something about your heritage." He had the children's full and undivided attention.

"Well, out of the lumber he sawed up out of the ole hoe handle, he built a six-bedroom house, with a kitchen bigger than this church! He built a barn for his twenty-two horses, a silo for his grain, and a toilet big enough to sit thirty-five people, all at once!"

The laughter had to die down before he could finish. "Then one day," he hooked one finger into a finger of his opposite hand, looked at the audience, and began slowly, "my great, great, great, great, great, great, great, Granddaddy just got tired of the good life. He had lived a long time in that big house, and had planted every single tree you see in Western Virginia, all through Calhoun County, on down the Little Kanawha, down below Creston, up Booger Hole and Hog Knob and Fingerboard, and clear out the West Fork. He planted every tree you now see when you are out in these woods."

His stance was one of a tired, tired man as he continued, "But he was tired of it. He just wanted to move on. So he sold his land and his huge house to a city slicker from up north. Well, he never thought to tell them folks the history of that house. So the fancy pants city slickers wanted to paint the house, of course. Nothin' would do 'em but to bring their pretty colors down and paint the inside of the house the colors of every spring flower you can think of! Well, that's ok, but the problem is, they brought a big can of turpentine with 'em, so's they could clean their brushes, and don't you know? They spilled that turpentine, and it spread out all over the floor. And the more they tried to clean it up! The farther it spread! And you know what it did? It pulled the poison right outa that wood and..." CRACK! He clapped his hands so loudly that everyone in the room jumped and one baby began crying. "Just like that," he said, "that house collapsed back to the size of a hoe handle, and killed everybody in it instantly."

The crowd took to their feet, cheering, whooping, whistling, and clapping their hands as he stepped down off the soap box, indicating his story was finished. They had found their Biggest Liar and the old timers knew he would be hard to beat in the years to come.

Chapter Thirteen

The day was over, the children were exhausted, the women wanted just to get home to sit down, and the men were so full of fine food they had a difficult time keeping their eyes open.

It seemed everyone was talking simultaneously on the way home. Ira and Little Ben were boasting about how they were going to tell the biggest lie the next time, because they had months to figure out what they were going to say. The adults wondered who their next preacher would be, and Grace, Cali, and Bessie were chatting about how ridiculous the boys from their church were.

Suddenly, as a lull fell in the conversation, Little Ben was overheard saying something about a little, dark skinned boy he had seen recently. All eyes were on him. His Papa looked at him and asked what he had said.

"Nothing," Little Ben said, just wishing the sleigh would open up and swallow him. He wanted everyone to stop looking at him, go back to their conversations, and just forget what he had said.

But instead, his Papa said, "I asked you a question, young man." The stern look on his face frightened Little Ben more than answering him did, so he chose his words quickly.

"I saw a boy, about my age when I was going down to the Bensons' Friday."

"Why didn't you tell me about this, Ben?" His father's face was equally as stern, if not more so rendering Little Ben incapable of speech. His Papa had never been really angry with him before, and now, it was in front of Maxine, and Ira, and everybody else in the sleigh. His chin quivered and huge tears slid down his face.

Ben regretted his tone and said, "You aren't in any trouble, Son," he started, "I just need to know where you saw this young man."

"In the cave. Where we stayed that first…"

"Yes," Benjamin interrupted him in mid-sentence, "that first time we went walking down in the valley and it rained. I know the cave. Was anybody with him?"

Little Ben had to think about that. He remembered the boy looking over his shoulder into the woods, but he never saw anyone back there, so he just said, "I don't know, Papa."

Benjamin, Abram, Elias, Kevin, and Denzel exchanged knowing glances, and Denzel clicked to the horses to pick up their pace. Before long, the Waters family was deposited safely in their cabin, except Benjamin, who was outside saddling Grace's mare. Sarah took a large package out to him, told him to be careful, and he rode off to catch up with Abram.

The next morning, Benjamin was home and the world continued as it had for the last year. Little Ben wanted to ask his father what happened, but knew better. He just kept his fears and curiosity to himself and left to do his chores.

Over the next few days, Little Ben heard whispers he tried to understand. Like, "the Bensons went." He also heard things that would not have been whispered normally, like, "ham," which piqued his curiosity painfully. Only an hour ago, a man came to the door, and with knowing looks, Kevin and Benjamin had left with him. Little Ben was certain his Mama knew where they were going, but she said nothing to him about it.

Suddenly, there was a knock on the door, and a huge man, who was dirty and smelled so badly Sarah did not want him in the house, asked where the man of the house was. "I'm sorry, my husband is out, but if you want to leave your name and where you can be found, I will tell him you called."

The man took his right arm and with a wide swing, pushed Sarah out of his way, entered the cabin, and began looking in all the rooms.

"I have children here," Sarah shouted.

The man turned to look at her, spit on the floor, and said, "What are you hiding here? I think you got what I want, lady, and I don't feel like playing games! Now you tell me where them niggers are…"

"Get out of my Mama's house," Little Ben said.

At the sight of him, Sarah moved quickly to Little Ben and stood behind him, leaving the area between the man and the front door open.

"Well, look at that! You got a boy to defend you?" he said as he laughed and took a step toward Little Ben. He froze in the middle of his step when he heard the hammer click on the single action gun the boy was aiming right at his heart.

"I may be a boy," Little Ben said, "but I don't have any problem shooting a man who would hurt my Mama. Now I am going to count to three, and the minute I say the word, three, I'm going to pull this trigger. I shoot squirrels every day, and they are a lot littler than you, so I figure I can put you down with one shot."

The man wiped his mouth with the back of his hand and opened his mouth to say something when…

"One," Little Ben said.

"But you haven't even heard what I…"

"Two," the little man said again. "Mama, will God forgive me for killing this man?"

"Yes, Ben. He will forgive you because you are protecting your family."

The man didn't wait to hear, "three," but he did stay just a second too long. As he ran through the door, turned the corner of the porch and dove headlong into the snow off to the right, he heard the crack of gunshot, and felt the bullet as it passed by his left shoulder, ripping the back of his shirt.

There were three other men waiting outside for him and one of them handed the man the reins to his horse. He swung his leg over the mount and said, "That little bastard tried to shoot me!" The men did not stop to ask questions, but galloped off full speed toward anywhere but there.

Another shot rang out as Little Ben stood in the yard, making sure they understood not to lurk about, waiting to come back in and hurt his Mama and his sisters.

When he went into the house, Sarah and Grace looked at him with new respect. Ben had no idea what the big deal was, but apparently it was a big deal, and he felt both proud and embarrassed.

"You were going to shoot him, weren't you, Ben?" Sarah asked.

"Yes, I was. I am glad he ran, because I wasn't hankering to kill a human being, but I would have if he hadn't of left when he did."

"Well," Sarah said with a smile! "I am grateful we have another man in the house, Ben. I am impressed with how you handled yourself, and thankful you were here. How did you know what to do?" She said as she began to set the table.

"I just did exactly what Papa told me to do if we were ever here alone and someone came in on us. He said to tell them to leave, to tell them I was going to count to three, and when I got to three just to shoot, and not think a thing about it. He told me to keep the gun pointed toward the door in case others came in and just shoot them without warning, because there could be several of them. He said I was to protect you and Grace when he wasn't here, and I told him I would."

Grace looked at him as if she had never seen him before. "You are growing up, Ben Waters, and I am so proud of you."

This was the moment he realized what he had done. His sister was proud of him, and instead of her taking care of him, he had protected her. They were equals now, he felt. The time for being a child was over. He was a man now, and he needed to act more like it.

When Kevin and Ben returned from wherever they had been, the family met them at the door, chattering about what Little Ben had done. Little Ben recognized immediately the look on their faces; the look of respect, and realization that the boy was becoming a man.

As the men took off their hats and coats, Sarah asked how they had found things, and they only replied, "Warmer."

Little Ben was tired, and as soon as he had eaten his dinner, he asked if he could go to bed. Just as he approached the bottom of the ladder, he turned and looked at his father and asked, "Papa, what is a nigger?"

Ben looked thoughtfully and said, "It is an ugly name, that ugly people call other people who have darker skin than we do. And I don't ever want to hear that word come out of your mouth again. Do you understand me, Son?"

"Yes, sir," Little Ben said. "And you sure are right about that! He sure was ugly."

Grace and the adults laughed and agreed, then spoke softly about what a good job Little Ben had done taking care of the household until they felt Ben had fallen asleep. After they felt the children were settled, they looked at each other with great concern.

"Are they alright?" Sarah asked. "I hate thinking about that boy down there in the cold. Oh, can't we bring them here to hide them?"

Kevin said, "You saw what happened today, Sarah. If they would have been here, that man would have found them, and think of what might have happened then. It is against the law to hide runaway slaves."

"Kevin is right, Sarah," Ben said, "We cannot risk someone finding them here. And no one would suspect they could survive outside in this weather. No, they are going to be searching homes everywhere, so the safest place for them to be is in that cave."

"Do they have enough food?" Grace asked.

Both Kevin and Ben laughed at her question and Kevin said, "Midgie took food to them yesterday so they may not need food for three weeks. I never saw such a passel of baskets!"

"But they did appreciate the blankets we took them today. Jeb did good in giving us that batch of blankets. They have well served their purpose!"

"Who is going there tomorrow? And won't those slave hunters see the tracks and follow them?" Sarah asked.

"No, everyone knows to go down to the valley either up or down stream of the cave, and then on in to the cave by way of the creek where our prints don't show." Ben added.

"Surely, they can't stay there forever without getting caught. If they tracked them this far, they can find them just a mile or so from here!" Grace said.

Ben said, "Well, I guess they didn't exactly track them this far. Someone saw them coming up from Bull River, or starting up Bull River that is. It appears they may have gotten a ride to Hog Knob, and then took off running up Bull River."

Kevin asked, "Where is Bull River, Ben?"

"On yon side of that hill right there in front of our cabin. If you just follow on down that holler, you will be in Bull River. Go on out, and you will come out in Bugger Hole. Then you just make a left and go up that hill to Hog Knob. That is where the Bealls live, you know Dan Beall, don't you?"

Kevin smiled at the unusual names of the areas around here, but made a mental note as to where each one was located. This was his home now, and he needed to know his way around.

Before they closed up the cabin and blew out the candles, Kevin said, "Ben, I need to ask you a favor of sorts."

Ben said, "Anything, Kevin."

"Well," Kevin said, "I have been thinking that I no longer live in the arms of the church, protected and safe, so to speak. I was thinking that it might behoove me to learn how to shoot a gun, just in case I am in the situation Little Ben found himself in today."

"Yea, that was something wasn't it?" Ben beamed with pride.

"It certainly was," Kevin agreed. "And to be honest with you, I am not certain Sarah would have fared as well had I been the only one here to protect her."

"First thing in the morning," Ben said, clapping his hand on the side of Kevin's arm.

"All right then," Kevin said. "In the morning then." He waived good night to Ben and the men went to their rooms.

Chapter Fourteen

The shooting lessons went well, considering. Kevin was a patient man and had no problem lining up the sights on the gun, and he practiced the art of squeezing the trigger instead of pulling it. Just for good measure, Benjamin had balanced a small coin out on the end of the barrel. It was Kevin's job to practice squeezing the trigger in a manner that would allow him to shoot the gun without knocking the coin off. As Kevin understood it, if you *pulled* the trigger, the coin would fall off long before the gun discharged.

Kevin had even become fairly decent at hitting the target and occasionally even hit dead center. The problem came, however, when there was a living, breathing animal in front of him and he had to aim to kill. According to Benjamin, Denzel, Abram, Elias, and any other man who was certain he could take Kevin hunting and be successful in bringing home game, the problem was that Kevin had a bad case of Buck Fever.

"Buck Fever," Abram began, "is a serious situation where hunters think they have pulled the trigger when they haven't. I knew one man who would swear he had heard the gun go off and felt the kick against his shoulder! But the weapon had never been fired!" It did indeed sound serious to Kevin, so why were they all grinning?

"I gotta say," Abram said finally, "I know a man can't help it, but danged if it ain't the funniest thing I ever did see!" All the men laughed at the unusual sights they had witnessed over the years. One man would hold his gun right on the prey, then suddenly, without firing a shot, begin shouting, "I got it! I got it! Where did it go!"

The men threw back their heads and laughed at the story they had told dozens of times. In fact, that had become a commonly used phrase over the years whenever someone lost something. Good ole Shy Codder. He made the best bows and arrows you ever did see, but he couldn't have shot a gun if his life depended on it!"

Kevin was mortified to know that he was one of the men the others were laughing at! They were not being malicious, but still, he had wanted to fit in with the local men since this was his new home. The problem was that Kevin not only had Buck Fever, he had his own particular brand of humiliation. He always stood with a tree at his back to lean on while waiting for the game. Invariably, and sadly, publically, he would aim his gun, take a deep breath and blow it out silently, point his weapon, concentrate on 'squeezing' and not 'pulling' the trigger, then slowly slide down the tree, mumbling incoherently, and eventually shouting, "Did I get it?"

Now he understood why the men shouted, "I got it! I got it! Where did it go?"

His humiliation was complete when Little Ben came to where he was sitting and said, "Don't worry, Uncle Kevin. You and I will go out tomorrow. You will be fine."

Kevin smiled weakly and said, "Thank you, Ben. I look forward to it."

Finally, the subject was changed when Benjamin stood and asked Kevin for his help with a project he had been working on outside. Little Ben announced that he would check the mare, but what he really wanted to do, was go see what his Papa and Uncle Kevin were doing.

Just as Little Ben stepped up to the back of the buckboard his father had been working on, he saw his Uncle Kevin picked up the boards revealing a false bottom underneath the wagon bed. "What is that for, Papa?" Little Ben asked.

"Nothing you need to concern yourself with, Ben. Go help your Mama."

"Papa, I am not a little boy anymore. I stood up to those men who came into our house, and you know I can keep a secret."

Kevin and Ben looked over the buckboard at each other. Kevin raised his eyebrows and tipped his head sideways as if to say, *he has a point*, so Benjamin relented and said, "Come on up here, boy."

Little Ben jumped up onto the buckboard and stopped. "Lie down in there," his Papa said.

"In this little box?" Benji asked.

"Yes. We want to see if a boy about your size could lie in there comfortably," he said, looking at his son with great respect.

Little Ben realized they were planning on hiding the runaway slaves in the bottom of the buckboard in order to take them somewhere. He immediately grasped the seriousness of the situation, and felt great pride that he had been entrusted with the information.

He jumped down into the box and stretched out. "Now, we are going to put the cover on top of where you are. Are you ready?" Ben asked.

But before Little Ben could answer, Kevin said, "Here, take my coat and put it under your head. I want to see if there is room for a pillow." The top fit perfectly, and it was made so that it could not be seen, even if the wagon were empty, although they planned to have it well loaded.

"What about the other side?" Little Ben asked.

"Benjamin, I believe you are more like the build of the man, why don't you climb in and I will see how it looks from here.

Both the man and they boy were well hidden from the naked eye. When they came out of the boxes they were so pleased with themselves they were laughing and slapping each other on the back until Grace interrupted and said, "What if someone asks you why each side is lower than the rest of the wagon?"

Kevin and Benjamin smiled at each other and said, "Follow us."

The men then revealed doors on the outside of the wagon, that, when opened, revealed another false back, so the human beings could not be seen! And the little boxes it created were filled with tools! They said they would simply explain it was a new invention, and if someone wanted to have their wagon equipped with it, they could certainly oblige them.

Now all they had to do was wait until the roads were passable from the spring thaw, and then continue with their plan.

Little Ben awakened with the smell of coffee and biscuits, and immediately became aware of the commotion downstairs. His Mama was loading books into a box, along with biscuits, a jar of apple butter, and a tub of butter. She turned as she remembered the ham slices she had prepared, and glanced up at Little Ben before loading them into the box.

Mama was going away again today, but this time he suspected she knew where she was going. She had taken the books she had used to teach him, and his sister, Grace, how to read. He realized that his Mama was teaching the man and boy hidden in the cave, how to read, and he loved her all the more for her kindness. He smiled at his Mama, and she understood that he had caught on, and saw the pride in his eyes, warming her heart.

"What are you going to do today, Benjamin, AFTER you take Dusty out?" Mama said to him.

"Oh, I coming, Mama!" He scurried down from the loft, and proceeded to get Dusty to go outside. As he opened the door to go outside, he said over his shoulder, "I am going to take Uncle Kevin hunting." At which Kevin dropped his head and groaned. "Everything is going to be fine, Uncle Kevin. You will see."

"Well, I certainly cannot do any worse than I have in the past. That is the great thing about doing poorly. At least the only way to go is up!" Kevin laughed and took a sip of coffee. Sarah patted him on the back and said, "You will do fine! All in good time, Brother, all in good time!"

Before long they were dressed and ready to go out into the woods. Little Ben tied Dusty to the porch so he would not go with them and chase away their game. It was still dark as they picked their way along on the well-known path with Little Ben in the lead. They were far from where they were going to actually hunt, a deer trail Little Ben had found last summer, so Little Ben started a quiet conversation with his Uncle Kevin. "I sure do miss Granny," he started.

"I know you do, Ben," Kevin began. "Tell, me," he began in order to allow Little Ben to talk about his beloved Granny, "Why was she so special to you? Did you two have great talks? Or did she just spoil you, as Grannies do?"

"All of that, I guess." Little Ben walked along for a minute, then continued, "She always had time for me, and I liked that. But she taught us things, too. There was no boy's work, or girl's work, there was just work that needed doin', and she wanted us all to know how to do it!"

"That is an amazing way to look at things, don't you think?"

Little Ben said, "Well, I didn't think so when she was making me cook and sew, but Grace took right to climbing on the roof and plowing the garden with the team!"

There was a comfortable silence between them, and then Little Ben continued, "You might find it interesting that Granny taught me how to hunt!"

"Really?" Kevin said surprised that the old homeless woman he had fed and cared for on the street had any idea how to hunt or shoot a gun.

"Well, really, my Papa taught me how to squeeze the trigger, and aim the gun, but, I just couldn't shoot for some reason."

Kevin was getting the idea of where the conversation was going and smiled to himself.

"What she said was, that killing an animal was new to me, and that in every man's life there comes a time when they have to realize that they are no longer boys, and have a responsibility to feed their family."

Kevin sobered up at that bit of information. He had never considered that part of his role in this family was to actually supply fresh meat for the table. Before, he had seen hunting as a way to prove himself to the other men, as well as for protection. But the thought that he was being asked to step up and take his part in feeding the family had never crossed his mind. He listened more seriously as Little Ben continued.

"Of course, Granny knew I didn't want to shoot anything because I was just a boy, then!"

Kevin smiled because it had only been a few months ago. But then he thought of all Little Ben and Grace had been through and considered the idea that, though he was small, he really was becoming quite an outstanding young man.

"But, I think," Little Ben continued, "that it just might be that since you have spent your entire life as a Priest… that… well… maybe the act of killing something might just be so hard for you, that you are not able to do it." Little Ben stopped in his tracks and turned to look at his Uncle Kevin.

Kevin looked at the boy and realized that his desire to belong to this family and community was indeed in direct contrast to his beliefs and upbringing. Perhaps that *was* the source of his Buck Fever. And perhaps he needed to bring those two belief systems into focus before trying to hunt again.

"You are an amazing young man, Ben," Kevin began. But it appeared that Little Ben was afraid he was going to bring up the events that occurred in Parkersburg and became a little restless. So Kevin said quickly, "In fact, I believe you are right! I do not know how to overcome that, but I do, in fact, believe you may have something there."

Little Ben was pleased that his words hit home as Granny's did with him, and that Uncle Kevin was not going to bring up the Parkersburg incident, so he was encouraged to say more. "Well, what Granny told me was that we have a family to feed." He counted off on his fingers as he said, "There is… you, Mama, Papa, Grace, me, and Aunt Florence. She isn't really my aunt. She is an elderly lady Ira and I met out in the woods. I guess everybody around here calls her Aunt Florence. We take turns providing fresh meat for her now. And all of us have to eat, three times a day!"

Kevin was impressed that a boy of his age would assume that much responsibility at such a young age and again, he looked at Little Ben with growing respect.

"The way Granny tells it; God gave us that food. He gave us deer, and squirrels, and pheasants, and wild turkeys. All so we could eat. Now killing a deer just for fun would not be right. But when you have a family to feed, you need what God sends. When you see it, you thank God for his provisions, take aim, and squeeze the trigger."

The thought of actually killing a living thing was heartbreaking to Kevin and Ben saw it on his face. He just said, "You have a family to feed Uncle Kevin. Just don't take more than you need, and be grateful for what you get."

Little Ben motioned for them to be quiet, as they slipped down the rest of the path. He waved for them to stop and get comfortable. Little Ben sat down on the ground, his gun across his lap, and Kevin leaned against a sturdy tree and stared at the path in front of him that appeared to be a major route for deer.

It was nearly an hour before they saw anything, and Kevin was grateful for the time to clear his head, and to pray about what he was about to do. "Father, I have spent my life sheltered by the church. I have eaten many meals, unaware of what had to be done to provide the meat that I so willingly ate. Now, I have a family to feed, and ask that you forgive me for doing what I must. I understand that it is your way of providing for us, and many times I have spoken of Jehovah

Jireh, our provider. And yet it has not until now, occurred to me just what sacrifices must be made to make certain our family has enough to eat. I do give thanks for the life of the sweet animal I may or may not slay today. And I thank you for this opportunity to feed my family."

His prayer was interrupted by a tug at his pants leg, which brought his eyes to where Ben was pointing. There stood a magnificent buck, with a rack of horns like he had never seen. He paused for a moment taking in the splendor of the animal, but another tug from the seated Ben, brought him back to reality. He slowly aimed his gun, relaxed his entire being, squeezed the trigger, and prayed that God would forgive him for killing the beautiful beast. The sound of a gunshot exploding against his right ear surprised Kevin, and the kick was powerful. But when he lowered his gun, he saw the rack of horns lying on the ground, and realized he had killed his first animal.

Little Ben was filled with joy at his success, then remembered how he felt after his first kill. "Are you alright, Uncle Kevin?"

Kevin walked up to the animal and said, "Thank you, you beautiful beast, for providing meat for our table. Your sacrifice will not be in vain. You will be blessed, and used for the glory of our Lord."

It was only then that Kevin realized what he had accomplished. "I did it! I did it, Little Ben! And we have Granny to thank for that!"

Little Ben was pleased. It felt like Granny had been there with them that morning, and it lessened the sting of her absence. Little Ben showed Kevin how to remove the scent glands on the hind legs, the male parts of the deer, and how to gut and prepare him, then they began the long process of dragging him out of the woods.

"Oh, wait," Little Ben said. "You need to reload your gun before we go any farther. You never know who or what you are going to meet out here, so you always gotta be prepared."

Kevin made a note of that information, loaded his gun and proceeded to help drag the deer out of the forest. Their walk was celebratory as they laughed about how clean the shot was, and replayed the kill over and over. Kevin had to admit that he was as excited as a child about telling the family all about it.

As they stepped into the clearing where the cabin stood, they stopped to rest. The remaining walk would be easy compared to the trek they had taken through the thick underbrush. Kevin removed his hat to wipe his brow with a handkerchief, when Little Ben screamed, "Dusty!"

Kevin looked up and saw what had alarmed him so. A black bear stood over the dog, just ready to grab Dusty in its teeth. Little Ben took off running toward the dog, but Kevin just managed to grab his shoulder and knock him to the ground. At once and without thought, Kevin brought the loaded weapon to his shoulder, aimed, squeezed, and shot as he said a prayer that the dog would be spared.

A squeal of pain was heard from the puppy as the bear came down on his little body. "You shot my dog!" Little Ben shouted at Kevin with tears falling from his chin. He hit Kevin in the chest with his fist and ran to be with Dusty.

"Ben, wait!" Kevin shouted as the boy got closer and closer to the bear.

But by the time Kevin got to the porch, Little Ben was trying his best to roll the bear over by pushing, shoving, or leveraging it with his feet. Kevin dropped his gun and grabbed the bear's hair, hoping it was truly dead and not just stunned, and aided Little Ben in his attempt to roll it over. It was no use. The bear was too heavy and even the man and the boy together could not budge it. Surely, had the dog been spared the bullet, it would have suffocated by now under the weight of the massive bear.

Little Ben sat down on the edge of the porch and wept. He rocked back and forth in rhythm with the sorrow that was pounding through his little heart and soul. He cried for Rev. Morrison, Dusty, the sorrow of what had happened with his sister, and now his beloved Dusty. His heart was broken and he was tired of all the losses. His sobbing broke

Kevin's heart, and he prayed that when the bear was moved, there would be no trace of a bullet in the puppy Ben loved so much.

Little Ben was crying so hard he hardly noticed when his shoe string disappeared under the edge of the porch. But when the puppy tried to pull his sock underneath the porch as well, he jumped and fell onto the ground to see if it was really there.

"Uncle Kevin, look!" Ben shouted. "Dusty is under the edge of the porch!" The problem was the bear was lying on the rope that held the puppy tightly in place. Very carefully, Kevin had to lie down and try to cut the rope as close as possible to Dusty's neck, without cutting the little guy, and without being able to see what he was doing.

Finally, the puppy was bouncing around in the yard, happy as could be, Little Ben right behind him laughing and playing with the dog as if nothing had ever happened, while Kevin sat on the porch trying to recover from the heart stopping events. He was white as a sheet, and a good bit nauseated if he were to admit it. But he was greatly relieved that, first of all, he had not shot Little Man's dog, and that he had not frozen in place as he had done before. No room for Buck Fever in this part of the country! He had a family to feed and protect.

Chapter Fifteen

By the time Sarah and Ben got home, there was a deer hanging from a nearby tree, gutted and ready to skin, and a dead bear lying in the yard. Kevin was aware that it would feed the family, as well as Aunt Florence, for quite some time, and that pleased him because as much as he liked squirrel, ham, and rabbit, he was ready for a change. He was pleased with himself. Not quite proud of what he had done, but he was pleased that he had done his part to feed the family he would give his life for.

But he in no way saw himself the hero, until the telling of the story by Little Ben, of how Kevin had singlehandedly killed the bear and saved the dog from a certain death. The story had to be told over and over, and with each telling, the danger became far more fearsome, the bear bigger, and the shot more perfect. This was the stuff families were made of. Stories of valiant men saving lives, and the everyday things they did… together.

The cabin smelled like home that night as the venison cooked in the roaster on the stove, the coffee perked, and the bread baked in the oven. Yes, this was his family, and he felt more a part of it than ever before.

Finally, the door opened and Little Ben and Dusty entered breathlessly from a long day of playing outside. "Papa," he said, "That man is out there again, standing on the top of the hill."

Both Ben and Kevin went to the window to look out at the stranger who would, from time to time, appear at the top of the hill, but leave before they could approach him to see who he was, and what he wanted.

"Stay inside, Ben," Benjamin said to his son. It is almost dark, and you need to clean up for supper."

Chapter Sixteen

It was finally time to go to church and meet the new Preacher. All of the Bensons and the Waters were excited, except their loyalties kept them from immediately liking the idea of a replacement. They were torn, with mixed emotions about the entire subject. Only Sarah expressed a completely open mind on the subject.

"Well, I am going to like him, and his family, just fine. I was a newcomer here one time, and everyone accepted me with open arms, and I intend to do the same thing," she said positively.

At this, Midgie and the others felt appropriately ashamed, but were still unwilling to be, what they felt, was disloyal to Preacher and Bun.

The church yard was abuzz with news of those who had met the new minister, talk of the war, and joy about spring planting. The ladies were excited about the new crop of herbs they would soon be gathering, since last summer's supply was now depleted. The men were talking about plowing their fields in time to catch a great deal of the water that was coming their way. This year the snow had been so great, they could not prepare their fields as they wished, but still, there was time before planting to get their fields plowed and open to the rain.

The huge bell that sat atop the church, began ringing, calling the congregation in for worship. It was the responsibility of Russel Selmon to greet the new Preacher and make him feel at home in the nearby parsonage. A hush fell over the crowd as Russel stood up and said, "I am sure you are all ready to meet our new Preacher. So without further ado, I will introduce, Rev. Carroll McCauley."

They were not sure what they expected, but it certainly was not the man who stood before them. Instead of authoritative, he looked, well, jolly! Instead of having the aura of a stranger, they felt they had known him all their lives. They could not help but love him instantly as he introduced his wife, his three little girls, and his only son.

He had a contagious laughter that filled the building and evoked chuckles from everyone within hearing range. When his children trotted across the floor in front of his podium it did not faze him in the least. He would smile down at them with the love of a father, and continue with the introduction of his life and experiences.

But when he stepped into the pulpit, no one doubted that he was filled with the Holy Spirit. He began by saying that often when he started in a new church, people would come and tell him of arguments they were having with others in the church. "I want you to know, that if you do that, I will turn you around and take you to the foot of the cross. I do not want finger pointing in my congregation. I do not need to hear what this one has done and that one did. This church is about the love of Jesus Christ! He continued to express the hurts and heartaches of everyone present, and God's promises to heal their pain and ease their suffering.

There was not a dry eye in the congregation when he led them in prayer, and dismissed them, long before they thought the service should be over.

On the way out, everyone waited in line to shake hands with their new leader. In the front of the line was Midgie, carrying little Roy Paul, then Cali, carrying Nancy, or Wheat as her brothers called her. Then came the stair steps of children, all named Benson. With every child that was introduced, Rev. McCauley laughed harder and harder! He hugged each and every child except the older ones, but instead shook hands with each of them, girls and boys, with great respect.

At the end of the line came Abram, who was followed by Ben Waters and his family. When it was Abram's turn to shake hands, he did so with a hearty grip. Then he said, "I am so glad to hear your sermon on how we should not finger point," then he pointed right at his friend and said, "Benjamin here, needed to hear that!" Then he briskly walked away, leaving a confused and babbling Benjamin in his wake! Rev. McCauley immediately got the joke and laughed a hearty belly laugh, before grabbing Benjamin and hugging him.

"I take it the two of you are great friends!" Preacher said with a smile that would warm you on the coldest of days.

Benjamin was happy to be relieved of the embarrassment, and mumbled, "I reckon we are, Preacher. I'm Ben Walters, by the way." Preacher shook his hand and put his other hand on Benjamin's elbow. There was an immediate connection between the two men that would last a lifetime.

After church, the men met to discuss the pending trip to Parkersburg in the new wagon Ben had built. They worried over whether it would call attention to them to have several riders with them, or if it would be safe for just one rider to take the wagon alone.

"The problem is, when whoever does this, gets there, they will have to actually sell the slaves to the man coming down from New York. He has purchased several slaves from the south, and gives them a piece of his land, and sets them free," said Earl Bush. Earl and his brother, Glendon, had volunteered to take them to Parkersburg. Another brother, Don, had offered to ride along if they thought it wouldn't be too suspicious.

Benjamin was relieved to know that he would not be asked to appear in Parkersburg. Because of his leg, he was too easily recognized, and it had not been long enough for people to forget the reward that was on his head.

"I have to say," Don said, "I do not feel real good about selling two human beings, even if it is for their own good!"

"I have a thought," Ben said, "why don't you just sell him the wagon! That way he could get them out of town, then he could claim they were his slaves later on."

"That sounds like a good idea, Ben." The three brothers looked at each other, clearly far more comfortable with this idea than with the actual selling of slaves.

"What would you take for that wagon, Ben?" Abram asked.

"Well, I really just rebuilt an old wagon that Madison Harper gave me. I guess six dollars would cover it," Ben said.

The men thought that was quite a generous offer and said so. "But what if the man wants the horse, too?" Earl asked.

No one had a horse they could do without now that it was time to plow, so they decided to send a message to the man asking him how he felt about the plan, and could he bring a horse to pull the wagon himself.

The plan was set in motion, so the men broke up their group to head out to their own families who were waiting to go home. As Ben limped over to his wagon he noticed a young lady, speaking to Sarah. She was someone he had never met, so he took off his hat and nodded to her.

"Ben, this is Lacey McClelland. She wanted to attend church here this morning, but she did not realize it started so early, so she missed the service today," Sarah said. "I have asked her to come to dinner with us, because everyone else has left, and the ride back to town takes so long."

"It would be our pleasure, Miss McClelland." He wanted to ask where she was from, because his mother had been a McClelland before she married his father, but that might start questions from the children that he was not prepared to answer.

The ride home was rather rowdy. They were all excited about the new minister, and the fact that Denzel was driving Lacey home in her buggy was plenty of fodder for gossip. Sarah kept looking at Grace to see if she showed any signs of jealousy, but Grace seemed as if she hardly noticed.

Sunday dinner was delicious, as Lacey had expressed several times. She appeared to be enjoying herself, and seemed to pay particular attention to Benjamin. Sarah was quite certain she could not turn his head, but still, she did not like the way Lacey hung on his every word.

Lacey looked at the children with great interest, and a look that was kindred to pure love. Benjamin and the children were quite oblivious to the special interest Lacey took in Ben, but Sarah was not. And she was not happy.

By the time dinner was over, a rain was settling in and it seemed cruel to expect her to travel back to town for the night. So Ben said cheerily, "Why don't you just stay here with us for the night?"

Kevin chimed in with, "I would be happy to take the bed Granny slept in before she had her room, and give Miss Lacey my room."

"Oh, it is settled then," Lacey said, laying her hand on top of Ben's. "I will stay the night, and thank you, Ben for asking. It was so kind of you!" Ben moved his hand quickly as his eyes darted to Sarah's. He knew instantly that she was not amused about the situation, but there was nothing to be done now.

Kevin saw the sparks flying between Ben and Sarah, and suggested that he walk Miss Lacey out to the outhouse and wait for her so that Ben and Sarah could have a moment. Then when he realized how inappropriate that would be he added, "Little Man, perhaps you should come with us and take Dusty for a walk. He has been shut up in here all day."

The rain was pouring down now, and the sky had darkened. The clouds looked angry and bruised, while the wind was rocking trees back and forth, whipping dead limbs off and tossing them through the air. Kevin was about to knock on the door to the outhouse door and inform Lacey of the downturn the weather had taken, when she opened the door and stepped out.

He called to Little Ben and the three of them made their way back just as lightning struck and the thunder shook the earth. When the door flew open the three of them and a soaking wet dog poured into the room, and froze in place. Clearly, they had stepped into a situation. There was anger in the air, and for one uncomfortable moment, Kevin thought they might continue their argument in front of God and everybody.

"Perhaps I should show Miss Lacey her room," Kevin said with one hand signaling to Lacey that she should proceed to the back of the cabin. But after a quick look at her quarters, Miss Lacey McClelland insisted on helping with the dishes. As Sarah washed, Ben dried and, much to Sarah's chagrin, Lacey assisted him.

"Little Ben, I believe it is your turn to dry the dishes," Sarah said with a look that left Little Ben no room to argue. He retrieved a towel from the cupboard, and became the third person drying dishes. Little Ben's eyes went from his Mama, to his Papa, to Grace, to his Mama, and then to Lacey. There she was smiling that goofy smile at him again. He looked at his Papa for some relief, but none came. The tension was so thick it was difficult to move around in the room.

Finally, the dishes were washed, dried, and put away. Dinner was not taken up, so eating supper would be very easy to do. Sarah left the room to get her sewing, leaving Ben alone in the kitchen, pouring himself a cup of coffee.

In an instant, Lacey was beside him, and far too close for his comfort. She glanced at the room where Sarah was, tugged on Ben's shirt, tiptoed and whispered into his hear, "Jesse?"

Ben dropped his cup and spilled it on the floor. Dusty ran over to lick up the spilled coffee and Sarah rushed out to see what had happened.

Lacey turned so she could look Sarah in the eye, and said, "I am so sorry. Ben was getting me a cup of coffee, and when I took it, I did not realize how hot it was. I am afraid I have always been rather clumsy."

Ben was feeling pressure in the pit of his stomach. He had to go to the outhouse immediately, or he would embarrass himself. He said,

"Excuse me." Grabbed his hat and coat and left before any questions could be asked of him.

When he returned, he stepped into the room and said, "Miss Lacey. Could I speak to you privately for a moment out on the porch?"

Sarah's face turned the color of the coals in the fireplace. She was red from her collarbone to the top of her head, so Kevin tried to intervene by saying, "I think I need to get some fresh air as well. I think I will go with you!"

He stood to get his hat, but Benjamin said, "If it can wait, I would appreciate it, Kevin. I need a moment with Miss Lacey." His eyes went to Sarah's face briefly. He was well aware of the storm raging inside her, but he had to find out how this woman knew his real name, and he could not figure out a way to do it without the privacy the porch offered.

The second the door shut, Lacey's arms went around Ben's neck and she kissed him on the cheek. "Now, wait a minute here!" Ben said as he grabbed her wrists and pried her arms from around his neck. "Why did you call me Jesse? My name is Benjamin. Benjamin Waters."

She stepped back, straightened her coat, and said, "Why Jesse McFay! Don't you recognize your little sister, Sarah?"

Ben's mouth dropped open. He brought to mind the image of the little girl he had last seen as they took him away the night he beat his father to death for abusing his mother. Then slowly, the face of that child emerged and changed into the lovely face of the young woman standing before him. It was Sarah, his sister! How had she found him? They threw their arms around each other, laughing and talking simultaneously when suddenly the door flew open and Sarah stared at them with so much anger in her eyes that Ben had to laugh.

"Sarah Waters, my wife, meet Sarah," he stumbled, not knowing what to say for his last name. If he used McFay, there would be many questions. So he chose to use his last name now, and hope his sister did not object. "Uh, meet Sarah Waters, my little sister!"

He winked at his sister as he looked down at her, and she hugged him tightly and said, "I'm sorry I didn't say anything sooner. I just wanted to make sure that J, I mean, Ben wouldn't be ashamed of me before I announced who I was."

Sarah pulled her shawl around her shoulders and pulled the door shut behind her. "You said, J, and then changed it to Ben. What were you going to say?" Sarah asked.

"It is ok, Sarah. Tell her my real name," Ben said as he looked at his sister.

"Jesse," she said. "Jesse McFay. He is my brother, Sarah. I have been looking for him for months! When I saw that he was known as Ben Waters, I had to devise a way to let him know who I was, so in the kitchen, I tiptoed and whispered Jesse in his ear."

"Yes, you did! And then I dropped the coffee and ran out of the house like an idiot!"

Sarah looked at the two of them standing side by side, and thought to herself that she would have seen it in their faces, had she not been so blinded by jealousy. Suddenly, she enveloped Sarah in her arms and welcomed her to the family.

"Now, we have some explaining to do once we get inside," Ben said smiling at his beautiful wife. The multitude of secrets they had invented would have to be reinvented in order to explain the children that could not possibly be Ben's, and... well it could wait. "Let's get in out of the storm before we 'citch our death a cold,' as Granny used to say."

"Who is Granny," Lacey asked innocently.

Ben and Sarah looked at each other over the top of her head, and smiled. "All in good time," Sarah said. As they turned to enter the door, Sarah stopped and said, "Having two Benjamin Waters in the house is confusing enough. Having two Sarah Waters would be impossible. Do you have a middle name we could use?"

At the same moment, Ben and his sister both said, "Elizabeth."

Sarah smiled and said, "Well, then. Welcome to the family, Elizabeth Waters!"

Sarah went back in and Benjamin pulled the door closed leaving them on the front porch alone. "Elizabeth, I am so happy to see you. I have spent many hours picturing your face, so I wouldn't forget. But the only image of you I could remember was of that horrible night when they took me away." Tears gathered in his eyes, and Elizabeth hugged him.

"Don't think about that night any more, Jesse," she said squeezing his hand.

"No! You must never call me Jesse, Elizabeth!" Ben said as he took hold of her upper arms and pushed her away from him. "Don't call me anything until you get used to the idea that I am now called Ben, or Benjamin. I am Benjamin Waters as far as this community, and this family knows."

"This *family*? This *family* doesn't know who you are?" She stepped back and shrugged his hands off her. "Jesse, what is going on?"

The second time she called him Jesse, it set off alarms inside him. He was so thrilled to see her, it never occurred to him that she might be a threat to their lives. He looked straight at her and said, "Do *not* call me Jesse, Elizabeth." He clearly pronounced her name in a way that communicated to her that their new names were going to be permanent, and there was no room for negotiation.

His sister was a little frightened at his tone and his demeanor, and realized he was not the innocent brother she had known so many years ago. They looked at each other with an emotion akin to panic, and both felt the bitter disappointment that their reunion was not as joyous as they had hoped it would be.

"Elizabeth," Benjamin started, "I have loved and missed you every day of my life. And you know that." Her nod encouraged him to go on, "But I cannot have you put my life, Sarah's life, and the children's lives at risk with your being here. And what is more, I will not allow it."

"Are you threatening me, Jesse McFay?" She said stubbornly.

This time his grip on her forearm was not as friendly as it had been before. He turned with her and headed for the wagon.

"What are you doing?" She was extremely surprised at his actions. What had happened to the brother that she could manipulate into anything? Why was he being such a bully now? "Stop! Stop it right now!" she said, expecting him to acquiesce as he had always done in the past.

"I'm not going to stop until I have you far from here," Ben said. "This was a mistake." He lifted her up onto the wagon she had rented, walked around the horse and pulled himself up beside her, taking the reins to turn the team.

He was so angry he could hardly breathe. He was afraid he was going to upset the wagon because of the mud and wet grass, and paused long enough to think about what he was doing with it. He had to get back over on the path, and slow down while going down the hill, or else he was going to injure, or possibly lose control of the horse.

They rode in silence for some distance. Ben was beginning to wish his sister could stay with him, then wondered if she was sent to find him by the bounty hunter. After all, he had no idea who she had become. But her unwillingness to call him Ben… something as small as that, but as critical as that… well, she could not be trusted. He gave the horse a slap on the back with the reins to punctuate his resolve to get her as far away from him as he could possibly manage.

"How did you get here?" he asked.

"In the wagon you are driving!" She spat back at him.

"Did you drive it all the way from Parkersburg?"

"No." She was pouting now, a technique that had always worked with her brother. He had adored her since the day she was born, and he was not only her loving brother, he had served as her father as well, because he had often been there for her when her own father was drunk and too dangerous to be around.

"Then how did you get here from Parkersburg?" He shouted out of frustration, which prompted her to become absolutely silent. He knew there was a period of time in the spring when the ice was melting and it was not safe to travel by sleigh on the river, and yet the ice had not melted enough to allow safe boat travel either. Therefore, there were a couple of weeks or more, depending on the weather, when folks either postponed travel, or caught a ride on a wagon that was headed that way. It was too far to go on Shank's Mare, and Ben certainly knew his delicate sister had not walked.

He was flooded with memories, long forgotten, of how she would pout when he wouldn't buy her candy, or take her with him when he went out with his friends in their neighborhood. The homesickness was unbearable, and her sitting there beside him combined and cracked his armor. He drew the wagon to a halt.

"What do you want, Elizabeth?" He stared at her, then continued, "What is it that you want from me?"

She locked eyes with him for a moment, then broke eye contact and stared at her hands. Ben sat looking at the landscape without seeing it, and his sister sat staring at her fingers. Finally, he picked up the reins and clicked for the horse to continue.

"No, wait," Elizabeth said, "Could we just start over?"

Ben stopped, but said nothing. There was nothing on this earth he wanted more at this moment, than to spend the next few weeks reminiscing with his sister. To have her here for a lifetime would not be enough to make up for all they had lost. But he could *not* risk the lives of his family. He took a deep breath to clear his head. This decision was not one he could afford to make hastily.

"What do you mean by start over?" Ben asked, tired of her games.

"Well," she said as she held out her hand for him to shake, "my name is Elizabeth Waters. I am here looking for my brother, Benjamin Waters." He is as handsome as I remember him, but far too grown up to treat him like the boy I used to know." Her smile reeled him in.

He looked down at her extended hand, shook it, then pulled her into his embrace. "I have missed you so much, Elizabeth."

"So, you are not going to call me Sarah, even when we are alone?"

"I cannot afford to, Elizabeth. And you cannot call me Jesse, ever! EVER!" He backed up to see her face. "It is a matter of life and death, Elizabeth. Forget that name and never say it again."

"Alright." She thought about it for a minute and then said, "Not even when we are alone?"

"No! You must get into the habit of calling me Ben, and you can't do that if you have two names for me."

"Alright! Alright! I understand!" She looked at him with the smile he remembered, and said, "I do not like it, but... I understand and I accept it."

"I am not sure you do. Our children only know me by Ben. I do not ever want them to hear that name and make the connection with who I was."

"Does Sarah know who you are?"

"Elizabeth, what are you doing here?" He had to ask for his own safety. He had not seen his sister for fourteen years. Plenty of time for her to have changed into a completely different person.

"Well, Mama was sick by the time word came to us that you had escaped. She so wanted me to come find you, so she could see you one more time before..."

"Before what? Is she dying?" Benjamin asked with a knot in his stomach.

Sarah looked up at him with tears in her eyes, and nodded her head yes. "Ben, she is already gone. I am so sorry."

Benjamin turned and jumped out of the wagon. He began walking in big circles in the field, stomping clumps of grass, and looking up at the sky. Slowly, he walked back to the wagon, put one hand on the seat, and asked, "When?"

"About a month ago, Jes – Benjamin," she had caught herself, but his look of warning registered with her clearly.

"A month?" he asked through his tears. "I missed hugging Mama again by a month?" He kicked the side of the wagon and yelled, "Why didn't you come get me before this? I could have seen my Mama if you would have come a few weeks ago!"

"Ben," Elizabeth said sweetly, "I had no idea where you were. Her last wish was that I find you. So I boarded the train in New York, and took it all the way to the end of the line in Parkersburg. I intended to start here and then work my way back. I got off and asked around for nearly a week. I thought about heading west in case you had, and I thought about going down one of the trails, but someone mentioned that many folks traveled up the Little Kanawha to settlements up here. To be honest, I was afraid to travel alone, so I hired a man to drive me here. He tied his horse to the back of the wagon, and returned to Parkersburg the day he brought me."

Ben's head was spinning. He was exhausted and found it difficult to separate the loss of his mother from the loss of Granny. His heart was so filled with grief from the losses, and joy at seeing his sister, he could not process any more information. He stood in the field with his hands on his hips, trying to breathe and figure out what he should do next. Finally, he turned, readjusted his hat, and climbed back into the wagon.

He drove the team in a big circle and headed back to the cabin. "Elizabeth, if I take you home, you are going to hear and see things you do not understand. If I can trust you to just hold your questions until we are alone; to go along with whatever is going on without betraying my trust..."

"Benjamin, I wanted desperately to find my brother. The one I trusted and loved more than life itself. I wanted it to be the way it was before everything went horribly wrong. I guess I thought we would go somewhere and start a new life, with just the two of us and life would be just like it was."

Ben looked at her and appreciated the fact that she did not say, "Before you beat our father to death with your bare hands."

"Now I have found my brother, and for that I am truly grateful." Her smile brightened her face. She locked arms with him and continued, "But never in my wildest dreams did I ever dream you would have a family of your own. One that you loved more than you love me. And one that you would turn me out to protect."

He looked at her, not knowing what to say.

She continued, "All I remember of you is that I was the only one in your world. At least that is how you made me feel. I thought you were the grandest when you stopped him from beating..." She breathed deeply, then said, "And I could not understand why they had taken you, because what you did was so good for us. I never had one bad thought about that, Benjamin. Not one."

He felt a load lift from his heart. He put his right arm around his sister and cried silently as he drove the wagon homeward. "Thank you for that, Freckles." He looked down to see if she remembered, and she hit him on the chest in mock anger.

"Oh, how I hated that nickname," she said laughing. "I prayed that my freckles would go away, but they never did!" She rolled her eyes and made him laugh again.

"Do you remember when you thought you could hide them by putting Mama's rouge all over your face?" They both giggled like children at that thought, then Ben said, "And Mama was so mad at you because…"

They both fell silent, caught up in the memories of how abusive their father was. The names he would call their Mama when she dared to wear makeup, the times he found her meager stashed of those things that makes a woman feel pretty, and would throw them out in the street and dare her to go after them.

They were approaching the cabin, so Ben stopped, lifted his sister down from the wagon and said, "Sarah really is my wife. We are legally married. Kevin is her brother, and Granny was her Mama who died a few months ago. I know you can figure out they are not really my children, although this community believes they are, and I won't have them thinking anything different," he said with a look of warning in his eyes.

She nodded in agreement as he continued, "That is all I am going to say about that. If something else comes up that you do not understand, just play along and I will fill you in later, ok?" He turned and headed toward the cabin to let them know he and Elizabeth had returned. "Oh, and one more thing. Our parents' names were Lloyd, and Juanita. It is a long story that I will tell you later." He began walking toward the house.

"Does Sarah know you have been in prison?" She asked, stopping him in his tracks.

"I believe she does, although we have an agreement not to speak about our pasts to each other or anyone else. None of us speak of our pasts to each other, or anyone else. Do you understand, Elizabeth?"

It occurred to her that Sarah might also be on the run. Had she escaped prison as well? She had paused a little too long to process these questions and was startled when Ben took a menacing stop toward her and said, "Do you?"

She quickly said, "Yes, I understand."

Ben said, "You are not to ask her about where we met, or where she is from. You are not to ask the children anything about their lives, or Kevin either for that matter. It is a matter of life and death that you do not speak of this to anyone else. If you want to be a part of my life, and I hope you do, you are just going to have to live without knowing any of this."

That stopped Elizabeth in her tracks. "Never?" she asked.

"Never." He watched her face for a sign of recognition, but she was still processing. He said, "I want to apologize in advance for misjudging you, if I *am* misjudging you, but I have to say this as well."

She looked up at him as he walked closer to him, curious as to what he would say next.

"If you do any of the things I have told you not to do, or repeat this to anyone, or put my family in danger in any way, I will send you packing and tell this community that you stole from us. You will NOT be allowed back!" Even he was shocked at the way he sounded.

The love in her face withdrew leaving only the look of pain in its place.

"I'm sorry, Elizabeth! I want you here so badly, but I cannot endanger the lives of my family. And to be honest, I do not even know you! Please, Elizabeth, try to understand the position I am in."

She was hurt beyond words, but she did understand his dilemma. If she wanted to be a part of his family, she was welcomed. But she had the responsibility of protecting them from harm as well. She decided that was not too much to ask. "I would not expect anything less from you, Ben. I would expect you to protect your family at all cost. I just hope that in time, I can become a part of that family as well."

He hugged her so hard she thought her ribs would break. "You *are* part of our family, Elizabeth Waters. So come on in and let me introduce my sister."

"Wait, Ben!" She stopped just short of the front porch. "What will they think of me for lying about who I was. I mean, how will you explain to them that I said my name was Lacey when it is really Elizabeth? I am so ashamed. I want to be someone they can look up to, but now they will think me a liar!"

Ben laughed a hearty belly laugh at that one. He said simply, "Oh, believe me, that will *not* be a problem."

Chapter Seventeen

The next few days were priceless. Everyone accepted Elizabeth's presence without question. In fact, nobody even flinched when Ben introduced her as his sister whose name was Elizabeth, and not Lacey as she had introduced herself earlier; they just accepted her as part of the family and got on with life, much to her amazement.

For now, she was sharing a room with Grace, who had always wanted an older sister, and finally had one since Elizabeth was only four or five years older than Grace. Besides, she was secretly pleased to share her room, because after sleeping in the orphanage, and then in the crowded cabin with all the others, her room seemed a little lonely.

As they brought the covers up to their chins, they rolled toward each other and Grace asked, "So, where did you and Papa grow up?"

Elizabeth was immediately on full alert. Benjamin had not filled her in on what he had told his family regarding his background, so she was determined not to say a word. "I am really too tired to talk much," she said faking a yawn. "But I could listen if you don't mind talking for a while. Have you always lived here?" Elizabeth asked.

Having no idea what her Papa had told Elizabeth about their pasts, Grace stated that she, too, was too tired to talk, and said, "Sleep well!" The two women turned away from each other and stared wide eyed at the walls before finally falling asleep.

Little Ben knew what to do with a Granny, or an Uncle Kevin, but he wasn't quite sure what to do with an Aunt. But Elizabeth fell head over heels in love with all the children, so it was only a matter of time until they became friends.

"What is that you are doing?" she asked Little Ben.

"Whittlin'," he said without looking up. *Dumb question,* he thought to himself. *I'm sitting here with a knife, carving on wood! What did she think I was doing?*

"Well," Elizabeth said as she pulled up a stool, "I like to whittle, too!"

Little Ben stopped what he was doing, and stared at her dryly. He had never heard of a girl who liked to whittle, and thought she was just saying that to get on his good side. But within moments, he realized she not only liked it, but was good at it as well!

"So, what are *you* doing?" he asked with great interest.

She had taken a bar of soap, and whittled off the top right portion of it. Then she began smoothing off the edges of the remaining part, revealing the back of some kind of animal. As she carved the top part, a small chunk was kept intact were the ears would go later, and then the flowing hair of a horse's mane came into view. Within an hour, she had a horse running at full gallop, standing on the shelf facing one fascinated, wide eyed, little boy!

"Can you teach me how to do that, Aunt Elizabeth?" he said eagerly.

Elizabeth had Rebecca sitting on her lap, braiding her thick red hair into two pigtails. "I call these piggy tails because her hair is too short to have real pigtails!"

"How do you know when they turn into real pigtails?" Little Ben asked with such sincerity that Elizabeth giggled at him.

"They *are* real pigtails, Little Ben," she said with a sweet smile. "I just call them piggy tails because she is just like playing with a little doll, and the name piggy tails sounds cute," she said in baby talk.

Little Ben rolled his eyes at all that silliness, and wondered when girls turned from silly little things, to down to earth people like Granny was. Piggy tails! He hoped she didn't say things like that in front of Ira and his other friends.

As Benjamin entered the front door, he passed Little Ben who was rolling his eyes as he exited the front door. As the door slammed shut, Ben asked his little sister, "How are you doing?" He pulled a chair up, turned it around backwards and sat down in it with his arms up on the back of it.

"Alright," she said as she turned Rebecca around and smiled at her adorable little face. "Grace asked me last night where we had grown up."

Benjamin placed his hands on top of his head and asked, "What did you say?"

"It's ok, Ben," she said patting his knee. "I just said I was too tired to talk much." Ben looked relieved until she said, "and then I made a mistake."

Ben had to stand and walk around this time. The tension of having her here was almost unbearable, and yet the thought of losing her was equally disturbing. He had had too many losses in too short a time, and just could not cope with losing her now.

She rather enjoyed watching him torment himself so she remained quiet. That is what he got for not trusting her. Instead of asking her what happened next, he assumed the worst, and his sister chose to just sit there and let him.

"Ok, what did you do? Is it fixable? Tell me what you said! I am telling you, Elizabeth, if you do anything to…"

"Oh, sit down, Benjamin Waters! You always did take yourself too seriously! Do you want to hear what happened or would you prefer to just keep telling yourself scary stories until you whip yourself into a tizzy that results in your having to run to the outhouse?" She crossed her arms and looked at him with raised eyebrows and her head tilted to the side.

"Well, you sister sure does know you, doesn't she?" Sarah said with a laugh as she and Grace entered the house with empty baskets. They had been outside hanging up clothes and were flushed from the spring sun, chilly wind, and hard work.

"Yes, she does unfortunately," Ben said. "And she remembers all too well how to drive me crazy, too!" He walked past Grace and gave Sarah a look that told her they would talk about it later as he took the laundry baskets from her.

Suddenly, Elizabeth was startled by a soft moaning sound and turned quickly to see where it had come from. Grace, Sarah, and Ben chuckled at her and Grace said, "That is a sound you had better get used to! It is the wind howling as it comes through the cracks in the walls. Nothing to be afraid of."

"Well, that is some wind," Elizabeth said warily. "Oh, do you remember when you used to make me kites, Brother?"

Ben smiled at the name she had called him when she was a child, and said, "I had forgotten that you called me Brother when you were little." It occurred to him that using that nickname just might be the solution to the problem of his name change. "Would you please call me that more often? It makes me feel like we are kids again."

Elizabeth immediately recognized the opportunity and said, "Well, Brother it is then. But do not think I have forgotten my request for a kite!"

"What's a kite?" Little Ben asked as he once again entered the cabin, with Dusty running past him to check the kitchen for crumbs.

"OH! You don't know what a kite is?" Ben asked with pure joy on his face. "Well, we are going to have to fix that!"

Elizabeth was delighted to see what a great father her brother had become. He picked up Rebecca and danced around with her while singing an impromptu song about flying a kite. Sarah looked on with great love in her eyes and Elizabeth was touched by the love they shared. It became clear to her why her brother wanted to protect this. This is what they had both wanted for their own family, and now he had it. It was her hope that she, too, would someday have a husband and children, and that their family would be as happy as this one.

Before long everyone was looking for all the items needed to build a kite and Elizabeth was surprised and pleased at the relaxed and celebratory feeling in the air. Just as they were wondering what they could use for a tail, Kevin entered with the seeds he had just purchased at Jimmy's and asked what all the commotion was.

"We are building a kite, Uncle Kevin! Do you know what a kite is?" Little Ben asked.

"Why, I believe I do, Little Man," he said with a smile as he looked around at the faces of this little family he loved so much.

"Do you have anything we could use as a tail for it?" Little Ben asked, looking up into the face of his uncle with so much hope, it prompted Kevin to say yes! "I believe I DO have something you can use. Stay right here and I will get it."

When Kevin came back, he had with him a long strip of material that was actually two pieces sewn together, back to back, one making a lining for the other. Benjamin looked at it, considering its length and finding it a bit too long, which was of course fixable.

Sarah looked at it as a beautiful piece of needle work with fine stitching, and thought it might be too beautiful to cut up for a kite tail. Perhaps a cloth to drape over the mantel?

Grace and Little Ben were just wanting to get it onto the floor where it could be sized and attached to the kite, and Rebecca was trying to get it into her mouth so she could chew on it.

But Elizabeth was so struck by its similarity to a Priest's stole, that she simply stood there looking at it for a moment. She held out her hand and felt the satin on the back of the piece, turned it and looked at the embroidery on the front of it, and looked up at Kevin who quickly cleared his throat, handed the cloth to Little Ben, then pulled up a chair to watch their progress.

"Come on, Aunt Elizabeth!" Little Ben shouted, arousing her from her stupor. "This is going to be as fun as the snowball fight!"

"What snowball fight?" That was all it took for the entire story of that wondrous winter day to come tumbling out. They were laughing and talking over each other, telling the story and being corrected by the other team. Elizabeth knelt down and sat back on her feet and watched as they interacted. *This is worth fighting for,* she thought to herself. I must tell Brother that I do understand now. I can live without knowing anything at all about these people. But I know I cannot live without them.

Before long, Ben was displaying his expert ability to fly a kite while the children clapped and asked for turns. Rebecca was too little to hold onto the string, so Benjamin tied it around her waist so she could hold on to the string and pretend she was really flying it.

Little Ben held his coat open, and ran as fast as he could to see if he could get airborne in the strong wind while Grace was watching her Mama and Papa hold hands. Kevin was showing Elizabeth how she could see their church from where they were standing when they heard Sarah scream. Turning, they saw Rebecca lifted into the air! Her feet about three feet off the ground, and she was traveling at an alarming rate of speed above the edge of the hill toward the treetops!

Benjamin tried to run to her, but his leg prevented him from catching her in time. Little Ben tried to catch her, but as the hill below her fell away, he could only run farther and farther down the hill with Dusty on his heels, while making attempts to jump high enough to catch her, but missing each time.

Sarah screamed as Kevin and Elizabeth both ran after her shouting, "Rebecca!" as they ran. Youth was on Elizabeth's side and she was the first to attempt grabbing the baby's foot as Rebecca bobbed up and down in the wind. But it was Kevin's height that saved the day as he lunged toward the skirt of the child, pushing Elizabeth down onto the ground roughly. She started rolling down the hill, screaming as she rolled over and over and Kevin had to jump over Elizabeth's foot to make the final leap and catch Rebecca's clothing in midair.

Kevin hit the ground with Rebecca sitting, happily on his fat belly, and the entire family burst into laughter at the comical sight. Rebecca, however, had thoroughly enjoyed her adventure of flight and was still hanging on to her kite string and jerking on it, hoping it would magically lift her high into the air again.

They surrounded Rebecca to be certain she was alright, then remembered Elizabeth and turned to find her covered from head to toe in mud and wet hay, her hat now on the side of her head, and her dress twisted half way around her body. They stood, frozen in place wondering if they should apologize or laugh, when her own laughter answered their question.

They laughed as they sat down on the cold, wet, ground and told what they were thinking, what they thought about doing, and how shocked they were to see the child twirling around at the bottom of the kite string. Finally, one of them said it could have had a tragic ending, and that thought sobered them completely. The thought of Rebecca flying off over the treetops, far from their care and being deposited somewhere far away – perhaps in the top of a tree was too much for Sarah to bear.

The tears flowed as she said, "What were we thinking? Here we are with four adults and none of us considered that possibility!"

"Well, it didn't happen," Elizabeth said as she sat down by Sarah and patted her arm. "It could have, but it did not. And since we will never let that happen again, there is no need to play it over and over in your head, unless you just *want* to frighten yourself!"

Ben remembered his mother saying those exact words, and smiled as he felt a renewed gratitude for Elizabeth's presence. "Come on everyone. We need to get into the house and get dry and warm." It was getting colder now that nighttime was coming, so Benjamin walked over and offered a hand to Kevin who was still lying flat on his back, and pulled him up off the ground in spite of Kevin's groaning and moaning.

"I am too old for these shenanigans!" Kevin announced as they headed toward the cabin, his hand on his back as if his it was hurting him.

But just as they turned and looked down the hill at their little home, the strange man who had been watching them from the top of the hill for several weeks, exited their cabin, closing the door behind him. He stepped off the porch, looked up at them, mounted his horse and rode away.

Ben and Kevin wanted to run after him, but they both knew he was too far away, and besides, neither of them had it in them to run again. They were exhausted and just walked along in silence.

"I'm going to run down to see if he took anything," Little Ben said.

"No, you are going to stay right here with us," Ben said. Little Ben clearly was not happy about it, but he stayed close to his father, eventually holding his hand as they walked.

Elizabeth was impressed at how well Little Ben listened to her brother. The boy did not seem to be afraid of him, and yet he obeyed him immediately. *Respect,* she thought to herself. *He respects his father. That is what I see. Respect, not fear.*

Benjamin grabbed the ax, stepped up onto the porch, and entered the house with Kevin close behind. Finding the cabin empty, he motioned for the rest of them to enter. Slowly, they all looked around and found nothing missing.

Kevin and Benjamin looked at each other with faces that said they would talk about it when the children were not there, and Sarah asked Grace and Elizabeth to help her heat up supper. Her glance at Benjamin clearly spoke of her concern, but she did not want to speak about it in front of the children either.

There was tension in the air and Elizabeth wanted desperately to ask who that man was, why he was there, and why were they not talking about it. But she knew better. Finally, she knew to hold her tongue.

When the children were tired, Benjamin asked Grace to take Little Ben with her, to sleep in her room. Grace did not know they wanted time to talk without having to worry about Little Ben overhearing them. But she knew them well enough to know there was a reason, and she did not need to know what it was. She simply said, "Sure, Papa. Come on, Ben."

Benjamin said, "Thank you, Sweetheart," when Grace tiptoed to kiss him on the cheek.

She smiled at him with great love and respect in her eyes, and said, "You are welcome, Papa!" She gathered up her sewing, turned and said, "Good night, all." Then she kissed her Mama and went to bed.

The adults spoke quietly about the day's events. They discussed the impending trip to Parkersburg and the decision to sell the wagon instead of actually selling the human beings inside it. No one was comfortable doing that, even for the good of the runaway slaves.

Sarah admitted she was upset that the young boy would no longer be her student. "He was a brilliant boy!" she said, wiping away the tears. "He learned to read faster than anyone I have ever tried to teach. And his father could have learned much faster, but I don't think I ever fully earned his trust. Or maybe he was just shy. But he was very, very bright. I only had to tell him once and he had it. But both of them learned to write their names, and both could read, so now it is up to them. I just wish I could have had more time with the boy."

"I think you would have brought that boy home with you raised him as your own!" Benjamin said, teasing her a little. "And he was very attached to you, too. That could be why you are sad."

The entire community had chosen not to use the runaway slaves' names, for fear that they might be said accidently, in the presence of those who would use that information against them. However, the two were well loved and cared for, and they all felt they had done their best to do what God would have wanted them to do. Their love would travel with them, and their prayers would accompany them to safety.

The subject of the mysterious man came up and they vowed to keep an eye out for him, and go after him the next time he appeared. They recounted all the times they had seen him, and told Elizabeth this was the first time they knew about, that he had actually been inside their home.

Benjamin announced that one of the men should be at the house at all times, but Kevin did not answer. They turned to him only to find that he had fallen sound asleep. Sarah put her hand on his shoulder to awaken him, and realized she could feel heat coming through his shirt. She jumped forward and placed her hands on his head to check his temperature and jumped to her feet announcing that he was burning up with fever.

It took both Ben and Sarah to get him into bed, then Ben sent her to get Little Ben to come help him get him undressed. In an instant, a sleepy boy stepped up beside his father to help undress his Uncle Kevin.

By the time they had him undressed and under the covers, Sarah was back with a pan of cold water and several rags to wash Kevin down. The back of his shirt and pants were still wet from lying on the damp ground, but the rest of his clothes were damp as well, and his skin was clammy.

"He was running behind me," Elizabeth said. "Perhaps he was sweating before he lay down on that wet ground. He could get pneumonia," she said with a worried look on her face. "Is there a doctor we could get?"

"No," Ben said, "The nearest one is in Parkersburg. I don't know what we should do."

"Midgie," Sarah said. "We need to go get Midgie! She will know what to do."

Ben was half way out the door before she finished her sentence.

"Be careful, Ben!" Sarah shouted at his back. "Watch out for the cave!"

Just then Sarah looked up and saw Little Ben standing and looking in horror at his Uncle Kevin. "Go to bed, Ben," Sarah said to the boy, and then added, "I will have to sleep tomorrow and will need you to take your turn watching your Uncle Kevin."

Little Ben stood a little taller, rubbed his eye and turned and returned to his sister's room.

Sarah was wetting a cloth and washing Kevin's face, neck, shoulders, chest and arms. She looked up at Elizabeth and nodded toward the dry rags. "Elizabeth, we need to keep him cool. Throw those covers back and wash his legs." Sarah waited for Elizabeth to move, but she simply stood and looked horrified at the man in the bed.

"But, I can't! I can't uncover a man's legs!" Elizabeth said looking appalled at the very thought.

Sarah stood, grabbed Elizabeth's arm and jerked her toward Kevin's head. "Oh, alright!" she shouted. "You keep his head, chest, and shoulders cool. Keep rewetting the cloth and wash him down! We have to get rid of that fever!" Sarah threw back the covers and began washing Kevin's legs briskly.

Elizabeth turned her back to Sarah and began the task at hand. She kept the cloth cool and wet, and washed him systematically from head to chest, arms to hands. The longer they washed him, the warmer the water became, until Sarah decided to get Grace out of bed to keep the cool water coming.

The three women were working diligently when Ben returned with Midgie in tow. She set about covering him with a blanket so as to prevent chilling, and encouraged them to keep wiping him down. She began brewing a tea with healing herbs in it, and pulled out a bottle of something called, "Lightening Hot Drops."

She made the cup of tea, stirred in a little molasses, then stirred in a few drops of Lightening Hot Drops."

She wanted to be certain she did not burn Kevin, so she let it steep for a while, then took it in for him to drink. "You're gonna have to hold him up, and put just a little in his mouth at a time," Midgie said as Ben lifted Kevin's upper body, and moved in under him so that Kevin was sitting up in his arms.

Sarah tried to give him a drink, then said, "Maybe this would be easier with a spoon, Grace, would you…"

"I got it, Mama," she said as she headed to the kitchen to get a spoon.

Sarah dipped a spoonful of Midgie's concoction into the spoon, then touched it to her lips to see how hot it was. "Whew!" Sarah said, turning her head away farm the smell. "What is in this!"

Midgie said, "Oh, just a few dried herbs I had from last summer, and the Lightening Hot Drops." She shook her head back and forth quickly and shrugged her shoulders as if there were nothing out of the ordinary.

"Well, what is in the Hot Drops, then?" Sarah said, smelling the strange mixture again. "Because it has something that… whew! What is that?"

Midgie got up, went over and retrieved the bottle for Ben to read, "Well, it is 50% alcohol, Chloroform 48 minims, Ether 48 minims, Fluid Extract Myrrh, Fluid Extract Capsicum, Tinct, and Lavendar Compound," Ben said, his eyes growing wider with each new ingredient.

No one was quite certain exactly what all those things were, but Sarah had heard of Chloroform and Ether, and was shocked that both of those were mixed in with the alcohol! "Are you sure about his, Midgie?" Sarah asked as she smelled the spoonful once again.

"As certain as rain," Midgie said. "It'll cure what ails you! Why my youngin's have had this very cup of tea many times in their lives. Now go on, make him drink it all!"

Sarah lifted the spoon to his lips and shook Kevin to awaken him. "Kevin, please sip this tea. It will make you feel much better," she said to the seeping man.

"Oh, honey," Midgie said with a shove, "move outta my way. She sat down with a plop beside Kevin, lifted the spoon and poured the liquid into the side of the mouth. "Now look here, Sarah," Midgie said. "You put the spoon in the side of his mouth so his cheek keeps the tea from running out. You put the tip of the spoon right on his tongue, then lift it, pushing the tongue down out of the way, and pouring the liquid right down his throat. Now there you go!" She said as he swallowed sip after sip."

"But he is sleeping!" Sarah said, "Won't he choke?"

"You swallow spit when you're asleep, don't you! It is just like that. And before you know it, the entire cup is empty."

Sarah had to admit that it was working. She was not sure of what was in the drink, but she found it interesting that a man would drink a cup of tea in his sleep.

"Now, we just wait," Midgie said. "I have a few more remedies in my bag, but we won't use'em lessen we have to." She folded her arms, leaned back in the chair, and said, "So how did he get this sick so quick!"

They explained to her about the day's events, flying the kite, and the mishap with Rebecca. Then explained that Kevin had caught her in midair, and was so hot and sweaty that he just lay on the ground for a while to cool off.

"Land's sakes!" Midgie yelled! "Don't you know that is where pneumonia comes from? The cold wet ground! It is *in* the ground," she said, pointing downward to the ground for emphasis, "and when you sit on it, or lay down on cold, wet ground is how you catch it!"

She shook her head and mumbled something about these young fools today, then added, "And there is sickness in the night air, too. So don't be out in it unless you have to be!"

She sat in the rocker Ben had made and rocked back and forth as if in deep thought. Then she said, "Glendon Yoak, Ivy and Paul's brother, went out one time to watch the boys plow the garden. He did not even put on his boots, and just walked around on that wet dirt in a pair of house slippers, and he got pneumonia and died from it! Yes, indeed! Forty-seven years old! Healthy as a horse! You gotta stay away from that cold wet ground!"

In the silence that followed, Midgie began picturing that child in mid-air, and the tizzy they must all have been in. She said, "I reckon that was scary, seein' your youngin' sailin' above the ground like that!"

Sarah was glad to speak of something else, so she said, "It was scary! Can you imagine?"

Midgie laughed heartily at that, and said, "With ten children, you see a lot of things! Why, one time when we was pluckin' chickens, Elias saw how red his hands got in the hot water, so he put Denzel in the apple butter kettle, filled it with water, and built a fire under it to see how red he would get! Abram just happened to see them or he would have cooked him done!"

Benjamin said, "Why didn't Denzel just get out of the water?"

"Well, apparently, he tried! But Elias had a big stick and would just push him back down, or hit him with it!"

Midgie was laughing at the event, so, in spite of themselves, they laughed as well. "Then once," she continued, "the gypsies camped near here, and stole our corn, beans, pots, pans, chickens, anything they could get their hands on. So my boys decided to sceer'em off!" She had to wait until she could stop laughing to finish the tale. "Well, them gypsies were camped over yonder," she said, indicating with her hand that it was south of them, "and my boys slipped up there and put two whole tin cans of black powder in a tree near 'em, lit the fuse and ran. There was the most earth shaken explosion you ever did hear! And when the boys looked up, that whole tree was gone! AND the dirt it was sitting in!"

Grace was fascinated, and naïve enough to believe every word Mrs. Benson said. So she asked, "Where is that hole? Is it still there? I would love to see that!"

Midgie said, "Well you have seen it, girl! It is full of water now! It's the lake Abram fell into!"

Finally, the family figured out that Midgie was exaggerating a bit, and broke into laughter at the trick she had pulled on them. This lying thing was a great pastime and proved itself a wonderful way to cut the tension in the room as the time dragged by.

As the night wore on, Kevin's fever would rise and break, soaking him and his covers in perspiration. But the fever always went back up, and around 3:30 in the morning, he seemed to be struggling for his breath.

Midgie went immediately to her bag and brought out several small black tablets which she crushed up, put into water, and fed to him with a spoon. The pieces had not dissolved entirely, so they caught in his throat and made him cough and choke.

"What did you give him this time?" Ben asked, almost afraid what the answer would be.

"Creosote," was Midgie's answer. Ben's feet hit the floor and he smelled the spoon, looking immediately at Sarah whose eyes were asking if it were true. Ben nodded at her confirming that it was indeed creosote, and both of them looked immediately at Midgie.

Suddenly, Kevin began to cough. He seemed to cough for a long time, on and on without breathing. Then when he tried to inhale, he found himself incapable of taking in air. It was as if his throat had swollen shut and his effort produced a sound like he was inhaling a whistle.

His eyes opened and he stared with panic on his face that was as red as a beat. Slowly they watched the color drain from his face, and he began turning blue around his lips, and under his eyes.

Sarah stood up defiantly, looked toward the ceiling, and shouted, "NO! NO, GOD! NOT THIS TIME! NOT MY BROTHER! I CANNOT BEAR LOSING ONE MORE PERSON!" She stomped her foot at God and asked, "DO YOU HEAR ME? NOT ONE MORE PERSON!" Her chin quivered as she finished her rant, and she fell to her knees and burst into tears.

But Midgie was far more practical. "All of you grab onto him wherever you can get him. We have to wrap him up and get him outside, right now!" she shouted.

Benjamin and Sarah feared that Kevin was already dead because of the combination of odd "cures" she had put into his body, and were not about to take him out into the cold.

She almost had him in a sitting position by herself, when Abram walked into the room. "I brought a cow," he said, then realized what Midgie was trying to do, and grabbed Kevin's shoulders, while shouting, "Ben, get his feet!"

Ben was not about to argue with his friend, Abram, so he did what he was told and lifted Kevin off the bed. Midgie turned to Grace and said, "Build up that fire, I want it real hot in here when we come back in! And boil a lot of water, in little pans so it boils real quick!" Then she stepped out of the way so the men could get through the kitchen and out into the cold.

"Keep him warm," Midgie shouted as she tugged and pulled on his blankets to cover his neck and ears. "Abram, go get that wagon," she said, "We will put him in there!"

Sarah and Ben wondered where they were taking him, but Abram and Midgie just placed him in the wagon, then stood watching him as if they expected him to speak.

Elizabeth, came outside with coats or blankets for everyone, then went back in to stoke the fire even more, and set more pans to boil.

Just as Sarah had had quite enough, Midgie said, "Alright, let's get him inside, near the fire! He is starting to chill!"

They obeyed although they were frightened that Kevin would never survive the night. They placed him by the fire, then Abram tapped Ben on the shoulder and indicated for him to follow him. They retrieved Kevin's feather tick and carried it back, picked Kevin up, put the mattress as close to the fire as was safe, then lowered Kevin onto it.

"Do you have another tick?" Abram asked.

"Yes, on our bed, Ben." Sarah said.

They followed the same procedure with the second tick so that Kevin was almost as high as the fire. The room was uncomfortably warm, and the air so moist that it was difficult to breathe. But Midgie insisted that more pans of water be set out. "Fill that cast iron pot and put it right in these coals," she ordered, and Elizabeth did what she was told.

Midgie turned to Grace and said, "Go find something else we can put into that fire! Little pans, big pans. Keep them boiling."

They were suffocating in the steamy room, and their clothes felt wet and sticky on their skin. But the blueness around Kevin's lips had gone away, so they were hopeful he was getting enough air. Just when they were beginning to relax, Midgie did the unthinkable.

"Back outside!" she shouted!

"No! His clothes are soaking wet! We can't take him outside in this weather! It is raining and cold outside!" Sarah shouted in protest, but Abram had already picked up Kevin's head, so Ben grabbed his feet.

Sarah grabbed the dry bed clothes off the floor where they had fallen when Abram got their tick, and took the wet ones off Kevin, and replaced them with the dry ones.

For about twenty minutes, they went in and out of the house, from heat to cold and back again. Finally, when they entered the house and put Kevin down on the bed, Midgie walked over and began pounding him on the back in rapid succession. Kevin began coughing and coughing until his chest began to gurgle. He coughed so hard he could hardly get his breath, and eventually began vomiting. By the time he had finished vomiting, he was breathing deeply and steadily.

He coughed a few more times, then lay back absolutely exhausted. His face was filled with color, and he slept soundly, with a strong and steady breath.

"There you have it," Midgie said as she washed his face and hands. "He will be fine now. You just gotta keep him warm and let him rest for a week or two. If he gets 'til he can't breathe again, just do what we did, steam up the house, and take him in and out." As an afterthought, she turned and said, "And you can keep that creosote. Give him two at a time, two or three times a day."

Midgie was packing up her things as if she saved lives every single day, while the Waters family felt they would never be able to sleep again! They were stunned by what they had just witnessed, and experienced physically, mentally, and emotionally.

As they went to the door, Midgie said casually, "Oh, and the cow is for milk. Give Kevin warm milk, straight from the cow every morning, noon, and night. It helps with Consumption, and it will help with pneumonia."

'Thank you's, were said, hugs given all around, and before long, Midgie and Abram were out the door, headed for home.

Chapter Eighteen

Monday, May 11, 1863

Little Ben was the first one out of the house that morning. He had awakened at the sound of the Whippoorwill singing in the distance. He remembered clearly, his Granny explaining to him that the Whippoorwill's song brought the sap up into the Maple trees, and they would soon be ready to tap for Maple syrup. He was excited, and decided that as soon as he finished at the outhouse, he would awaken Uncle Kevin so he could hear the song as well.

Kevin had not snapped back from the bout of pneumonia as was expected. He seemed to be cold all the time, and still napped most afternoons. But Little Ben had decided that all he needed was some good spring weather, and that by the middle of summer Uncle Kevin would be fine. It was this goal that gave Little Ben something to do besides miss his Granny, and he had decided to go at it full force.

He stopped before stepping up onto the porch and listened as hard as he could to see if he could hear the Whippoorwill one more time. Instead, he heard the church bell ringing.

"Papa, Mama, wake up!" he shouted as he entered the house.

The bedroom door opened and Ben came out, pulling his pants on over his long johns. "What's wrong, Son?" Ben asked sleepily.

"Church bell's ringing!"

Ben got to the door with four long strides, grabbed his hat off the nail beside the door, and went out onto the porch to listen. It rang three times, and stopped. In about five minutes it began again, rang three times and stopped again.

He went back into the cabin and announced that there was going to be an assembly at the church at 3:00 this afternoon.

"Why?" Sarah asked as she pulled on her house robe.

"I don't know, the bells didn't tell me, Sarah! I don't think Preacher knows Morse Code!" He enjoyed his joke, and Sarah was looking at him with a silly grin when he scooped her up in his arms, and gave her a long, sweet, kiss.

The children giggled with embarrassment, but secretly reveled in the display of love between their parents. Elizabeth smiled at her brother's gesture, and hoped that someday she would be loved that much.

The ridge they lived on was shaped like an S. They lived on the south part of the S, and the church was in the middle. When the bell rang, it went out to all those on that ridge, for miles around. But Ben was not certain those down off the ridges, toward Leafbank, could hear the alarm, so he saddled up Patsy, Grace's mare, and headed out to spread the word about the meeting.

On the way, he ran into Bernie Siers and mentioned how much he appreciated the loan of the cow. Bernie asked how Kevin was doing, and waited patiently while Ben explained how grateful they were that he had survived, but they were quite worried that he was not recovering as they thought he would.

Bernie encouraged him to keep the cow, and keep feeding him warm milk as long as he would drink it. At that, Ben laughed and said, "Well, he is down to one glass a day, and only if we threaten him with no food!"

"It gets old really fast, Ben. I had to drink it when I was a boy because my Mama had Consumption. She was sure it would keep me from getting it. But it was a long time before I could look a glass of milk in the eye after that, I can tell you!"

"Well, I thank you for the loan of the cow, Bernie. How can I repay you?"

"Well, I will tell you that when our girl, Susan, lived here, we had that cow because she loved milk. But now that she is married, and off with her husband clean out in Ohio, we don't much need that cow anymore." Ben noticed the sadness in his eyes.

Bernie continued, "So, you could save us the cost of feeding her if you would just take her off our hands, Benjamin! I am sure those youngin's of yours could use the milk."

Ben didn't know what to say. He was already eaten up with guilt for keeping the cow the last few weeks, but this was something else alltogether. "Now, I couldn't do that, Bernie," he said, feeling at a loss for words. "Well, you'd be doin' us a favor, Benjamin! Think on it, and talk to the Missus about it. I am just too old to have to get up early just to milk a cow for milk we got no use for."

"I will think on your offer, Bernie, and I do appreciate it."

That was enough for Bernie, so he nodded his head in agreement.

"Did you hear the church bell this morning?" Ben asked.

"No, I didn't. But we slept late. What is going on?" Bernie looked appropriately concerned, knowing that the bell could mean anything from news about the war, to an outbreak of measles, to a death in the community.

"Meeting at 3:00," Ben said, then turned his horse and said, "I gotta go tell the others."

Within an hour he had either told all his neighbors, or recruited others to go out and spread the word so he headed on home.

There was standing room only at the church. The children were sent outside to play so the adults could hear what was going on without distraction. Kevin was not feeling up to the trip, so Grace had offered to stay home with him.

155

"We have news of the war," Preacher started. "And there is some news I know some of you have been waiting for, so after a word of prayer, we will get started.

The men removed their hats and bowed their heads, and Rev. McCauley held out his hands and began praying. "Father we thank thee for the fine people of this community. Although they may not be in the war, we know their hearts are, and we love their hearts, Lord. So bless them as they hear the news today, and help us all cope with the changes this war will bring. Help us to strengthen each other by leaning on each other, and getting our strength from you. In the name of Jesus, we ask all things, Amen"

The church followed with, "Amen." Then Preacher stepped down and gave the floor to the men who had brought the news.

"Thank you, Preacher," the tall, thin, man began. "The first news I want to bring you is that on May 9th, well, last Saturday, the Confederate Army launched an all-out attack on our neighbors at Burning Springs. You know that that area is full of gas and oil, and the Rebels see it as a big advantage to the Union, so they have targeted it often."

Murmurs followed as the congregation began speaking about those raids, and predicting they had been as unsuccessful as before. Their attention turned to the Hamiltons, as their sons Victor and Roger were stationed there. The news of the attack sent fear through their hearts, and their friends were attempting to comfort them. Finally, someone from the back shouted, "Quieten down sos we can hear what them fellers have to say!"

With that the men proceeded to tell the whole story, about how "Grumble," which was a nickname for the Confederate General William Jones, and well over 1,400 men rode into Burning Springs and burned everything needed for the production of oil; all the barrels, the equipment, engines, wagons, wooden pipes, and engine houses had been burned to the ground. They had burned about 150,000 barrels of oil and the black smoke could be seen for miles.

The Hamiltons were worried about their sons and when asked about casualties, the men said there had been a few, but they did not have the names. Mrs. Hamilton cried softly into her hanky, while her husband hugged her to him and said she needed to wait until they got word. "It might not be so bad after all," he said with a hug around her shoulders. She patted her daughter on the knee, and the girl leaned against her Mama pitifully.

Another man, who was wearing more expensive clothes than they were used to seeing, stood to give them an update on the status of statehood. "As you know, last March the voters approved the state's amended constitution to allow western Virginia to become a separate state from Virginia." Although the congregation was aware of this, a cheer broke out as they celebrated the freedom from the unreasonable and controlling laws and taxes Virginia had imposed upon them.

"Now, President Lincoln has had some reservations about signing this proclamation, and he must sign it before we can become a state."

"Why wouldn't Lincoln sign it? He would have one more state in the Union. I would understand if we were trying to succeed from the Union, but...," Paul Yoak was interrupted when the crowd began to murmur and arguments broke out as to whether or not Lincoln should sign it.

"There are many of us who don't want to split with Virginia, so it would be a good thing if Lincoln just refused to sign it at all!" a lady in the back shouted.

The crowd erupted into a loud din, as argument after argument ensued. Finally, Caleb Rogers stood up front with his hat in his hand, raised his hand and shouted, "Alright, quiet down! Quiet down!"

Finally, everyone found their seats and gave him their attention.

Caleb nodded in gratitude, and began, "Right now, we are sitting ducks for the Union. We are cut off from Virginia by the mountains to the east, and Richmond doesn't care what happens to us. They are not going to waste military forces on protecting this part of the state!"

Heads nodded in agreement so he continued, "So if we don't break with Virginia, we are going to be bordered on the west by Ohio, which is a Union state, and to the north by Pennsylvania, which is also a Union state, with no military support to back us." Even those against statehood saw the logic in that, and waited to hear more.

"Besides," Caleb continued, "our rivers flow north and west, so that is where our trade is! With Ohio and Pennsylvania! And about 10 years ago, the B&O built that train from Harper's Ferry to Baltimore, not to Richmond! Our economic future lies with the North, not the South! What do we have if we remain with Virginia? Nothing."

Silence hung in the air for a moment.

Bernie Siers stood and asked, "Why would Lincoln *not* sign it?"

"It is against the law! That's why!" an angry man shouted from the back.

"What is against the law? What law says we can't become a state?" an angry woman challenged.

The man in the suit who started this held up his hand to quiet everyone. "There *is* a law," he began, "that says a state cannot split from another state without the permission of the other state."

The majority of those listening wanted desperately to have their freedom from Virginia, and felt as if the prize that had been within reach, was now being snatched away. Angry shouts emanated from the group, and Preacher stood to quiet them.

Preacher held up his hand and the people quieted out of respect for their minister, but the anger seethed.

The pastor interlaced his fingers over his chest and said with a smile that comforted everyone, "You know, arguing amongst ourselves won't change what this man came to say." He smiled at everyone in the room as if he was hearing a joke in his head, which simply and easily made everyone feel foolish of their behavior. "And if we keep arguing over every point," he continued, "it will take him three weeks to say it!" His belly laugh was contagious and had everyone smiling and some actually laughing. It was said with the same kind of exaggerations that Liars used to make a story funny, and the anger dissipated as the day's events were brought into perspective.

The suited man nodded his gratitude to Preacher and began again, "Yes, the Constitution says a portion of one state cannot form a new state without the permission of the state they are leaving. In your case, Virginia. However, the questions Lincoln asked last December when this reached his desk, were these: First of all, does Virginia still fall under the protection of the Constitution now that it has left the Union?"

Head nods and smiles spoke of relief, people clapped and stomped their feet in joy as their prize was placed once again within their reach. Then, they again turned their attention to the speaker. Things were going their way and they wanted to hear more.

"And secondly," the gentleman continued, "Lincoln wanted to be clear that this was actually a good thing for the Union. He wants to be certain it is legal, good for the Union, and good for the people of this part of the state, and not just an expedient means to an end."

"I heard the name of our state would be Kanawha for the rivers that run through here," Abram said loudly.

Some of the names considered were, Kanawha," he said with a hand gesturing toward Abram, "Western Virginia, New Virginia, Allegheny, and Augusta. But the name that was settled on, is West Virginia."

People nodded and looked at each other approvingly. Some said the name aloud, liking the strength of it as if flowed off their tongues.

An old timer, named Indianapolis Yoak stood up and said, "In March of '56 we split from Gilmer County and became our own county and named it Calhoun after John C. Calhoun who, as you know, was a great supporter of the South, slavery, and state's rights. Now, here we are seven years later seceding from the South all together and becoming a Northern state! I never heard tell of the like!"

John Ball stood and said with a twinkle in his eye, "Well, that will make that cabin my brother-in-law, Sam Barr, built across the river from the Simon Stump farm, be located in three counties, and two states, without ever moving!"

People nodded their heads and laughed at that truth, and began discussing how odd it would be to live in a different state than Virginia. West Virginia. They said it over and over.

Then Ben asked, "When do you think President Lincoln will sign this? Or will he even sign it at all, in your opinion?"

"Well, time will tell, time will tell." The man then asked for any other questions, and when there were none, he turned the meeting over to Preacher.

Chapter Nineteen

As soon as the family had left with the Bensons to go to the church meeting, Grace put Rebecca down for her nap. Certain that Rebecca was asleep, Grace went in to where Kevin was reading and asked him if he would like coffee. "Why yes, I would love that, thank you," Kevin responded, laying his book aside. "It seems I have not been warm since the day I took ill." He sounded discouraged and exhausted, and again, Grace wondered if he had acquired heart problems, or if he had caught some other disease that may have been lurking in that damp ground along with the pneumonia.

He had been wearing gloves every day to keep his hands warm and still they were as cold as ice. Grace felt his ice cold touch as she placed the coffee in his hands. Alarmed, she went to the nails by the front door and retrieved a scarf which she placed around his neck. As she stoked the coals and added small pieces of wood to start a fire, she asked the question that had been hanging between them for some time. "Uncle Kevin, did you talk about what happened in Parkersburg with Mama and Papa?"

Kevin swallowed the hot coffee he had just sipped, and said, "No. I did not, Grace."

Grace turned her back to the fire and looked at him as if she had never seen him before. "Really?" she asked. "Why?"

Kevin replied simply, "It was not my secret to tell."

Her expression changed from suspicion, to respect. She thought about what he had said.

"Besides," he said with a smile, "I *was* a Priest you know." He took another sip and said, "Keeping secrets has become a habit." Then he smiled to put her at ease.

She was completely prepared to chastise him for telling something so personal, and had worked out the conversation so as to be ready for anything he said in his defense. So she was completely caught off guard by his faithfulness to her situation and immediately burst into tears and sobbed with gratitude.

Kevin did not react in any way, other than to hand her his handkerchief. Although he wanted to draw her into his arms and let her cry all she wanted, his experiences with abused women told him that was not a good idea.

"I feel so silly," Grace admitted. "I never do this." She finished crying, straightened up, gained her composure, then immediately burst into tears again. She turned her back to Kevin and cried sorrowfully.

Kevin stood and walked up behind her, and said, "I would like to put my arms around you if I might. But only if you are comfortable with it."

Grace turned and nodded her head quickly. As Kevin's arm encircled her, she began to sob in earnest. He loved her as his own child, hugged her tightly to him, and whispered, "You are safe now, our precious Grace." As she sobbed he encouraged her to cry and let it all out.

Grace cried for the childhood she had lost, for the loss of her Granny and her birth Mom, for the abuse she had suffered, and all she had endured. Finally, the tears subsided and she found peace and comfort in her Uncle's safe arms.

"Am I?" she asked. "Am I safe now?" she said with a long deep sigh.

He placed his hands on the backs of her arms and pushed her back so he could see her face, "Of course you are, Grace." He paused and thought for a moment about what she had asked. Then asked, "You are not frightened of me are you? Because you know I would never hurt you or…"

"No! I am not frightened of you," she said with a fleeting smile. She stood and went to retrieve a clean hanky to blow her nose. "I am just afraid he is going to find us! I am afraid now that we have been spotted and identified that the Sheriff will come and take us away. I'm afraid I have led the authorities to Mama and Papa! I have not slept well, or gone outside without looking around for someone coming to get us, since we were in Parkersburg! I know I should have told Mama and Papa, but I was afraid they would be ashamed of me, and angry for leading the authorities to them! I don't want to have to leave here because of me!"

Kevin was appalled at how well this child hid her emotions. He had not seen one indication that she had any residual feelings about what had happened in Parkersburg, and as much as he wanted to talk about that, he wanted nothing more than to simply listen right now, to truly hear what she had to say. So he wisely sat in complete silence.

She got the coffee pot and poured more coffee into his cup, poured a small amount into another cup, then filled it with warm milk, pulled her chair over to the fire, and sat down to warm herself as Kevin returned to his rocking chair.

Kevin swished his coffee around in his cup, then took a sip and waited for her to continue. Her first words were, "I have been so happy, and so safe in this house. For the first time in my life, I have felt completely safe." Tears welled up in her eyes until they fell softly down her face, her chin quivered and she said, "Now it is all ruined. I feel like I should run away again."

Kevin leaned forward in his chair and hesitantly placed one hand on hers. She gripped his hand and held on tightly as she wiped her nose with the hanky she had in her other hand.

"Ok. Let's talk about that," Kevin said as he stood and stretched his back and shoulders. "Tell me why you do not feel safe."

"Because the Sheriff knows *who* we are, and *where* we are. It is only a matter of time until he comes to get us!"

Kevin moved the rocking chair he had been sitting in, closer to the fire and directly across from her so he could see her face. He leaned forward with his elbows on his knees and held out his finger tips for her to take hold of. She was leaning with her elbows on her knees as well, playing with her hanky, which she put into her lap before taking his hands.

Sitting toe to toe, elbows on their knees, Kevin insisted that she look him in the eye. When she did, he nearly wept, for the defeat, fear, and exhaustion he saw in her eyes.

"First of all, dear Grace, the Sheriff you spoke of is a lifelong friend of mine. Had he wanted to take you into custody, he would have detained you right then and there. Instead, he simply told me to take you back to my sister's family, and did not request any information as to where you could be found in the future."

She looked at him and said, "But…"

"He is a lifelong friend of mine, Grace. I know him well enough to know that he was giving me permission to take you back to your family, that he has no plans on returning you to New York. It was a gift he gave you because he understood the situation and clearly sided with you. This is not just between a helpless little girl and the man who runs the orphanage anymore, Grace. You have family now! And besides, the entire world sides with you. Can't you see that?"

Grace's eyes shot up and met with Kevin's. "Are you sure?"

"Yes. I am absolutely positive. Morris was almost as angry with that man as I was!" Kevin laughed at his display of an anger he had no idea he was capable of.

Grace smiled and said, "You *were* pretty mad!" And laughed with Kevin at the memory of what had happened.

Kevin said, "Yes. I was angry. Sheriff Morris was angry. And the jury Dunge will have to face will be angry as well. He is going to prison for a long, long time, Grace, and the Sheriff knows you have a stable home to be in. There is no way he will try to take you back to that horrid place."

Grace was nearly convinced, and drew in a deep breath. "It was so frightening to see how quickly life could change. One minute I was Grace Waters on a great adventure with my Uncle, and the next I was that tiny, little, nobody that was completely under his control!"

"Oh," Kevin said smiling, "You were never a tiny, little, nobody, Grace. I am sure there were times when you felt like that, but the truth of the matter is, you were just a patiently waiting, very angry, giant, preparing for a time when you would rise up and fight!"

She smiled at that image, so he continued, "And the difference in then and now is, you are not alone now. You have a jury of people who are going to hear what he did, and side with you! They are going to be very angry, as angry as you were at him for doing this despicable thing to a child, or many children I believe you said. You have a community, and parents who love you and will protect you with their lives. You have a brother who would shoot anyone who came near you, and if he didn't have a gun handy, he would take them to the ground, and then the two of you could stomp on him some more!"

They both had an extremely freeing laugh over that memory, then Kevin continued, "And you have an Uncle Kevin who did not leave any information with the church, or anyone else, as to where he could be found!"

Her head shot up and her arms went around his neck, hugging him so tightly he thought he couldn't breathe! She sat back in her chair and said, "You are a very kind, very smart man, Uncle Kevin!"

Kevin took that as a supreme compliment, then said, "See? We are all here to protect you, your brother, and Rebecca, with our very lives if need be."

"About Rebecca," Grace said hesitantly. Kevin waited.

"Do you feel differently about me, now that you know she is mine?" She could not bring herself to look at him when she asked.

"Not at all! Not at all," Kevin said without wavering.

She turned and looked at him suspiciously. "How can you not think…"

He knew she did not want to have to finish that sentence, but he did not speak. Did not let her off the hook.

"What, Grace?" he said. "How can I not think what?"

She turned defiantly and looked at him with anger in her eyes. "How can you not think I am a whore like Mr. Dunge said." She lifted her head defiantly in a way that made Kevin even prouder of her.

"Because I know who you are, Grace. I know the kind of woman you are. You had no choice in the matter. It was done to you, and not with your approval. You were a *child!* A child who was abused and mistreated by that…" His words drifted off as he felt the anger return.

He walked the floor for a moment, then said, "Tell me who you think you are, Grace."

"Well, I tend to measure myself through my Mama's eyes." She thought about that for a moment and then said, "The Mama who left us at the orphanage." She looked at Kevin to be certain he understood her meaning, then continued, "She was dying you know. She did not have any other option."

Kevin realized she was defending her mother, and said, "She must have loved you a great deal to have put your needs ahead of her own."

She smiled, content that he did not blame her mother. "I believe I did everything she asked of me, and with God's help, I believe we have the life she wanted for us, finally." Kevin nodded and she continued, "I think I am a great deal like Granny. I am strong and able to do things others find daunting." She looked at Kevin for approval, and then finished by saying, "And I believe God loves me, and is proud of me, just the way I am."

Kevin felt tears in his eyes as he said, "That is the most wonderful self- evaluation I have ever heard, Miss Grace! It was powerful, and to the point, and yes, I, too, believe God is proud of you, because of the way you are."

They sat in comfortable silence for a while, then Kevin said, "You asked me if I felt differently about you after I knew Rebecca was your daughter. I knew you meant, did I think badly of you, so I said no, to reassure you. But that was not entirely true. I do feel differently, but in a good way. Let me explain."

Grace held onto the phrase, "in a good way," so as to not let her heart sink while she waited, and soon he began again. "I traveled to Parkersburg with three children, but I came back with a woman I admire unbelievably, a young man who took a great deal of responsibility for another person, and a very loved baby. I think of you differently, but the change came from an awakening in me. I had the privilege of getting to know you better, and I loved everything I saw. I am even more in love with this family now than before we went, and I am truly impressed with your strength, and your courage. You have not had an easy life, and because of that, you have every excuse in the world to be bitter, and angry. But instead, you have chosen to be compassionate, loving, and kind. You even extended God's Grace to that horrible man who abused you. Yes, I think differently of you, but certainly not *less* of you. No, I quite admire you, Grace Waters. You are already what I have striven a lifetime to be."

Grace was beaming, her face aglow when Kevin finished speaking, then he realized the time and said, "But we are both going to be in trouble if we don't get supper on the table! They should be home soon!"

Both leapt to their feet and began preparing the evening meal, for soon the family would be home, sharing the news and events from the day.

Chapter Twenty

Spring had finally come to the Waters' home. Little Ben decided that Uncle Kevin needed to get out in the warmth and told him so. In fact, he insisted on telling Uncle Kevin he had to get up and go out with him to "let the sun beat the orneriness out of ya!" He had taken to quoting Granny almost verbatim as often as he could. This particular morning, he took Kevin to choose the right tap for tapping the Sugar Maple trees, and insisted he learn to whittle.

Although Kevin's body demanded sleep, he had grown very fond of the boy, and tried his best to keep up.

Denzel had become a regular at their home. He was there to plow the garden, and taught Grace how to walk behind the team and plow, yelling Gee and Haw to turn the horses right and left. He helped Grace and the others with planting, offered to help add another room for Elizabeth, and some nights, even stayed for dinner.

Caleb, on the other hand, seemed to always think Grace needed help with things. No matter what she was going to do, he insisted that it would be no trouble to come help her with it. The more he tried to help, the angrier she became with him.

"I seem to hold your attention to a great degree, Caleb Rogers, but I do not understand why. Why would you be interested in what I am doing if you think I am a complete idiot? Completely incapable of doing anything on my own?" she said before turning away from him and climbing onto the Benson's wagon to go home after church one day.

Caleb was frustrated, but determined to get some time with her, and he thought he knew how to get it. But it would take some doing, and some help from Little Ben. The next Sunday was the annual Boxed

Lunch dinner, and he was determined to know in advance which lunch Grace was bringing. The ladies would pack a lunch with their name on it, for two people in beautifully decorated boxes with spring flowers, or something they had knitted, roses from an old hat, or simply colored paper to make their package look attractive. Then the men would bid on the boxes, and have lunch with person who had brought it.

As long as he knew which box was hers, he could bid on it and finally have a quiet time with her. So before the family left, he approached Little Ben and said, "Hey, Ben." He thought he would gain some edge with the boy by not calling him Little Ben, so he said, "I was thinking, Ben, that a boy like you could use a new shiny penny!"

Ben looked up at him feeling both impressed at that shiny penny he was holding, and suspicious at what the older boy's motives were. "What do I have to do to get it?" Little Ben wanted to grab that penny and look at it, but he knew Caleb would lift it over his head, so he shoved both hands deep into his pockets and waited.

"Well, I thought it would be nice if we all made Grace feel good by paying a lot of money for her boxed lunch next Sunday. So, I was thinking that if I knew which one it was, I could buy it at a fair price!"

Ben looked up at him dryly, and Caleb said, "Ok, three pennies!" He reached in his pocket and brought out the remainder of his money and held out his hand with the pennies in it.

Little Ben could not bear to say no to Caleb, but he was not about to betray his sister for any amount of money, so he gritted his teeth, closed his mouth tightly, turned, and walked away.

Later in the day, Little Ben announced at the dinner table just what Caleb had done explaining every detail vividly, completely oblivious to the fact that Grace was embarrassed to the bottom of her soul. She looked at her family and said, "I don't know why he won't just leave me alone!" and stomped off to her room to be alone. Kevin smiled silently and continued eating.

Knowing looks passed between the adults, then smiles brightened their faces and Little Ben said, "I don't get it. What?"

Benjamin walked by his son and messed up his hair. "You will get it someday, Ben. Just not yet."

A knock on the door surprised Elizabeth and she dropped the bowl she was filling onto the floor. She stooped to clean up the mess she had made as Benjamin opened the door to reveal the man who had been watching their house from afar.

Ben's hand went up to the man's chest as he pushed him out onto the porch, closing the door behind him. In an instant, the door opened again and Kevin appeared beside Ben with a loaded gun.

"Who are you, and why are you watching my family?" Ben asked angrily.

The man slowly took his hat off and looked down at Ben with an air of superiority that made Ben even angrier. Ben's fist balled up the man's shirt as he said, "Who *are* you? And what are you doing here?"

"The name is Oak Ferrell. Although some folks call me Oaky. And in answer to your question, I own this cabin and the land it sits on."

Ben's knees went weak as he remembered what Midgie said the first time they met, "You must be a friend of Oaky's, and if you are a friend of Oaky's, you are a friend of ours!"

His mouth went dry and he had a sudden urge to go use the outhouse. Kevin found himself once again clueless as to what this meant, and Ben had no time to fill him in, so he turned to Kevin and said, "Please go back in, Kevin, and tell them everything is fine. Mr. Ferrell and I are going to take a walk."

Kevin turned to go into the house, and Ben added, "Tell them it is just a man about some business, would you Kevin?"

Kevin nodded quickly, then said, "Stay in sight, will you?"

Ben nodded and Kevin went inside closing the door quietly behind him.

"First of all," Ben said, "I want to apologize for my treatment back there, I had seen you several times and felt you were a threat to my family."

"And *that* is what you want to apologize to me for? After living in my house like you own it for more than a year? You apologize for treating me *roughly*?" Oak asked.

Ben said, "The night we came here, it was snowing and bad, and we just took refuge in the only place we could find shelter. I can promise you we meant no harm. We had no intentions of…"

Oak stopped and turned toward Benjamin. Ben thought how appropriate the name, Oak, was as he stood there towering over Ben, solid as a giant oak tree, and hoped Oak had no plans to beat him into the ground like a tent peg.

Oak recognized the fear in his eyes, relaxed his shoulders and said, "First of all, I am Oak Ferrell. Call me Oak," he said as he offered his hand to shake.

A very confused Ben took his hand and shook it vigorously, then said, "I am pleased to meet you, Sir."

"Sir?" Oak said with a laugh. "You must be awful scared of me to call me Sir!"

"Well, we have been trespassing on your land, and living in your house for over a year, as you said! We came here Christmas Eve, 1861."

"I know when you came here!" Oak said with a laugh! "Don't you think folks around here have let me know what is going on? Small community, Son. Everybody knows everything."

"Well, what do we do now?" Ben asked. He could stand the suspense no longer.

"Will you stop looking so frightened? I'm not going to hurt you! See, this cabin was my Mama's. She lived here most of her adult life, even after my Pa died, she stayed here until the day we found her in her rocking chair in front of the fire."

The men walked along in silence as both men thought of their Mama's, who had died in that cabin.

"After she passed on, I could not bear to go back in it. My boys went in a cleared most of her things out of there, but I just couldn't go back in."

"I understand that," Ben remembered how difficult it was the first time he entered the cabin after Granny died, and saw her little apron on the nail in the kitchen, and her sewing lying on the arm of the rocker.

"So we just moved to the West Fork, and I never looked back. When I heard there was a family living here, I asked if they were fixing the place up, and they said you were, so, I just let it be. I have kept a close eye on the place. Been here from time to time, just to make sure you hadn't burned the place down." He looked at Ben and smiled.

Ben could wait no longer, "So, why are you here now? Do you want us out?" Ben was trying to skip right over the part where he might call the Sheriff of Wood County to arrest them for trespassing, and tried to plant the idea that they would just move out if he wanted them to.

"No. I don't want you out, Ben." Oak said. "I have to tell you that it feels better to me to have someone looking after this place than it did when it sat empty. I know there is a lot of love in that house, with all them youngin's." Again he smiled at Ben, then continued, "You know, my Mama had a flower bed out front just like you had last summer. In the same place and everything." His smile had a glimpse of sorrow in it.

Ben said sadly, "That was Mama's flower bed. She passed a couple of days after Christmas this past winter."

The news seemed to grieve Oak when he heard it, too. He must have enjoyed seeing an elderly lady tending to her flowers from time to time when he rode up onto the hill and looked down at his Mama's house. He was quiet for a while, and Ben just gave him that grace.

Oak stopped on top of the hill, and turned to look back at the cabin. He stood there for a time, remembering playing on these hills as a boy, then he drew in a deep breath and said, "Ben, I have come here to make you an offer."

Ben nervously waited to hear what he had to say. It seemed that Oak expected him to say something, so he replied, "Yes, Sir?"

"I had two boys. One of them was killed in Arnoldsburg last year in that raid, and the other one is... well, he went off to war, and we haven't heard a word from him in over a year."

Ben said, "I am really sorry, Oak."

Oak nodded his appreciation, then continued, "I am too old to farm for a living," he said sadly, "and without my boys to help, well... It is just me and Clary now, so I was thinking. Since you and your family seem to be real happy here, I just thought you might want to buy it from me, land and all."

Ben was shocked, pleased, and terrified all at the same time. How could he make payments? And why would Oak offer to let him buy it after what they had done? Yet the thought of owning this home and some land was the dream of a lifetime! When Ben came to his senses he said, "I don't know what to say, Oak."

"Well, first off, do you want the place?"

"Yes, I do!" Ben said without hesitation. "But I am not sure of how I would make the payments, or even if I can afford to..."

"Now, we can work all that out if you want the place."

"I do," Ben said. "But why? Why would you do this for us?"

Oak said, "Well, I admit, when I first heard of you moving in, I was fairly miffed. But then the snows came, and before I had a chance to get over here, I had gotten used to the idea. The first time I came to check on you, as I crested this hill, I looked down there and saw lights on, and the window steamed up from cooking, and…" Oak removed a bandana from his back pocket and blew his nose. "Well, it felt good to see Mama's house like it was before. You had patched the roof, and I could see you had done a lot of work on the place, so I just left. But then I came back in the summer to speak to you about leaving, and I saw that little flower garden. I thought to myself, nope. I can't do that. This is what Mama would have wanted."

Oak decided he had had enough sentimentality, so he cleared his throat stood tall, and said, "Ok, here is what I was thinking. I want $250 for this house and the ten acres I own. I figure you have put about $100 worth of work into it, but then you owe me about $50 in rent. So I will settle for $200 from you for the farm and the house. I will take $5 a month for forty months if that is agreeable." He stopped and turned toward Ben, who was dumbstruck.

"I appreciate the offer, Oak," Ben stepped back, his mind spinning, and finally said, "I have to speak to my wife about it first." He felt a little silly saying that, and wondered if most men would have said yes, or no, without having had to discuss it with their wives. But he had no intentions of agreeing to tie himself and Sarah into that kind of obligation without first discussing it with her.

"Of course, you should discuss it with her first," Oak said. "I will be staying with Aunt Opal for the next few days, so I will check back day after tomorrow if that is alright with you."

"That is just fine, Sir," Ben said offering his hand in gratitude. Would you like to stay for supper?"

"No, I finally got up the courage to go into the house the other day when you were flying kites up here. And I am glad I did. I liked what I saw in there, but, well, it was hard on me to be there without Mama.

I don't think I will ever go back. I said my good-byes. But thank you for the offer!"

"Well, if you change your mind, just know that you are always welcome," Ben said with a smile. He took a deep breath and added, "But I have women folk living there. I would appreciate it if you would knock the next time."

Oak laughed a deep belly laugh and said, "I was certain you were all out of there before I went in. But you have a good point. And rest assured that after this day, I will just be one more neighbor."

"Well, I hope sometime you will come for dinner. After all, it is your home place," Ben said sincerely.

"Thank you, Ben. It is good of you to ask," The men shook hands and went their separate ways.

That night in bed Sarah and Ben tried to wrap their minds around Oak's offer. Occasionally, Ben sold a piece of furniture, or repaired something that kept them in grocery money. But taking on a $5 debt every single month was a huge responsibility. And the thought of having to meet that payment every month for the next forty months seemed an impossible task.

They slept very little that night and it was noticed by all the next morning. First of all, they slept later than they usually did, and when they did come out of their room, Ben was unusually quiet, and Sarah was snapping at everyone around her.

The children quickly decided to go outside and look for worms for fishing, in the hopes that Ben and Sarah would be in a better mood when they came back inside. Kevin looked at the two of them and asked, with a smile on his face, "Sleep well?"

"No, we did not," Sarah said with a laugh. "How could you tell?"

Kevin knew better than to answer, so he just took a large drink of coffee into his mouth as an excuse for not answering, and watched them fill their plates with cold, leftover eggs and bacon.

When they sat down at the table, Ben said, "You know the man who was here yesterday?" Kevin nodded, so Ben continued, "He is the owner of this cabin and the ten acres it sits on. He offered to sell it to us for $200, and we were up all night discussing what we should do."

Kevin asked if he wanted the money immediately, and Ben explained about the $5 payment each month for forty months as Kevin listened carefully. Then he said, "Do you want to stay here? I mean, are you planning on moving away?"

"Oh, no!" Sarah said bringing her hand to her throat. "We would love to stay here. But it is the idea of being in debt, and owing that much money every single month for forty months that is the problem."

After much discussion, the three of them decided on one thing. They definitely wanted the house and the land. Now they just needed to decide how to afford it.

"Good morning, sleepy heads!" Elizabeth said as she came in from the outside with an empty clothes basket. Apparently she had been up, had done her laundry, and had just finished hanging it on the line. Sarah, who was facing the door held up her hand against the bright sun and said, "Would you please close the door?"

Elizabeth did, then breezed through the room and said, "I am stripping beds this morning. It is a beautifully clear day, and clothes are drying so quickly that I just thought it would be a great time to wash sheets and blankets." Within minutes she came from the room she shared with Grace, arms full of sheets and blankets, and headed out the door to the wash tub.

Sarah was the one who returned the conversation to the purchase of their home. "I still have some savings. Maybe we could find a used sawmill, and you could set up a business making furniture for people, or supplying wood for building or repairing homes."

Kevin said, "The furniture you make is unbelievably beautiful, Ben. I am sure I could sell it in Parkersburg. I know of several people in our parish who could place your furniture on consignment in their shops."

"I must admit that I like the idea of wood working for a living," Ben said. "And I do like the idea that it is something Little Ben can learn and make a living at when he grows up as well. But building a business takes time, and we would have a $5 payment due within weeks! We would have to find a sawmill, get it moved here, put out the word. And even if you took some of my work to Parkersburg, there is no telling when it will sell. I don't know how we could do it."

"Well, I have a proposal," Kevin began. "I have some money saved that I can put toward the purchase. It would be enough to get you by until you are established anyway."

"No, Kevin, we are not taking your money," Ben said.

"Why not?" Sarah asked. We are all family, Ben. This is Kevin's home, too. So why shouldn't he invest in it if he wants to?"

Kevin placed his hand on Sarah's and said, "Thank you, Sarah."

The three of them were silent as they refreshed their coffee and Sarah made another pot, while Ben looked out the window. Finally, Kevin spoke and said, "Aright, I have an idea. Would the two of you please sit down and listen to what I have to say? After I am finished, you can ask all the questions you want, but I need for you to hear me out first."

Ben and Sarah walked over to the table and sat down. Kevin went to the door and asked the children to stay outside until they were called, because they had something to discuss that was very important, and they needed to be able to speak uninterrupted.

Elizabeth was nearly finished with her laundry, so she decided to help the children look for worms.

Kevin looked as if he were a Priest about to give a sermon as he walked around in deep thought, rubbing the palms of his hands together. Finally, he turned toward them and said, "All my life, I have been cared for. First by my parents, then by the Monastery. Then I moved on to being a Priest in a Parish, and again I was fed, housed, given my clothing and medical care. I had absolutely nothing to spend my money on."

"Now here I am again, being cared for. My food, my lodging, the sewing of my clothes, all are provided for me by the two of you, and I find myself wanting to invest in my own life!"

Ben knew where he was going, so he said, "Now, Kevin, as much as we apprec...."

"No, hear me out, please," was all he said as he held his hand in the air to indicate his desire for them to wait until he was finished.

"Now, I have nearly $300 in my bank account in Parkersburg." Ben opened his mouth, but again, Kevin held the palm of his hand toward Ben and said, "Please?"

"I could pay for the farm, outright, and still have nearly $100 in the bank for medical needs, or to help out in an emergency, AND BEFORE YOU SAY ANYTHING!" Ben had risen to his feet in protest, but Kevin was prepared. Ben sat down and listened, although clearly not with an open mind.

In exchange, I would like to be able to build my own house on this land, and you could supply the lumber, and the labor to build it."

Ben began calculating in his head as to what kind of exchange that would be. "But a new cabin would not be worth $200, Kevin. You would be cheating yourself. I won't do it. I'm sorry, Kevin, and I do thank you, but, well, it just isn't right."

Kevin thought about it for a minute and said, "Well, in the first place, I would put the deed in your name so your children could have it when they are older. I have no children, and do not see children in my future, so we should do that for Grace, Ben, and Rebecca." Again, he kept talking so that Ben could not have time to object.

"I would not have a house payment, or a rent payment for the land I was living on, and we could share the gardening and the hunting for the food we ate, so basically, I would be eating your food, from your land, for the rest of my life. Usually Priests work until they can no longer hear confessions, then they go to a retirement home and sit and play checkers all day. You will have given me a family, a home of my own, with land all around me. No Priest I know has ever had so much. Please, let me do this. I want to pay my own way, just as much as you do, Ben."

Sarah was already convinced, and looked at Ben to see if he was going to accept the offer. He still was balking at the idea, and said it wasn't fair for Kevin to use his money to purchase the land, and put Ben's name on the deed.

But Kevin reasoned with him, saying, "You have a use for this farm that I do not. You have children to build a life for. I do not. But I would like to share in that life with you, if you would let me. It is a small price to pay for all that you have done for me."

Ben shook his head from side to side, then said, "I don't understand why you would do that, but if you want to, then we have a deal." Sarah clapped her hands and stood to hug Kevin. The three of them decided to purchase a saw mill anyway, and together, Kevin and Ben could build a business that would sustain them financially for the rest of their lives. It was a joyous day as the Waters' house was filled with excitement, joy, and celebration. They began discussing where Kevin's house would be, and plans for the sawmill. They were daydreaming about what furniture pieces would be easiest to ship to Parkersburg, and which would sell the most locally, when they heard a knock at the door.

Sarah opened the door and saw Elizabeth, Grace, and Little Ben huddled together on the porch, soaking wet from the downpour of rain Sarah was unaware had even started!

"Can we come in now?" Little Ben said with his teeth chattering. "We are freezing!"

All three adults realized they had forgotten to tell the children they could come in, and had no idea it had started raining.

"Oh, my!" Kevin said, jumping to his feet to get towels to dry them. "I do not want them to get pneumonia like I did. I cannot believe we forgot the children!"

While the three went to their rooms and stripped out of their wet clothes, Kevin built up the fire and Sarah made hot chocolate for everyone. Ben gathered the wet clothes and hooked them over every chair back, nail, or bed post he could find to let them dry. The storm raged on, outside that little cabin. The rain pounded down on the tin roof and the thunder rolled in the distance, but those inside were safe, loved, and excited about their future.

Kevin looked around at his family's faces in the fire glow, the children with their wet hair, in their night clothes and snuggled up in blankets. He felt himself to be the most blessed man on earth, and said aloud, "Life more abundant… indeed."

Chapter Twenty-One

Word spread that Benjamin had bought the farm and had paid cash! He was looked at with great respect when he entered the church. After all, he not only bought the farm outright, he was going to be a business owner, and he was a hard worker. Although many questioned privately where he had gotten the money, most felt happy for the family who had come with so little, but now were making a go of things.

They liked Ben and were impressed with his woodworking skills, and everyone liked the family as a whole. They were known for being there for anyone in trouble, donating whatever was needed when a crisis occurred, and most important, they loved the Lord.

Ben was, for the first time, proud of who he had become, and you could see it in his demeanor. He looked men in the eye, and shook hands with great confidence. He was often asked for his opinion on the war, and other local problems that occurred.

He still had worries, however, and he decided that worries are a part of every man's life, no matter how happy that man was. He had found out at church today, that they were taking the runaway slaves to Parkersburg the next day, when the church had had a special prayer for their safety, and the success of the attempt to free the man and boy. Although Ben was not going with the men, he had a nervous stomach anyway, for fear they may be caught.

He looked over at Sarah and she smiled at him, then placed her hand in his, it was a tiny little fist that his hand completely covered. His eyes then went to Grace, who much to his chagrin, looked more like a grown woman than she did a child. Suddenly, someone in the far right row of pews caught his eye, and he realized that it was Caleb

Rogers who had also been looking at Grace. Ben drew down his eyebrows at the boy, and nodded toward Preacher, indicating that Caleb should be paying attention to the sermon. Caleb's head snapped around, and Ben could see the red creeping up Caleb's neck as embarrassment made his face glow like a hot ember.

Ben thought about all the changes that had occurred in the last few days and felt a little nervous. He was going to be a land owner, a business owner, the father of a young woman who might be married soon, and his sister was back. All that took some getting used to. He liked all those things, but missed, painfully, the simple days with just Granny, Sarah, and the children. Life certainly did change quickly. His mind drifted to Caleb and he turned to see him staring at Grace again.

Preacher was finishing up his sermon early because everyone was excited about the fact that after church, there was going to be the Boxed Luncheon. Caleb had worked chopping wood, mending fences, and hauling rocks for a neighbor who was building a well, so he had nearly $3.00 to spend on Grace's lunch box. The question was, which one was hers? He hated to spend that much money on one lunch and not have it be Grace's.

Denzel sat in the pews on the left with his family. He had to turn completely around to see the Waters, so he just sat there stewing about the lack of funds he had. He had also been willing to work hard to buy a lunch, but he had a full day's work just to keep his family's farm up. Besides that, he had done a lot of free work for the Waters' family this spring, like plowing the garden for them, so he did not have spare time to work for money like the other men did.

Everyone gathered around Preacher before the auction, the women's eyes were sparkling with secrets, and the men jingled the money in their pockets. After a brief prayer, lunch was started by way of the auction.

The first package to go up for bid was Cali's. It sold for 30 cents to the boy she had called goofy before in the wagon on the way home.

Her smile said she was rather happy that he had purchased it, though, as they headed over to where the ladies were pouring coffee and sweetened tea.

The money raised this day was to enlarge the church just enough to have a dry place to meet for meals like the one today. So everyone was as generous as they could manage to be. There were no boxes going for less than 25 cents, and Denzel was certain he could never compete for the one he wanted. He was so embarrassed about his limited funds, he untied his horse from his family's wagon and went home on his own.

As the auctioning continued, Sarah Waters' highly decorated lunch went up for sale. Just for sport the men bid against Benjamin, partly to tease Ben, but partly to raise the amount of money the church would receive. Penny by penny the men would outbid Benjamin, and the entire church would laugh loudly at Ben's frustration, but he finally won the prize by paying the unheard of price of 40 cents! The crowd cheered as he stepped up and received the lunch, and Sarah rewarded him with a kiss on the cheek.

Sarah tugged at Ben's hand to leave, but just then, Little Ben stepped up beside his father and looked up at him through his eyebrows. Ben smiled down at him and said, "Just a minute, Sarah. There is something we men have to do."

Little Ben bent forward and looked through the crowd at Maxine Benson. She smiled at him, her face as red as a beet, and nodded toward the next lunch that was up for sale. Ben picked Little Ben up and placed him on a chair so he could be seen. The bidding began with five cents, and Little Ben raised his hand as he had seen his father do.

One of the boys next to him said, "Six cents!" Little Ben looked at his father in horror, and Ben whispered into the boy's ear.

Little Ben smiled, held up his hand, and said, "TEN CENTS!" as loudly as he could, and the crowd laughed at the boy's efforts to ensure that he get the prize. The smaller boy looked like he wanted to take a swing at Little Ben, then just turned and walked off, with his fists in his pockets.

When the lunch was handed to Little Ben, Maxine ran over to him and held his hand. "Let's go, Benjamin!" Her smile revealed the two teeth that were still missing, and Little Ben thought it was the cutest smile he had ever seen.

After several more lunches came and went, the auctioneer picked up a beautiful, blue box, with purple ribbons on it, and Caleb became aware that someone behind him was clearing his throat repeatedly. It was odd enough that Caleb turned to see who it might be, and there, smiling from ear to ear, was Kevin, who nodded his head toward the offering.

Caleb turned back to see the man holding the blue and purple box in the air to show how beautifully it had been packaged, when he heard an even louder clearing of the throat. He turned again and saw Kevin nodding toward the front, as if he wanted something. When the auctioneer began the bid at 25 cents, Kevin pushed Caleb forward, making him trip and push the man in front of him. "And we have 25 cents, do I hear 30?" the man said, pointing to Caleb.

When Caleb turned this time, he saw Kevin winking at him and shaking his head yes slowly, and it finally dawned on him that this was Grace's lunch. He smiled at Kevin, and Kevin smiled back, then turned him around and made a hand gesture that indicated Caleb should continue bidding.

Although several men bid on Grace's lunch, no one had the ability to pay more than the $2.60 Caleb bid for the meal. Grace's face was laughable to Sarah and Ben, because they knew immediately she was furious that Caleb had bought it. And for $2.60? She was humiliated by his show of unwarranted extravagance, and her face said she was going to make him suffer for being so bold.

She pulled her hat down until it was crooked and just barely hanging on to the side of her head, and stomped over to select which glass of tea she wanted.

"Why are you doing this?" she said as they sat facing each other at the picnic table. She had leaned far across the table so that she could whisper loudly to him.

He said, "I can't hear you, Grace," then went around the table and sat down beside her. Well, actually on her, until she scooted over to make room for him. As she did this, she looked around to see who was present and watching what he had done, jerked on her hat to stabilize it, and gave Caleb a look that would have frightened a grizzly bear. She was pleased when she saw no one looking at them, but what she did not realize, was that almost every adult was finely tuned to what was going on between them, and enjoying every minute of it.

As she snapped out the words, "Let's eat and get this over with!" he busied himself with opening the box, smiling and admiring the wrappers and the meal she had prepared. Her hat bounced in rhythm with her words as she admonished him for spending so much on a silly lunch, and one did not have to be anywhere near the table to know exactly what was happening. Ben and Sarah watched with great amusement as the two fought their way through the meal.

Kevin noticed that Eileen Rogers was one of the two ladies left, and when the next box was lifted to the auctioneer, she sat at attention as if to see who would buy it. When the men brought the bid to 50 cents, Kevin offered 75, and the lunch was sold.

Eileen and Kevin walked quietly into a shady spot and sat on the grass while they had lunch. Everyone was being so entertained by Grace and Caleb, they didn't seem to notice the two of them eating quietly in the shade of the old oak tree, laughing and talking as if they had known each other their entire lives. They had lived their lives, and had no time for being coy, or evasive, so they just talked freely and laughed heartily. Kevin had never seen himself as ever having a personal relationship with a woman, but this was wonderful for him because he felt more comfortable and happier than he had ever been.

Meanwhile, more people came to sit on the picnic table with Grace and Caleb, so the arguing had to stop. They both smiled at the others who were getting comfortable, and both took their turns at small talk when the occasion arose, but when everyone else was engaged in conversation, Grace turned to Caleb and whispered, "What do you want, Caleb Rogers? You treat me like I am a mindless being, and then you pay $2.60 for my lunch?" She glanced around to be certain no one was paying them any mind, and continued, "Did you do that just to embarrass me? Because if you did, it worked!"

When she finished, Caleb's mouth was full of her delicious fried chicken and he made no effort to clear his mouth so he could answer. He simply chewed and made faces to show her how delicious it was. He kept nodding his head in approval, then turned and lifted his glass in preparation to take a drink when he had swallowed that bite.

Grace was furious. She had spoken in a way that demanded an answer, then was made to wait while he slowly chewed his food. She looked around at others who were talking softly, then back at him. He was still chewing! She could feel her anger slipping and as he mimed that he was trying as hard as he could, she could stop it no longer, and burst out laughing. The two of them giggled like children as he finally took a sip of tea and cleared his mouth.

Grace said, "You did that on purpose!"

"I did not!" Caleb said playfully. "I had no idea you were going to yell at me when I took that big bite of chicken!"

"I did not yell at you!" She stopped and looked around to see if anyone was listening to them. When he leaned against her shoulder, she shoved him back and smiles broke out across the crowd of people before they then went about their business.

"So, I believe you asked me a question a bit ago," Caleb began, "that certainly deserves an answer."

Grace was impressed that he had gone back to that, seeing as how it would have been easy for him to ignore her question altogether. "Yes, I did." She said to give herself time to remember what it was she wanted to know.

"Ask me anything," he said confidently.

She briefly saw him differently for a moment, but brought her complaints back to the forefront, and said, "I just want to know why you keep following me around, and offering to help me." When he did not respond, she said, "I feel like you think I am incapable of even walking without your assistance!"

Caleb popped a bite of bread into his mouth, and wiped his hands and mouth on the napkin she had brought, because he needed a minute to think. When he had swallowed, he said, "Alright, I will tell you." He stood up, then turned and sat down straddling the seat she was sitting on, took a deep breath, and said, "I enjoy your company, Grace Waters. Although you made me madder than a wet hen when you locked me out of my Mama's house, I have not been able to stop thinking about you since that day, and I haven't thought of any *other* girl since, either. So I have been asking to help you, because I would like to see you more often."

Grace's mouth fell open and she sat straight up. That was not what she expected to hear from him, and her mind was reeling.

Caleb smiled because he had finally rendered her speechless. This time he put another bite of bread in his mouth, and sat, waiting for *her* to speak. He folded his arms, lifted his eyebrows, and smiled a cocky smile that unnerved her, and before she could even gather her thoughts, he grabbed another bite of chicken, pointed at her and said, "I am waiting!" and popped the chicken into his mouth.

Oh, that ridiculous smirk! Grace thought to herself. *What kind of a man would just say something like that, right there in front of God and everybody?* She looked nervously from side to side to see if anyone had heard what he said, and began planning what she would say to anyone who would dare ask her about it.

He tipped his head to the left and looked at her as a reminder that he was waiting to hear what she had to say, then turned back so he was facing his plate, and began spearing the fodder beans with his fork. Before he put the bite into his mouth, and without looking at her, he said, "Well, where is that little spitfire that dumped water over my Mama's head, now?" And then he had the audacity to laugh out loud.

Grace was madder than she had ever been. She wasn't sure how he had turned the conversation back on her, but she was sure she never wanted to speak to him again. He was infuriating, arrogant, and obnoxious! How dare he say those things to her and then laugh at her! Out loud! She began opening her little bowl of food, eating the chicken with her fingers, and staring straight ahead.

He turned, picked up her napkin and wiped a drop of grease from her lips. "I am not a child, Caleb Rogers! I do not need to be fed, I do not need you to wipe my mouth, and I do not need any help from you to do anything!" By the time she had finished the sentence she was standing and shouting so loudly everyone, including those who had chosen to remain inside the church could hear her.

She quickly gathered up her things, snatched a chicken leg out of Caleb's hand, retrieved his bowl and fork, threw everything into the box she had brought, and turned to walk away.

Caleb called after her, "Wait!"

Grace turned and looked dryly at him and said, "I believe you have gotten your $2.60 out of this meal, Caleb Rogers. Now your quiet time with me is up!" She threw her chin up and walked away from him with her nose in the air.

Behind her she heard Caleb shout, "I could yell what I have to say, if you don't mind everyone hearing it!"

Grace's mouth fell open. Everyone she could see was staring at the two of them and she thought she would die of embarrassment. Suddenly, anger replaced humiliation and her eyes narrowed as she stopped, turned, and stomped her foot at the impertinence of this man. She had no choice but to return to him to hear what he had to say. "What? What is so important that you must say this one last thing to me?" The look on his face dared him to answer.

"Only this," he said, smiling a beautiful smile, she had to admit, "tonight when you are all alone, if you do not think of me as well, I will leave you alone to find someone else."

Her mouth opened and the only sounds that would come out were, "Ah! Whe! Wha?" Finally, she stomped her foot again and screamed, "OH!" Then turned and marched all the way back to her family while trying her best to control her thoughts. She sat down beside Sarah and Ben, totally unaware of the humor in their eyes, and began making a mental list of all the reasons she disliked Caleb Rogers. But try as she may, she thought about him almost every minute of every day until she saw him again, and she could not for the life of her figure out why.

Chapter Twenty-Two

The men had returned from taking the runaway slaves to Parkersburg, and Abram had come to tell Ben all about it. When he rode up, Ben said, "Why don't you come on inside and have a cup of coffee. It is getting chilly again, and the family will want to hear anyway."

Abram removed his hat as he entered the house, and Sarah took him a cup of coffee which he accepted with gratitude.

"Abram is here to tell us about the slaves and what happened to them," Ben said as the children, Elizabeth, and Sarah gathered round.

Abram was not a man of many words, so he said simply, "Well, the trip was a success. Nobody stopped them and they went right through Parkersburg and met the man on the Ohio River. He liked the wagon you made, Ben, and when they told him they would rather sell the wagon to him than the slaves, he suggested instead that we just trade wagons with him. Now the wagon they brought back is a fine wagon. Big enough for you to take the family places in, and sturdy enough to haul rocks if you had a mind to. I hope you don't mind."

Ben was elated. "No, I don't mind one bit," he said. "I never expected to see that old wagon again anyway! Did he know how old it was?"

"Yes, he did," Abram continued, "but he said he don't care about that. He liked how you fixed it sos a man or two could be taken places without anyone seeing them. He even offered to buy more of these if you want to build them. He says he will take two more at any price you would ask."

Ben and Kevin smiled at each other as Abram finished his coffee. Sarah said, "How are the twins?"

Abram said, "Oh, as ornery as ever, I guess. That Wheat is growing like a weed, but that boy has some catchin' up to do."

"Try not to compare the two, Abram," Elizabeth said. "If you only had him you might not think him small."

Abram thought that might have some truth in it, but he was still concerned. "Midgie has a couple of small boxes she used to keep spices in. She put the twins in those and kept them behind the stove during the day, just to keep them warm enough. Now, Wheat has outgrown her box, but, now, that boy hasn't even filled it up yet. And that box isn't even big enough for me to put my foot into!"

Sarah had noticed the difference in the twins but had said nothing. She thought to change the subject by asking about Midgie, or the children, but instead said, "Summer is coming. Once he gets some sunshine on him, he will grow."

Abram looked thoughtful, but said nothing, so Sarah decided to go with the change of subject. "How on earth does Midgie cope with all those children? I have trouble with the three I have!"

"Oh, she manages," he said. "She gets up and hardly sits down all day, but she always is smiling, so I guess lovin' what she does gets her through it all. Same as all Mamas!" He smiled at Sarah as a compliment to her, then stood up, indicating his visiting time was over, and Ben and Sarah walked him to the door.

"I hadn't noticed anything odd about the twins," Ben said as soon as he was sure Abram had ridden far enough away that he could not be heard. "What is wrong with the boy?"

Sarah looked at him with an incredulous look and said, "How could you not notice? Nancy is twice as big as Roy Paul! He just doesn't seem to be growing. I am actually very worried about him," she said as she began to gather up the coffee cups to wash.

Kevin was playing with Rebecca, but something about him caught Sarah's eye. "You look tired, Kevin. Are you feeling alright?"

Kevin sighed and admitted he was not. "I just can't seem to get over whatever it was that I had. I was thinking of traveling to Parkersburg as soon as I am able, to see a doctor friend of mine there. I want to go retrieve the rest of my savings anyway, so I thought this might be a good time."

Sarah and Ben nodded in agreement, their concern clearly showing in their eyes. "But we cannot let you travel alone, Kevin," Sarah began. "One of us should go with you."

Benjamin looked at Sarah and both of them knew his limp would be too easily recognizable. Sarah felt a knot in her stomach as fear gripped her. She could not forget the terror she had felt when last in Parkersburg and was found by those thugs who intended to return her to her home. Kevin looked back and forth, watching first Benjamin's face, then Sarah's, then Ben's again. He had been a Priest too long to not recognize the conversation going on between them. He knew it was not possible for them to go with him, so he said, "I fear I will not be able to go at all for a few weeks. We could talk about it then?"

Relief flooded over both their faces, as Kevin watched and wondered what had happened to these people he so loved, that had left them so shattered.

Chapter Twenty-Three

A new day dawned on the Waters family. Summer had come early and the heat was boiling down on the newly planted garden. Little Ben had painstakingly shown Kevin everything about growing the garden his Granny had taught him. Kevin was just as fascinated by the cutting up and planting of the potatoes as they had been just a year ago, and was impressed by the knowledge Little Ben had about where to plant which plant so that the sun could shine on the entire garden. The boy's tails of the cucumbers not liking wet feet and explanations of God's role in the year's crops were both funny, and heartwarming, so Little Ben had a more than willing audience in Kevin, who sat every day, on a small stool Benjamin had made for the occasion watching Little Ben work in the garden.

"Uncle Kevin," Little Ben leaned on his hoe handle and began, "I don't want to appear to be disrespectful, but…" His voice drifted off as he lost his courage.

"Go on, Little Man," Kevin encouraged

"Well, you are just practicing being lazy by just sitting in that chair!"

Kevin had to suppress his shock and surprise at the statement, and recovered in time to say, "Go on."

"Well, I am afraid you will never get any better if you don't get up and do something. You go from bed, to sitting at the table in the house, to sitting up here watching me work! Now, don't get me wrong, I love spending time with you, but, well, the problem is, I can hear Granny in my head telling you, 'Git up from there! They's work to be done and you ain't special! Get off your fanny and do something!'"

Kevin had to laugh at Little Ben's imitation of Granny. It was dead on, and worse, he was right. He had been babying himself and needed to fight if he ever wanted to get better.

He looked at the boy standing in front of him, speaking the truth that no one else dared to say, and realized that Little Ben was no longer a child. He had grown taller through the winter and his upper body was becoming that of a man. The muscles in his chest and arms were more clearly defined, replacing the pudgy torso of a child, and he was beginning to show signs of a light, yet visible, mustache. Last summer he looked like a bear cub running about in the tall grass, but now all that had been replaced with the long gait of a young man.

"I'm sorry, Uncle Kevin," Ben said, "It isn't really my place to say…"

"No, Ben," Kevin said sincerely, "you are absolutely right. And I am impressed that you had the courage to talk to me about it. You are becoming a fine man, Ben Waters, and a man that I highly respect."

The last thing Ben expected was to be told he was becoming a man. Especially one that a man like his Uncle Kevin would respect! He had feared Kevin might reprimand him for speaking out of turn, or perhaps that his uncle might have laughed at him, but never, in his wildest dreams did he imagine that his opinion would have carried so much weight. He was a man, huh? Well, he had noticed that chopping wood was easier, that he could carry far more wood than before, and especially that he was beginning to look his Mama in the eye. When had he grown so much? And how did it happen without his noticing it?

His thoughts were interrupted when Kevin stood, stiffly, and said, "Well, I reckon I should start my fight to get better by gathering up these tools and carrying them back to the shed." He did not relish the thought of walking around in the hot sun, bending over to pick up the tools and struggling down the hill with them at first. But then he realized he was beginning to sound like an old man, and that was one thing he did not want to be at his age. So he stood up, waited until he was stable, then began doing exactly what he did not want to do.

By the time Kevin had gotten to the cabin, he was exhausted. His arms ached, his legs were weak and shaky, but it felt good to do something besides sit. He wanted to do more, but after drinking a long, tall, glass of cool water, he found instead that a nap was in order, so he went to his room to lie down. *Little Ben was right!* Kevin thought to himself! *I was working hard at being lazy! Well, as Mama used to say, "Tomorrow, I'll get up and be a better person!"*

The day was a scorcher. Sarah was so hot inside the kitchen that she nearly fainted several times, and had to stop and breathe deeply, then wash her face with cold water. The one window in the front room, the one in their bedroom, and the one in Kevin's room, did not provide any movement of air inside the house and Sarah was certain she was going to faint if she did not cool off.

Ben had read about a ramada when he was a little boy and built one for his family. It was basically a roofed building without walls, which provided shade with a breeze so they could sit outside when it was raining, or too hot for the sun to beat down on them, and string beans, or wash clothes.

Sarah became fearful for her health, and went out alone, because Little Ben, Elizabeth, Rebecca, and Grace had gone swimming in the lake with the Bensons. But the shade was not enough to conquer the nausea that nearly overwhelmed her as she walked in the boiling hot sun toward the pavilion. She simply could not stand the heat one minute more, and did not even realize when her knees buckled and she went down onto the ground face first.

Kevin had taken a walk as was his daily practice now in order to regain his strength, and Benjamin had gone to help a neighbor with his planting, so no one knew how long she had been lying there in the hot sun when Ben rode up.

"Sarah!" Benjamin was off the horse before it had stopped. His heart pounded as he rolled her over to see if she was still breathing. Her face was as red as a beet, so he tore open her collar to give her some air. Realizing she wasn't injured, but simply overheated, he moved her to the shade, and ran to the cabin for a bucket of cold water. His first thought was to pour water into her mouth, or should he wash her face and neck? In panic, he simply dumped the entire bucket of ice cold water into her face, causing her to sputter and spit while coughing as if she might drown!

"What are you doing?" she shouted at Ben!

"You are passed out! I didn't know what to do!" the frustrated Benjamin shouted back at her. "Are you alright? What happened?"

Sarah herself had no idea what had happened, and only a vague recollection of her attempt to get out of the house before she fainted. She sat up too quickly, and before she could stop herself, she vomited into her lap.

Ben ran around behind her and allowed her to lean on him until she could stop vomiting and relax into his arms. She began chilling, and with teeth chattering she closed her eyes and said, "I'm sorry, Ben, I don't know what is wrong with me. I feel so odd, as though my lips are numb." He knew the minute she finished talking and fell back into his arms that she had passed out again, and worry overcame him.

He picked her up and got her inside the house, stripped off her soiled dress as well as her underclothes, and put her to bed. The open window provided no breeze, but instead allowed an almost visible cloud of thick hot air to enter. Just as he closed the window he heard Kevin enter the door.

Ben covered Sarah with a sheet and stepped into the front room to tell Kevin what had happened.

"Perhaps I should go get Midgie," Kevin said. "I think this is more than we can handle, and I would hate to harm her by not knowing what to do."

"Are you sure you are up to the trip, Kevin?" Ben asked.

Kevin wanted more than anything to say that he was, yet he did not want to get halfway there and not be able to deliver the message. "I'm sorry, Ben," he said, "my ego wants to rise to the occasion, but I fear I may not be healthy enough to make that trip in this heat, and I would not harm Sarah for anything in this world."

Ben said he understood and asked Kevin to wait in the front room while he tended to Sarah. When Ben entered the bedroom they shared, he remembered that first night they stayed there, when Sarah was angry with him for leaving the children in her care inside the cave the night before. Just to make her angrier, he volunteered to take the bed with the children this time, and let her sleep on the hard floor by the fire and it worked like a charm! He could still remember the look she gave him over her shoulder as she entered the only bedroom and slammed the door in his face.

Now he loved her more than life itself, and she was lying there unconscious and helpless. *Dear God,* he prayed, *please don't take my precious Sarah away from me. I beg you God to bless her and protect her, because I can't...* He burst into tears and sat on the edge of the bed, holding her tiny little hand in his and looked at the delicate features of her lovely face. His prayers continued and he could not bear to leave her.

Kevin interrupted by saying, "You need to go, Ben. You can't help her by sitting here."

Ben snapped back into the reality of the situation and said, "Just keep washing her face with cool water if you would, Kevin." Then he turned and tucked the sheet and blanket snuggly under her chin.

"I will not leave her side for one moment. Now go! Fetch Midgie! She will know what to do."

Sarah had not awakened by the time Ben returned with Midgie, Cali, and Bessie in tow, so Midgie immediately took control and shouted, "OUT! Out, all of you!"

Kevin left the room, but Ben protested vigorously. He wanted to be there with her, to encourage her and to love her into regaining consciousness...

"OUT! I'm not telling you again! Do you want a dead wife, Benjamin?"

That did it. He left the room and glancing back he saw Midgie jerk the sheet off Sarah leaving her completely naked on the bed. "Stupid men!" Midgie mumbled. "We gotta get her cooled down, Cali!"

Like clockwork, Bessie handed the bucket to Ben and said, "Get a new bucket of cold water from the well, and keep them coming." Cali began to fan the front door in an effort to get a breeze started, while Midgie examined Sarah.

"Did she vomit?" Midgie stuck her head out the bedroom door and asked.

"Yes, she did," Ben answered, wringing his hands. "Is that bad?"

"Ain't none of this good," Midgie snapped back at him.

"She'll be fine," Cali said to ease his mind. "She may have had a heat stroke. It happens sometimes." She said that in passing as if everyone had had one or two in their lives, but Ben was not comforted.

Midgie poured cool water over Sarah's head and chest, then quickly spread the water over her fevered body with a cloth. She would soak rags in the cool water, and place them behind Sarah's head and under each arm. Before long Sarah began to twitch and moan as if her legs were cramping. She became restless and her arms flailed wildly.

"Benjamin! Git in here!" When Ben entered the room and saw his wife lying there naked in front of everybody in the room, he was overcome with embarrassment. "Git over here! Oh, settle down! She doesn't have anything I haven't seen before! Now sit down there and rub her legs when they cramp. She's got heat cramps. They don't last long, but they are mighty painful! I'm hoping we don't have to heat up towels and put on her legs. It would help with the cramping, but we gotta get her cool."

Just then her right leg began to draw up and Ben did as he was told. He rubbed the muscle in her leg until it relaxed and felt every pain as if it were his own.

"Bessie! Bring me some cold water with salt in it!"

Bessie obeyed, and as she entered the room, she was stirring the water to mix in the salt. "Give me the spoon!" Midgie barked out, and Bessie quickly did exactly as she was told.

Midgie began spooning the salted water into Sarah's mouth and although the cramps continued for some time, they eventually began to weaken, and finally stopped altogether.

"You're done now," she said to Ben, dismissing him with a wave of her hand. He started to protest, but thought better of crossing Midgie, and did what he was told. Within an hour or so, Sarah was beginning to chill, and the evening was cooling the place down, so Midgie gathered up her things, called for Cali and Bessie to help dress Sarah in a night shirt, then covered her lightly with the sheet and one light blanket, and prepared to go home.

The trip to the Benson's was done in Ben's new wagon, and the talk was easy in the cool of the evening, the tension of the day behind them. The day was still rather hot, but a breeze was blowing and the girls sat in the back, enjoying the cool coming up from the ground on their bare feet and legs as they dangled them from the back of the wagon.

"I had Bessie cut up some ham and pick some greens for supper. You can have sandwiches so you don't have to cook and heat up the cabin in the process."

Ben pulled up to the Benson's house, stopped the wagon, and said, "I don't know how to thank you, Midgie, for all you have done for us. I hope someday I can repay your many kindnesses."

"Oh, I think diving into a frozen lake and pulling out my Abram went a long way toward that, Benjamin. But neighbors don't keep score. We just do what God asks us to do, and leave it at His feet."

Ben smiled and went around the wagon to help Midgie down as the girls ran into the house ahead of their Mama. As soon as Midgie was in the house, Ben returned to his wagon to head toward the lake in order to pick up the children who were still swimming. But just as he clucked to the horse to move on, Midgie opened the door, stepped back onto the porch and shouted, "You need to keep an eye on Sarah in this heat, now that she is with child!" Then, with a wave of her hand, the door closed and she was gone.

Ben stared at the door for several minutes, but still it did not register. *What? What did she say? Did she say Sarah is with child? Is that why...?*

Ben forgot about the children and headed straight home. At times he tried to hurry the horse by flipping the reins against her back, but it was uphill all the way and he knew it was dangerous. He wished he was on horseback so he could go faster, but he wasn't, so he had to take his time and not injure the mare.

Finally, he arrived at home, jumped off the wagon, ran into the house and asked Kevin to tend to the horse as he ran to Sarah's room. When he entered the bedroom, he saw Sarah sitting up in bed, sipping on the cup of cold salted water Midgie had given her to drink. She smiled sweetly at him, and he thought she had never looked more beautiful. "Did she tell you?" was all she said.

"I can't believe it!" Ben said as he sat on the bed and hugged her to him. They were laughing and chattering at each other when Kevin entered the cabin, so he knocked on the bedroom door and asked if he could come in.

"Certainly, Kevin," Sarah answered, pulling the sheet and blanket up around her neck to cover her night clothes.

"Ah! There you are, all bright and happy! You gave us quite a scare young lady!" Kevin entered only as far as the doorway, but smiled a smile filled with relief at seeing her sitting up and laughing again.

Ben and Sarah looked at each other briefly, then Sarah said, "Oh, I think it was just one of those things that happens to a mother-to-be!"

It took a minute for the news to register with Kevin, but once it did, his face glowed. "Congratulations, Sarah," he said with a nod in her direction, "and Benjamin!" He nodded at Ben as well, and continued, "I cannot say how happy I am for you." He meant every word of it, and yet he was saddened as well. For the first time in his life, he wanted more. He wanted this kind of love as well. Certainly not children at his age, but he wanted the love of a good woman. He wanted companionship, and someone he could love and be loved by. His thoughts drifted to Eileen Rogers and the afternoon they had spent together on the day of the Box Luncheon and was surprised at his emotions when he pictured her laughing that day. He left the room quietly and noticed that Ben and Sarah did not even see him leave.

Chapter Twenty-Four

"Where are you going?" the ever present Caleb asked as he brought his horse in line with Grace's mare.

"Do you wait in the woods for me, or do you actually run into me by accident almost every single day of my life?" Grace said, followed by an audible sigh.

"Both," Caleb said just to annoy her. "I thought you could use some company, that's all!"

"Use some company for what?" she said as she pulled her horse to a stop. "Because I can't ride the two miles over to Mrs. Siers' house all by myself?"

"What do you want from me, Grace?" His stallion was prancing and eager to run, but he held it in place while he looked her in the eye. "I suppose you want me to follow you around like a whipped puppy, like Denzel Benson does, just doing whatever you want to do?"

"Actually, that would be nice! Denzel accepts me for who I am. If I wanted to climb on the roof and add on another room, Denzel would not blink. He would begin gathering the tools and asking me what the room was going to look like!"

"So you expect me to let you do men's work, and just not care about my wife's safety?"

"Oh!" Grace said as she kicked her horse into a gallop.

The stallion, Caleb called Scott, reared in the air and bolted out after Grace. When Caleb caught up with her he grabbed the reins in front of Grace's hands and pulled the horse to a stop.

Infuriated that he had called her his "wife," turned into her being livid that he had stopped her mare from running. "Caleb Rogers, I want to make myself perfectly clear. I am not now, nor will I ever be your wife! I absolutely detest you, and the sight of you makes a perfectly wonderful day turn into the most miserable moments of my life! Why do you torment me so? GO AWAY! GO FAR, FAR, AWAY, CALEB! I do not want you in my life! Why can't you understand that?"

A long, long, silence hung between them. For what seemed like an eternity, the two sat looking at each other. Grace regretted her stern words, and yet they needed to be said. She searched his face to see if he might possibly cry, or feel anger, or say something horrid to her in return, but he just sat there on his stallion, looking like the beautiful specimen of man that he was, and yet hurt. Deeply hurt.

Before she burst into tears, she decided to turn her horse and continue to the Siers' home for her time with Mrs. Siers; her guitar lessons, and comfortable talk between herself and a woman who desperately missed her daughter. She checked her feelings, and decided that although she had been rather harsh, it was better that it had been said. *Now I can go on with my life,* she thought, when from behind her she heard Caleb shout, "See you tomorrow!"

~~~~~~~~

Dorothy Siers was a beautiful woman. Never did she have a hair out of place, and her home was just lovely and neat as a pin. Grace had started visiting her because she could sense her loneliness, but continued to visit because she actually enjoyed her company. Besides, Grace was becoming quite accomplished on the guitar, and had achieved enough proficiency to actually play along on several songs with Bernie and Dorothy Siers. Her visit today was much longer than usual because it was so much fun actually playing, instead of just practicing guitar. At least that is what she was telling herself. The truth was, she did not want to run in to Caleb Rogers again today. She needed time to think, and just time to be. All she wanted to do was ride home and enjoy the beautiful summer day, although her finger tips were throbbing from all the playing she had done that day. The callouses on her fingertips were enough for rehearsing, but this was the first time she had actually played for so long without taking a break.

"Your fingers must be aching by now," Mrs. Siers said. "Let me fix you a cup of tea. I have some wild strawberry muffins if you like!"

Grace really wanted to get home before it got dark, but Mrs. Siers looked so thrilled to offer the tea and muffins that Grace could not say no. After all, she was certain she had made them just for her. By the time she left, it was dusk, and although she decided not to race home, she did keep a steady and even pace. She knew her Mama would be worried, and send out her Papa to look for her if she didn't get home soon.

As she rode out of the trees toward the clearing, a man stepped out in front of her horse and held up his arms which spooked Patsy at first. One of the reasons the Bensons had chosen Patsy for Grace, was that she was sure footed and hard to spook, which proved invaluable now. Instead of rearing and throwing Grace to the ground, Patsy simply backed away from the intruder, first raising her head and then lowering it to the ground, over and over and over.

It wasn't until Grace had the mare under complete control that she noticed it was not Caleb as she had first thought, but a stranger she had never seen in these parts before. Panic rose in her throat but she was determined not to give in to it. She kicked Patsy in the ribs and prepared to gallop past the man, but he caught her reins as she went by, spinning the horse around to face him.

He grabbed her by the left ankle, and when she reached down to free herself, he grabbed her wrist and pulled her off, into his arms. Her knee came up and caught him with a crippling blow, and she blasted him in the side of his head with her fist. But as he fell, he took her with him and began slapping her, saying, "You dumb wench! I wasn't going to hurt you until you pulled that little stunt! Now I'm gonna teach you a thing or two about men!" Her mind went to the boat docks in Parkersburg when the filthy man was trying to attack her and her Papa had come out of nowhere and lifted him off her. *Please God, send my Papa to me now! Let him be looking for me and bring him here, Father!*

She bit his lip until she tasted blood, then with her hands firmly planted on either side of his head, she dug her thumbs into his eyes as far as she could manage. Then, as if her prayers were answered, the man was lifted into the air, and she could breathe again. When she sat up, she could see the stranger being pounded in the face again and again, but not by her Papa. By Caleb. *Thank God Caleb did not listen to me; did not go away as I told him to. And thank God he did not give up on me!*

After Caleb knocked the man unconscious, he pulled his shirt up over his head to immobilize him, albeit temporarily, but still, long enough for Caleb to get the upper hand again when he woke up.

He walked over to Grace, knelt down and said, "Are you alright?"

Grace took several breaths while she did a quick inventory of her injuries. The back of her head hurt where she had hit the ground, and a sharp rock had been gouging her lower spine, but other than that she was fine. Caleb sat down on one heel beside her and tenderly brushed the hair out of her eyes. His concern touched her heart.

"You are sure he didn't... well... hurt you?" he said with great concern.

In an instant, panic and rage filled her so that she was no longer in control of herself. Her breathing was shallow and it appeared she was about to explode, when she shouted, "Yes, I am sure, Caleb. He did not *rape* me if that is what you mean!" She lingered on the word 'rape' as if to shock him with the word.

Caleb was taken aback by her anger, but had no time at all to process that information because without taking one breath, she spat out, "I have *been* raped, Caleb! I know what that feels like and he did not rape me! *That* I know for sure!" She was trembling with emotions and could not stop herself. "So, now that you know, you can just walk away from me and leave me alone! I am damaged goods, Caleb, and will never be a wife to anyone."

She shook so that he thought she would fall into little pieces. Her breath was halted as if it repeatedly caught in her throat, unable to reach her lungs nor escape her lips. She began humming a strange moan and rocked forward and back over and over, and he feared for her mental state. As the humming became louder and louder, she screamed a throaty scream and began sobbing through her fury. She jumped to her feet and began running to nowhere. She shrieked and ran in jagged circles as if she had no idea where she was supposed to be, while Caleb watched helplessly.

All he could think of was to hold her in his arms, to take away her fear by taking control of her physical being. As he approached her, she threw punches at him and fought to get away, but he persisted in getting his arms around her and holding her tightly. He rocked her back and forth gently as if dancing with her, and whispered, "It is ok now. You are safe with me. It's ok, Grace. Everything will be ok. Shhhhhh. Shhhhhhh. It's ok, now."

Before long, he felt her relax in his arms, and at that moment, her knees buckled. She would have fallen to the ground had he not gripped her tighter to him, and managed to wrap his arm under her legs and lay her gently on the grass in the clearing.

He left her there and collected the horses, took the man's belt off, secured his hands behind him, and with a grunt, threw the man over Patsy's saddle. As he walked out into the clearing leading the two horses, he saw someone approaching in the distance. It wasn't until the men were within speaking distance that Caleb could make out the forms of Benjamin Waters, and his son, Little Ben.

Rage was on Benjamin's face as he quickened his step to find out what had happened to his daughter. Caleb was certain his life was not worth a plug nickel if he didn't explain to Benjamin what had happened, and quickly. As Ben grabbed Caleb's shirt and raised his fist to bury it in

Caleb's face, Caleb blurted out, "This man tried to attack Grace. I just happened to be here to help." Then Caleb twisted back to reveal the man thrown over the horse.

Ben breathed deeply several times as the rage drained from his body, and he let go of the boy's shirt to calm himself. He remembered the blinding madness that possessed him when he beat his father to death, and he began to steady his breathing in an effort to not beat Caleb senseless. As he did so, he remembered his beloved Grace, and turned to see if she was breathing.

"She is fine, Sir. I think she just fainted."

Ben said, "Did he..."

"No, Sir," Caleb said, "he did not."

Benjamin's body suddenly deflated, and he fell on his knees beside Grace. Little Ben had watched the entire scene without saying a word, but finally walked up beside Caleb and said, "I am so grateful you were here."

Caleb wondered if the boy knew what had happened to his sister in the past, but just nodded his head in response.

Benjamin picked his daughter up from the cold ground, and carried her the rest of the way home. Caleb watched him carrying her, with his feeble leg, and thought what a fine man Benjamin was. With great respect, he decided when the time was right, he would ask to speak to him about his feelings for Grace. But he thought he would wait a while, until Ben calmed down and was certain Grace was alright.

With the cabin in sight, Grace awakened to the swaying motion of being carried, and looked up to see her father holding her in his arms. Tears ran from her eyes, and her Papa just held her closer. With Sarah right behind him, he carried Grace to her room and placed her on her bed. Caleb waited on the porch while Sarah and Ben got her calmed down, and made certain she was not hurt.

Benjamin stepped onto the porch with Caleb after Elizabeth and Sarah decided to help Grace undress. "What are we going to do with him?" Ben asked Caleb as he nodded to the man hanging from the saddle.

"Well," Caleb said, "I have never seen him in this neck of the woods before, so I figger he is a deserter. I thought I would take him to town, and have Hulse lock him up in that cellar house until we can take him to Parkersburg to the Sheriff."

Ben had not been able to look Caleb in the eye yet, but he did so as he offered his hand and said, "Thanks, Caleb." Then added, "For everything."

That was all Caleb needed to hear: that Ben did not blame him, or suspect him of any wrong doing. Before Ben could change his mind, Caleb left with the man slung over his horse and walked to town by way of Leafbank.

When Ben went back into the house, Sarah and Elizabeth were sitting at the table quietly, staring at their cups of coffee. He asked how she was, and Sarah said Grace wanted to be alone.

"Do you think that is a good idea?" Ben asked.

"Well," Sarah said with a knowing smile on her face, "I gave her a cup of Midgie's Lightening Hot Drops!" All those at the table smiled, knowing that soon, Grace would be fast asleep.

"He didn't hurt her," Ben said, wondering why their little spitfire was taking the entire thing so hard.

"Ah, but he did, Ben," Kevin said. "He took away her sense of security. He stole her perception that she could protect herself and was safe to be who she wanted to be here."

Sarah sighed deeply and tipped her head back to keep the tears from rolling down her face. "She has been so happy here! And now…"

"Now, we just need to love her more, to give her room to grieve the many losses she has had in her life," Kevin said. "And what we cannot heal, God can."

Sarah continued to cry and could not stop, which was uncharacteristic for her. Ben was wondering what the problem was, and he remembered Midgie's words, "You need to keep an eye on Sarah now that she is with child!"

Ben took Sarah's hand in his and said, "You are exhausted. Come on, I want you to lie down for a while." It was early in the evening, but after he convinced her to put on her night clothes and get under the covers, she fell into a deep sleep, and did not awaken until the sun was firmly set in the sky, and breakfast was over.

"Well, look whose awake!" Ben said teasingly when Sarah stumbled out of the bedroom looking completely confused.

"How long did I sleep?" she asked curiously.

Ben took a big drink of coffee, draining his cup, and said, "Two days!"

"Two days?" she shouted before she saw on his face that he was just teasing her.

He walked over and gave her a kiss on the forehead and said, "You must have needed the rest if you slept that long. Now what can I fix you for breakfast?"

"Just coffee," she said. The sound of food just did not sit well with her yet this morning, then her thoughts turned to Grace. "How is she this morning?" she asked as she blew across the coffee to cool it.

"She isn't awake yet either," Ben said as he suppressed a laugh. "How much of those Hot Drops did you put into that cup?"

"Well, not enough to kill her I hope!" She tried to rise from the table to go make sure Grace was still breathing, but Ben placed his hand on her shoulder to stop her.

"She is fine," he said. "Elizabeth is in there with her, reading and waiting for her to wake up. Just relax."

Sarah was glad to accommodate him, and leaned on the table with both elbows, happy she did not have to get up right at that moment. The hot, black, coffee hit the spot, so she drank it eagerly, enjoying the feel of warmth in her stomach.

"I have no idea what to say to Grace when she does come out of the room," Ben began. "I don't know if she wants me to hug her or stay away from her again. Kevin says we should just be the same we always were, but I don't know." He drifted off in his own thoughts until Sarah stood, knocking over her chair, and vomited all over the table. Ben grabbed the chamber pot and caught the rest of it, but Sarah had to sit down to keep from falling.

She broke out in a sweat and felt sicker than she had ever been in her life. Ben led her back to bed and she didn't even fight with him when he pulled the covers up under her chin. It was raining, mercifully, and the day was cool and wet. She listened to the rain hitting the tin roof, said a prayer for Grace, and fell into a deep, deep, sleep.

Little Ben and Kevin had gone hunting early that morning, but returned when the rain started pouring down in earnest. They entered the room soaking wet, and had to shed their clothes right there at the door. "Kevin," Ben shouted over the downpour of rain that was pounding on the roof, "I want you to get on dry clothes and go to bed as well. You cannot afford to risk your health by getting run down, and that wet won't do you any good either."

Kevin began to protest, but Ben insisted by saying, "Go on now. You cannot afford a setback."

Kevin saw the logic in it, and stopped only briefly to get an update on Sarah and Grace, then went off to bed as he was encouraged to do. "I'll bring you some coffee," Ben said, "do you want anything else?"

"No, *Mama*!" Kevin said in a teasing manner. "Coffee will be fine!"

After Kevin was settled, Ben turned to his son and said, "Now if we could only get Rebecca to bed, we could do some fine whittlin'!"

Little Ben said, "Papa, could we talk about something?"

"Sure," said Ben. "What's your trouble?" Ben asked as he sat down to give his son his undivided attention.

"Well," Little Ben needed just a moment to collect his thoughts, "I just wanted to talk over with you where I am headed in this life."

It took everything Ben had, not to laugh at such a statement from such a young person, but he managed. "Well, I think that is a fine idea, Son."

Little Ben said, "I don't know how old I really am," he began, and Ben realized that this conversation was heading in a far more serious direction than he thought.

"And if I don't know how old I really am, then how do I know when I am finally a man?" He looked at his father for answers that Ben did not have. But it occurred to Ben that this was indeed a serious thing for the boy. Was he 13 or even15? The boy had certainly grown a lot over the winter, and could have been much older than he looked when they found, due to malnutrition, so how old was he? He now towered over Ira, and seemed to be more mature now, than Ira, as well.

More important questions came to mind and Ben asked, "What are you feeling in your heart, Son? What I mean is, when you came here all in the world you wanted was a slingshot. But what is in your heart now?"

Little Ben looked at the floor and then at his father and said, "Well, Uncle Kevin and I have been studying the Bible a good bit."

Ben nodded his head, yes, and said, "Well, that is a mighty good thing, Ben."

Little Ben continued, "And I want to be a preacher. Granny and I talked about my being a preacher, too. She said God's hand was on me, and that I had powerful prayers." He waited for a moment and then continued, "That day I didn't want to water the plants because I didn't see them growing, you know, the day after Granny showed us how to plant the potatoes and such?"

Ben nodded again.

Well, that day she told me to carry the water up from the well, and water each and everything we had planted, as an act of faith. Faith that we had done the possible, and now we trusted God to do the impossible."

Ben waited for his son to continue.

"She also told me that I was a seed planted by God, and that she was watering me, so God could make me into a fine preacher." He smiled at her memory, then said, "I decided that if those plants grew, and she was right about that garden, that maybe she was right about me. I have spent a lot of time up on that hill, praying, and asking God why he protected me all those years when Grace was being abused so, and then when she had me and Rebecca to feed. Grace had it so hard," he dropped his head and sniffed.

Ben put his hand on his son's knee, and said, "You had it hard, too, Ben. Bad things happened to you, too. You were hungry, never knew a Mama and Papa's love before. You were cold, and frightened. You had it bad, too. But your attitude remained that of a child. That always amazed me about you."

Little Ben looked up at him and wiped his nose on his sleeve, so Benjamin continued, "You have an amazing spirit, Ben Waters, and I do believe that spirit comes from God. I believe your Granny was right about that." Ben sat for a minute and then continued, "But it is important that you feel led by God to become a minister, Ben. You cannot do it because your Granny suggested it, or because I can see that in you. It needs to be a calling, straight from God. A call on your life that you must decide whether or not you will answer."

"Papa?" Little Ben asked, "Would you mind if I did become a preacher, and not follow in your footsteps and be a woodworker?"

The question caught Ben off guard, and then Little Ben's wording sounded familiar. How many times had he said that he was building a business his son could step into and make a good living doing? For a brief moment, he felt a twinge of disappointment, he had to admit, but what Little Ben wanted out of life was more important. "Of course not, Son. Whatever you want to do with your life is exactly what I want for you. I want to see you a free man, happy, and healthy, and doing what you feel called to do with your life. One man cannot decide that for another."

Ben felt a great amount of pride when his father called him a man, then it brought back the first question he had no answer for. When did he know he was a man, when he had no idea what age he truly was?

"Uncle Kevin and I were talking about how much I had grown this winter," he said to his father. "And it got me wondering…"

Ben waited for a few seconds and said, "Wondering what, Son? What is it that is really bothering you?"

"Well, two things," he said holding out two fingers. "First, what if I want to get married, but I don't know if I am old enough?"

Ben sat up straighter and said, "Whoa, there, Son. I am not sure how old you are either, but you sure are not old enough to get married."

"But how do you know, Papa?"

"Because I know you are still a boy. You are going to have to trust me on this one, Ben. You are just beginning to grow, and you have a lot of finishing to do. You have to know how to support your family…"

"But I do know how to support my family. I want to be a preacher!"

"Whoa! Slow down, Son! Just because you think you know what you want to do with your life, doesn't mean you are ready to do it. It takes years of study and work to become a preacher. You can't just announce that you are one, and expect to be given a place to live and a church!"

Little Ben looked confused so Ben continued, "Why don't you talk to Uncle Kevin about what it took for him to become a priest? He can give you a far more realistic view of that than I can."

Little Ben agreed, then Ben said, "You said two things were on your mind. What was the second one?" Ben was relieved to change that subject.

"The second thing is, well, if I don't know how old I am, how will I know when I should go to war?"

Benjamin nearly fell off his chair. "You are not going to war, and that is all there is to it. Now you can just stop thinking about that, right now! You are not going to war if I have to sit on you until the war is over!"

Little Ben said, "But Caleb Rogers little brothers went to war. Maybe I am their age."

Ben stood and walked around in the room. He ran his fingers through his hair and clicked his teeth together in an effort to get a grip on his emotions. "Benjamin Waters, you are not going to war. That is the last I want to hear of it, too. Do you want to kill your Mama? And what about Grace? How could you put her through that? No! I won't hear of it."

Ben turned and looked at his son, then just for good measure, added, "And if you run off and enlist, I will join the Army and come looking for you! Do you understand me?"

Little Ben had never seen his father that upset. He decided to be supremely respectful, and replied, "Yes, Sir. I understand."

"And furthermore, I will have no more talk of this in this house! Your Mama is in a very delicate condition, and I don't want you worrying her to death with this talk of going off to war!"

"Yes, Sir," was all Little Ben could get out. He knew the subject was off the table, and unbeknownst to his Papa, Little Ben was thrilled about it. He had no desire to go to war, but was beginning to feel obligated. For now, it was enough that his Papa had said, no.

The rain fell outside the cabin, and Ben stood watching the water trickle down the window, running toward other drops as they passed. His anger passed and he turned toward his son and said, "I want you to feel you can talk to me about anything, Ben. I don't want you to fear talking to me, but I guess I wasn't ready for all this talk about your being a man. I still see you as my little boy, I guess. I mean, I am just a human being. I make mistakes like everyone else. So, I guess what I am trying to say is, I want you to be able to bring anything to me. You can tell me anything in this world. And I may get upset, or angry, or shout and yell, but if you give me a few minutes of being human, I will calm down and be the best friend and father I know how to be."

Little Ben's face split open into a wide grin. "I know, Papa. I know I can talk to you. And it is ok that you got all mad. I did not want to go to war anyway! I guess I was just feeling a little like other people might wonder why I didn't."

"Well, you do not make a decision about something as important as going to war, based on what others might think of you. You have to do what you think is right. As long as your Mama and Papa agree!" he said with a glint in his eye and a loving smile on his face.

They sat there in a comfortable silence for a while, each lost in their own thoughts, until Ben said, "So, did you have a particular girl in mind for marrying?"

Little Ben's face reddened and he nodded his head, yes. "Maxine Benson."

Ben grinned and said, "I can see that. You two have been smitten on each other since that first day in the wagon when you were making her laugh with those hot potatoes."

"I love her Papa, and she loves me, too," he said with no hesitation.

"Really? The two of you have discussed this?"

"Yes. I asked her to marry me, and she said she would!" Little Ben's face was red as wild cherries, and Ben knew this was an important moment.

"You know she is several years younger than you are, don't you? Are you willing to wait?"

"Yes, Sir. I will wait 20 years if that is what it takes. I am going to marry her someday, Papa."

Ben looked at his son thoughtfully, then said, "I believe you are, Son. And you will be a lucky man."

Chapter Twenty-Five

Caleb gave Grace a full week to recover before going to see her. He feared his presence as a man might upset her, and yet all he wanted to do was help.

Grace, on the other hand, did not take his absence as a patient thing to do. She saw it as rejection. After all, with news like that who would want to be around her. If he had ever thought of her as a wife, that was over now. And she was certain news like that would spread like wildfire throughout the community, so, she decided, she would never marry, and would forever carry the burden of one who was not fit for marriage.

That was fine, she decided. She would dedicate her life to helping others; delivering babies, tending to the sick, patching up broken bones, doling out herbs and medicines as she saw fit. Why, even her visits to Mrs. Siers were helping the poor woman cope with the absence of her daughter, Susan. That was what she would do with her life. She would help others as she always wanted to be helped.

She had not left her home since that day when she was nearly assaulted. She was not afraid, she told herself, but there was no need to leave… well, no really good reason to go out, in her opinion. Her family just loved her and let her be, so that was a comfortable, and safe place to be for now.

At Kevin's suggestion, Sarah had spoken to Grace about what happened, and told her that that was the last time it would be brought up to her. They did not want her to feel at any given moment, that the subject would be brought to mind and discussed again and again. However, if she wanted to speak about what happened, or how she was feeling, she was welcomed to bring it up at any time, and they were willing to help in any way they could.

Everyone thought she was suffering because of the attempted assault, but what bothered her more, was that for some unknown reason, she had trusted Caleb with her secret – an admission she now regretted.

Her long sighs, repeated bouts of isolation in her room, and wistful looks out the window were actually a deep longing that she could somehow un-ring the bell, so to speak. If she had a way to take those words back she would. The rest she could cope with.

A knock on the door sent Grace to her room. She wanted no company other than her family, but when she heard Denzel's voice at the door she thought it might not be so bad… sitting on the porch and talking to Denzel.

She stepped out of the room and looked around at the surprise on her family's faces, and said, "Hi, Denzel!"

Denzel took his hat off and smiled at her. *Maybe he hasn't heard yet,* Grace thought to herself. "Would you like to sit on the porch and talk for a while?" Grace asked.

"Sure!" Denzel said as he opened the door and replaced his hat. The two of them went outside and sat down in the new rocking chairs Benjamin had made. "These are really nice!" Denzel said. "I wish I could get one of these for Mama!"

"They are nice," Grace said. "Papa is going to paint them white, but he just hasn't yet. I think he has trouble painting them because someone is always in them!" She said with a smile.

"I'm sorry about what happened to you," Denzel said without noticing the sorrow that appeared on Grace's face.

"Well, news travels fast in a small community, I guess." Grace was heartbroken that Caleb had told everyone about that day. But whatever she was hoping to keep a secret was now out in the public eye for everyone to gossip about, and there was nothing to be done about it.

"Yea," Denzel said, "nobody has any secrets here, I am afraid."

Grace took that as confirmation that not only what had happened to her was fodder for the gossip mill, Caleb had actually told people what she had said to him. She was looking at her interwoven fingers in her lap when Denzel said, "Hey, you want to go swimming in the lake?"

Grace looked at him with new eyes. Whereas before she had seen him as a potential husband, she now saw him as a child, immature, and unaware of the real struggles in life.

"What? Why are you looking at me like that?" Denzel said.

"No reason." Grace said, knowing things would never be the same with the two of them again. "I'm just really tired, Denzel, and I have a lot to do before the day is over."

She stood to indicate his visit was over, and as he walked away he said, "Did I say something that upset you?"

Grace recognized he was incapable of understanding her, and yet he was a kind and good man, so she smiled and said, "No, not at all. I just really need to be here today with Mama. Maybe we can swim another day." Her smile was genuine. Just because she no longer thought of Denzel in a romantic way did not mean she no longer considered him a friend.

He stopped and turned to her with a big smile and said, "For what it is worth, I heard you nearly blinded that guy that attacked you. They sent for the Doc when they got him to Parkersburg. Don't know if they can save the eye or not!" He was proud of the way she fought the man, like an older brother who was proud of his little sister for fighting so well.

Grace had to admit she was pleased that she at least delivered one blow in her defense, and shouted, "Thanks for telling me," as he walked away, turning to wave goodbye.

As she turned and looked up the hill in front of the cabin, she saw a man approaching on horseback. She stood in the doorway and watched, feeling safe with her father, brother, and Uncle Kevin right behind her. As the rider got closer, she realized it was Caleb, turned and went to her room.

Benjamin watched Grace go into her room and met Caleb at the door. As Caleb stepped up onto the porch, he removed his hat and said, "Mr. Waters."

Ben said, "Caleb," and held out his hand.

Caleb shook his hand with a firm grip, and said, "Would this be a good time to speak with you privately for a moment, Sir?"

As Ben turned to grab the door handle, he looked at Sarah with his eyebrows up as if to say, *wonder what this is all about?* He grabbed his hat and closed the door behind him.

The two men walked up to the top of the hill on the pretense of seeing how the garden was doing, as Ben waited for Caleb to begin. "Sir," he started, "I guess you already know that I am interested in your daughter, Grace."

Ben grinned and looked at the ground. "Well, secrets are hard to keep around here, Son," he said with a laugh as he looked the very embarrassed Caleb in the eye.

It was Caleb's turn to look at the ground. Then he looked up and said, "I'm not sure Grace is as keen on me as I am on her, but I am a patient man, Mr. Waters. And I love her." He took off his hat and ran his fingers through his thick black hair and said, "And I want her to be my wife."

Ben thought about that for a minute, then said, "Are you ready to take on a wife? I mean, you have to have a place to live, a way to feed and shelter your family, because there will be youngin's you know."

"Yes, Sir!" Caleb said with a smile, "I sure hope there will be youngin's." The smile disappeared, then he said, "Well, in answer to your question, I am ready to take on a wife. I have my own farm, close enough to my Mama to tend to her needs with fixin' things and all, yet far enough away that we can have our own lives. We will be attending the same church we do now, which is with you, so you will be seeing her at least every Sunday. I am a God fearing man, who loves the Lord, and your daughter, Grace."

The thought he had put into the marriage almost brought tears to Ben's eyes. It was exactly what he wanted for Grace and he could not be happier. Again, Ben held out his hand and Caleb took it. "Well, you have my blessing, Son, but you still have to work it out with Grace, and that may not be easy. She is her own person you know."

Caleb put his hat back on, looked out into the trees, and said, "Whew! Don't I know it!" Both men laughed, then Caleb bit his lower lip and said, "But that only makes me love her more." He nodded repeatedly as if he was most certain that he loved her, cantankerous spirit and all.

Ben slapped him on the arm and said, "Well, let's get back down there so you can see the one you came to see!" And the two men started down the hill.

Caleb said, "Do you think she is ready to see me? I mean, I know this has set her back some, and I don't want to push her."

The words, "set her back some," made Ben wonder what he knew about Grace's past, but he said nothing. "Well, the one thing I do know, is that Grace is not shy about letting us know what she is feeling!" Both men laughed and agreed with that, then Ben continued, "All I ask is that you respect her boundaries. Don't force her into anything she is not ready to do." When he stopped walking, Caleb did, too. Ben looked him in the eye and said, "And that goes for *after* you are married, too." There was a long pause, then Ben asked, "Do you understand what I am meaning by that, Son?"

"Yes, Sir, I do," Caleb said, meeting the challenge up front. "And I promise you I will never do anything to hurt your daughter. Besides, like I said, I am a very patient man."

Ben stared at him, trying to look into his soul, because if he were lying, and if he ever did hurt Grace, Ben knew it was in him to beat him to death with his bare hands, and he did not want that to happen.

"You had better be," he said with a look that could have been a smile, but may have been a warning.

Chapter Twenty-Six

The men returned to the cabin with a new understanding. Caleb waited in the front room while Benjamin went back to talk to Grace. Sarah invited him to sit down, but he was too nervous, and continued to stand.

Ben knocked on Grace's door and waited for her to respond before entering. "Grace, Caleb is here to see you," he said sweetly as he walked over to the bed where she was lying, and moved a curl of hair out of her eyes.

"I don't want to talk to him, Papa," she said, and when she blinked a tear slid down her cheek.

"Did Caleb hurt you out there, Grace?" Ben had assumed Caleb was telling the truth until Grace did not want to talk to him.

"No. NO! Papa! No, he didn't hurt me. He saved me from that horrible man, and that is all," she said as she sat up and wiped her eyes with her handkerchief.

"Then why don't you want to see him?" Ben asked. "Please tell me if he hurt you in any way."

"No, Papa, he really did nothing wrong." She realized that was not a good explanation so she continued, "I… I'm just embarrassed, that's all."

"Embarrassed by what, Grace? How could his saving you embarrass you? Abram sure wasn't embarrassed by my jumping into the water to save him. There is nothing wrong with accepting help, Grace."

"I know, I… I just can't explain it, Papa."

"Well, let me say this. You can hide in this room for the rest of your life, hiding from people, and fearful of going out for any reason. Or you can use common sense to keep yourself safe and continue your life as it was. But I want you to choose which one it is going to be. I don't want you to just let it happen to you. Do you understand?"

Grace looked at him briefly and said, "So, what you are saying is that I shouldn't just sit here and hide? Unless I want to become that kind of person."

"Yes. That is exactly what I am saying. Do you want to spend the rest of your life living like you have lived this last week? Fearful? Sad? Worried?"

Grace thought about what he had said, and thought about how miserable she had been. She wanted the joy back in her life, and realized that she was going to have to fight for it if she wanted it.

Ben said, "I just had a good talk with Caleb, Grace. And I think he is a good man. Maybe he would be a good place to start if you want to get back into the world you lived in before."

Grace inhaled deeply and sighed a long slow sigh. "Ok, Papa. I am not sure how to find my way back, but I am going to try. I love you, Papa," she said before planting a kiss on his cheek, then standing, straightening her hair, and saying, "Wish me luck."

She decided not to be vulnerable. She decided to pretend Granny was with her, because she knew Granny would never tolerate her being a coward. She stepped out into the room, looked Caleb in the eye and said, "Hi!"

His face beamed, and he said, "Hi! Feel like taking a walk?"

"Sure," she said as her stomach clinched at the thought of going far from the house.

Ben saw her hesitation and suggested they go up and check out the new bench he had placed in the shade of the trees beside the garden.

Caleb seemed a little too interested in the new bench, but that was fine, Grace thought. She could come straight home if things got uncomfortable. No, her Papa had said to use common sense, and common sense told her that Caleb would never hurt her physically. But if he had told everyone about what she had told him…

"Grace?" Caleb said. He was holding the door open and waiting for her.

"Oh!" She said as she stepped back into reality. The two of them walked to the top of the hill, walked around the garden carefully, crossed over to the edge of the hill, and sat in the shade of the huge Oak tree on the new bench Ben had made for just that spot.

Caleb smiled and said, "It is so good to see you. It killed me to wait an entire week to come over, but I wanted to give you time to…"

"Time to what, Caleb? What did I need time for?"

"I don't know what to say, Grace," he said. "Tell me what you want to me to say, and I will say it."

She couldn't speak. She didn't know if she was angry, or upset, or… what was she doing up here with him anyway? She was angry with him for telling her secret, and knew in her heart that he fell below her standards of what she wanted in a man. She breathed in and out loudly as she tried to decide what she wanted to do. She fought the instinct to run home, but had no idea what she was doing there with Caleb.

"Tell me what you are thinking," he said. "I can't read minds, and I don't want to say something that will make things worse. I have never been in this situation before, Grace. I am new at this, but I want to learn. I want to know how to comfort you, but you have to help me understand."

It was true. Neither of them had been in this situation before and she saw the truth in what he was saying. She was angry with him, and he deserved to know why. She took a deep breath and began, "Denzel was over there earlier today, and he knew all about what happened to me."

Caleb had no idea where she was going with that, so he just said, "Yea?"

"Well, I didn't like that." There, it was out in the open.

Caleb felt he was walking over a lake, on very thin ice, but he proceeded with caution, "Ok, I understand that you didn't like that Denzel was over here earlier and knew about what happened to you." Grace nodded. "But, I don't get which part of it upset you. Did you not want Denzel here? Or were you upset because he knew about what happened to you?"

"YES! I was very upset that he knew what happened to me! That was private, Caleb. Why would you tell that to everyone in the community? Did it make you feel like a big man, saving a little girl from the mean attacker?"

Caleb was taken aback. Still confused, he said, "Wait. You seem to be getting angrier and angrier, Grace, and I have no idea why. Could we just calm down and take this one step at a time?" He waited until she was ready to speak again.

"Ok, if I have to spell it out for you I will," she said, standing, arms folded, and facing him. "I am angry because you told everyone my business."

Caleb stood and said, "Ok, that is a good place to start. I did tell everyone what happened, but not because it made me look like a big man. I told everyone because there might be more soldiers out there, and I wanted everyone to be aware of the danger. There are some beautiful children in this area, who go swimming alone, and walk to Jimmies, or to their neighbor's house by themselves because it used to be safe to do that. What I told them is that it is not safe to be out alone anymore."

The anger in Grace's face melted away as she totally saw his point, and was ashamed of her behavior. But why had he told about her past? There was still that question to ask.

"What?" Ben said, "What are you thinking right now? Because something changed in your face. What is it?" Unlike Benjamin, Caleb knew a great deal about women. He had watched his mother suffer the loss of his father, and her son whom she loved more that life itself. Oh, she loved Caleb and his twin alright, he had never doubted that, but Seth was the one who stepped up to replace their father. He had kept the farm running, hunted for food, and been their mother's confidante after their father died, and Caleb knew what Seth had meant to Eileen. His Mama had been broken, and Caleb had watched every tear, every smile, and every heartbreaking look of sorrow on her face.

Grace was not accustomed to being read so well. She felt her privacy had been invaded somewhat, and yet she trusted him with that; his ability to look into her soul. Or she would have trusted him, had he not told about her past. Even she knew that was not fair to condemn him for doing something, so unlike him, unless he told her to her face that he had.

"When I asked him how he knew, Denzel said nobody has any secrets around here. Does that mean you told everybody what I told you about my past?" Her chin held high, she was determined to have it out one way or another. At least she would know.

The look of shock on Caleb's face was priceless. He wanted to shout at her for accusing him of something so underhanded, but he knew by the look on her face that this was important; too important to risk messing up.

"You have to know, Grace Waters, that I would never, *ever,* under any circumstances, divulge something that personal. I said nothing to anyone about that, including your father, and would never in this lifetime have brought it up again if you hadn't." He stood and walked in a large circle with his fists on his hips, then said, "And just so you know, that had nothing to do with *your* past. That had everything to do with the past of the sick monster that did that to you. It was *his* sin, not yours!"

Her face told him that what he was saying was soothing her mind and heart, so he continued, "You are still the same girl you were before that happened. And I love that girl so much I would lay down my life in a heartbeat for her, right here, right now."

Tears came to Grace's eyes and relief flooded her entire being. He drew her into his arms and held her gently. He carefully placed his hand on the back of her head, and hugged her tenderly. She cried tears of relief, and gave up all that haunted her. As she pulled her handkerchief out of her sleeve, they sat down on the bench together.

Suddenly, Grace burst into a full body laughter. "Look," she said as she pointed to the part of the garden farthest away from them. There was her father, pouring water on one plant in the far edge of the garden. "He is checking on us," she said laughing.

Caleb waved at Benjamin and Ben waved back, then took his bucket and went back down the hill. "I love my Papa," she said. "And it is a good thing you were behaving yourself!" She looked at Caleb when she said that and then laughed again.

"Believe me," Caleb said, "the last thing on earth I want to do is make your Papa mad!" He looked down at her hand and said, "May I?"

"May you what?" Grace said, truly not understanding.

"May I hold your hand?" he said with the sweetest look on his face.

Grace understood the full meaning of his request. It meant that he wanted to be closer to her, but would not go any faster than she was comfortable with. She smiled and placed her hand on his. He covered her hand with his other hand, and said, "Ahhhhh! I have been wanting to do that for a long time," he said with that beautiful smile he had that drove her crazy.

"Caleb," she said, "I do not know how to thank you. For everything. For saving me, for hearing what I did not want to say, and respecting my privacy. For not judging me." She began to cry again.

"There is honestly nothing to judge, Grace. It was done *to* you, not *by* you. I get that." He paused and said, "Is it possible for you to just let that go?"

"I appreciate that you are a kind and understanding man, Caleb, but most men would not be as forgiving, and…"

"Oh, you don't have to be worrying about other men and what they think, Miss Grace! Because you are going to marry me!"

"What? I will do no such thing, Caleb Rogers! Who do you think you are to say such a thing to me?" He grinned, as the Grace he was more accustomed to, had finally made an appearance.

"Yep! Ask your Papa! He has already given his approval!" That grin again! She just wanted to slap that ridiculous grin right off his face! How dare he just make an assumption like that!

"Oh, you can fuss, and you can fight, but we are going to get married, Miss Grace! And I don't care how long it takes, either. Two weeks, two years! Whatever it takes, I am willing to wait because I love you, more than you can imagine."

Before she could protest, he kissed her. Right there under the big Oak tree, sitting on the bench her Papa had made. She leaned into the kiss, and nearly fell over when he pulled away from her. "Well, I am willing to wait two years unless you kiss me like *that* again!" he said, standing and putting his hat on.

"Unless I kiss *you* like that again! I believe *you* kissed *me*, Caleb Rogers!"

He headed for the Waters' cabin ahead of her, and shouted over his shoulder, "But you *liked* it!"

By the time they stepped into the front room of the cabin, Caleb and Grace were laughing and sparring with each other. Sarah, Kevin, and Ben were happy to see how lighthearted she was, and even Little Ben had noticed the difference in his sister and was relieved at the change.

Suddenly, they heard the church bell begin to ring. One, two, three. Three rings that late in the day meant that the community was to meet at the church at 3:00 PM the following afternoon. Although they were concerned about the reason, they felt there was no imminent danger or emergency so to speak, or they would have simply rung the bell 7 or 8 times and called them together tonight.

Caleb excused himself to go share the news with the neighbors down on Leafbank, and any other place that was not within earshot of the church bell.

"Did you enjoy your visit?" Ben asked.

The smile on Grace's face told him the entire story. She was in love with Caleb Rogers, and Ben could not be more pleased. She said, "Yes, I did, very much in fact. Thanks, Papa," and tiptoed to kiss him on the cheek again.

She started toward her room, then turned and then said, "Did you and Caleb have a chat today that I should know about?"

Ben smiled and said, "Oh, we had a chat, but I don't know that you need to know anything about it." He smiled at her, knowing that it was Caleb's place to bring up the subject of marriage. And he strongly suspected Caleb already had.

Chapter Twenty-Seven

Friday, June 25, 1863

The church bell had rung the day before, signaling a community get together at the church today at 3:00. Neighbors came from far and near to hear what the news was, and they were not disappointed.

Rev. McCauley stood before the crowd of people gathered in that small church. Not only were the pews filled, there were people standing two and three deep along the walls, not to mention those standing outside, as close to the windows and door as possible, all in the hopes that it was the news they had been waiting for.

"Alright, if I could have your attention!" The crowd quieted so they could be introduced to the strangers in the front of the church, and hear the much anticipated news they had hoped for. But as Preacher stood up, once he had everyone's attention, he said, "I think I am going to preach a sermon!" His laugh was contagious and soon everyone was enjoying the joke. When they quieted for a moment, he said, "I want to invite all you back on Sunday morning, you know we hold services here every Sunday morning, and now that I have seen all of you here, I know you know the way!" The good natured laughter resumed. Some of the regulars looked at the others and nodded their heads as encouragement for them to attend.

"I do want to open this meeting with a word of prayer, though. You know wherever people gather together, God is there." Rev. McCauley waited for a second then continued, "Whether this is seen as good news by some of you, or bad news by others, God is here. Many of us have loved ones who are gone from home, fighting this war, and I just want you to know, God is with them, too."

The crowd hushed as the Holy Man bowed his head in prayer. He held his hands in the air and said, "Our Heavenly Father, we have acknowledged your presence here in humble recognition of the honor you bestow on us by simply loving us, just as we are. We ask that you be with us today as this news is heard, that you bless this community through all the changes we must endure. We ask this Father in Jesus' name. Amen." Preacher then said, "I have one announcement before we start, I spoke to the Hamiltons today, and they said they have heard from their sons, Vick and Roger who were at the attack on Burning Springs. They are fine, and are planning on coming home to visit sometime this summer. The crowd cheered as those around them patted the Hamiltons on the back.

Then Preacher stepped aside and said, "This gentleman is Mr. Kinkaid, and he has come to share some news with you."

There was a soft murmur of voices as they waited for the gentleman bearing the news to stand before them. When he spoke, he did so with all the aplomb of a town crier – his words were high, loud, and clear as if he were introducing the Queen of England and his stance was such that it brought chuckles from the farmers present in the church. But as he began to read, his persona disappeared and all who were there became aware that they were witnessing the making of history.

So loudly that he startled the ladies on the front row, Kinkaid began, "As of June 20th, 1863, by order of the Congress of the United States of America, the State of West Virginia is hereby recognized as the 35th State of the Union."

A cheer went up by the majority of those gathered there, but two men pushed their way out using language some had never heard, and some began praising the Lord for His hand in deliverance from Virginia. No one noticed the dry look the speaker gave Preacher, which prompted the Reverend to stand and hold up his hands to quiet the crowd. "Could I have your attention again, please?" Preacher said.

The crowd quieted quickly, and the man continued, "There is a distinction to West Virginia's statehood that is unique to all other states. It is explained as this: The children of slaves born within the limits of this State after the fourth day of July, eighteen hundred and sixty-three, shall be free; and all slaves within the said State who shall, at the time aforesaid, be under the age of ten years, shall be free when they arrive at the age of twenty-one years; and all slaves over ten and under twenty-one years, shall be free when they arrive at the age of twenty-five years; and no slave shall be permitted to come into the State for permanent residence therein."

The rumbling of voices again distracted those attending from what the speaker was saying. Some agreed with the ruling, and others thought it completely unacceptable.

Kinkaid wiped his brow with his ever present handkerchief and said, "Rev. McCauley! I must insist that you maintain control over this mob! I have many communities to visit and I can ill afford these outbursts!"

Preacher, in an attempt to let folks finish their conversation, stood slowly, removed his handkerchief from his pocket, wiped his forehead and neck, folded his handkerchief again, replaced it in his pocket, then took a step forward and said, "May I again have your attention?"

Kinkaid looked at Preacher in a way that indicated he was weighing the sin of punching a minister in the nose against the frustration that was building inside him.

"There you are, go on now," Preacher said with a smile, and took his seat.

"Let it be known that Berkeley County, Virginia, and Jefferson County, Virginia have voted to also join with West Virginia, and Congress has recognized those counties in the Eastern Panhandle as a part of West Virginia."

The crowd began to rumble again because some had no idea what that meant, and others were trying to explain the importance of that statement. This time Kinkaid did not defer to Preacher. He simply took a step forward, raised his eyebrows and glared at the congregation down his nose until they fell silent.

Then Kinkaid continued, "This is a devastating blow to the Confederacy because the B&O Railroad runs through those two counties and will now disrupt the movement of Confederate troops and supplies since it is a northern state!"

Ahhhh! They said, as their murmuring went from a noise to a commotion, then elevated itself to complete pandemonium!

Kinkaid slammed his book shut, grabbed his hat and coat, motioned to his driver and left the church in a fit of pique! He would be saddened to know that not one person even noticed he had left.

After the meeting, people left the church and its mounting heat, and went outside to gather in groups and discuss the news. Caleb, however, wanted to speak to only one person, and she was just as eager to join him. As they walked through the crowd in search of a quiet, shady place to sit, Grace thought about the last time they were together there. How much life had changed since she stomped away from him at the picnic. She felt as if she had aged years since that day, and yet it had only been a couple of weeks. She felt strangely grown, mature, and very much in love. How did that happen? And when? Growing up was strange and magical matter, and she didn't even know when it had occurred.

She looked up at Caleb and saw him watching her intently. She smiled and he said, "You look beautiful today!"

She was pleasantly surprised at his statement, and suddenly could not look directly into his eyes. She looked at the ground for a moment and then said, "Why, thank you, Caleb Rogers! What do I normally look like?"

The two of them giggled, then Caleb gestured with his hand for her to join him under the ancient Oak tree in the cool shade with the others.

They spent their time there, under the watchful eyes of every single adult who had seen them fighting the last time they were together, sitting with their heads together speaking softly to one another. Some of the older ladies were discussing which kind of cake to make for their wedding, and Eileen and Kevin were smiling at the perfect vision of young love.

After a bit of small talk, Caleb took hold of Grace's fingers and said, "Have you thought any more about what I said, Grace?"

Grace was surprised that he would bring that up again so soon, that he meant it in the first place, and that he would bring it up here, in front of everyone. Her eyes darted around to see who might have overheard him, then said, "Oh, Caleb. You did not mean that. It was kind of you, but…"

"I did mean it, Grace! I want to marry you!" he said just a little too loudly for Grace's comfort. Her eyes darted around again so he lowered his voice.

"I asked Mama how she knew she wanted to spend the rest of her life with our Pa." he said.

Grace looked up at him surprised that a man would go to his Mama for such advice. Caleb grinned and said sheepishly, "She's my Mama! Who else would I ask?"

Caleb scooted around to get more comfortable and to be a little closer to her, then said, "Mama said she never looked at it like that. She never asked herself if she wanted to spend the rest of her life with him. But she knew in her heart, she did not want to live the rest of her life without him. That is how I feel about you, Grace. I do not want to live the rest of my life without you. Now, I am a patient man, and you do not have to answer now. I just want you to know my heart."

Grace's heart was ripped in two. Part of it soared because the man she loved, loved her, too! But the other part sank in despair because she did not feel she was worthy to be any man's wife. She said, "Oh, Caleb, you know what happened!"

Caleb said, "Yes, I do. Almost every minute of every day, I want to hunt that man down and… Well, yes I do. And I have feelings about that, too!" Grace braced herself. She could not stand his pity, or to feel he was taking her for marriage because he thought no other man would have her. "But all my feelings are about him. I want to hunt him down and…" He sat there trying to still himself, then continued, "I feel rage!! I am the angriest I have ever been, Grace, because I feel like you have been mine forever, and I wasn't there to protect you!"

Her mouth fell open and tears began forming in her eyes. He scooted closer and put his arm around her shoulders before saying, "But none of those feelings have anything to do with you. You are an incredible woman, Grace Waters, a one-of-a-kind, for sure! You are the woman I love and want to spend the rest of my life with. None of the other stuff matters to me. Please, believe me, and think about what I have asked you."

Suddenly a shadow covered them, and Caleb looked up to see Benjamin standing over them. Apparently, Sarah and Ben did not like that Caleb had his arm around Grace in such a public way, although in private would not have been acceptable either. Caleb pulled his arm away from Grace and stood to shake hands with his father-in-law to be, or at least he hoped so.

Ben saw that Grace had been crying, but said nothing. "So, Caleb, what did you think of the news today? After some idle chatter, Grace stood to join them. Before long, it was time to go home, and Grace's mind was filled with ways to speak to Denzel about her feelings for Caleb. It was not something she was looking forward to, but had to be done.

Chapter Twenty-Eight

Grace did not have to wait long for the opportunity to speak with Denzel, because first thing in the morning, he appeared at the door with some dresses for Rebecca that Maxine had outgrown. "Mama is doing some spring housecleaning and wanted Rebecca to have these. If they are still worth wearing, she could use them again for Wheat if you have a mind to save them."

Grace had met him at the door because she wanted to talk to him. She handed the dresses to Sarah, who thanked Denzel profusely for them, then said, "Mama, would you mind if Denzel and I took a walk. I can help you with the strawberries when I get back."

"Oh, I think Elizabeth and I can handle the strawberries, you two go and have a nice walk," Sarah said.

"Did I show you the bench Papa made for the Oak tree by the garden?" Grace said with great pride.

"Well, you did, but I would like to see it again!" Denzel was always the gentleman, Grace thought. *If only I could love him like I love Caleb,* she thought to herself.

"It sure is beautiful up here," Denzel said as they finished climbing the hill and approached the shady Oak to sit down on the bench.

Grace did not respond because she was so deep in thought, so Denzel said, "Is something wrong, Grace?"

Grace said, "I have never been in this position, Denzel, and I am afraid I am going to make a mistake and hurt someone's feelings. Someone I care for deeply." Grace looked at him and somehow the pity in her eyes told him this was not good news.

"Well, if you have something to say to me, Grace, just say it."

"Well, I, uh…" Grace has rehearsed this dozens of times, but when it came to saying it aloud, she lost her nerve.

"Grace, we have known each other for a long time, just say what it is you need to say. You are making me more nervous by not telling me, than you could ever do by telling me. Are you sick?"

"No! Nothing like that," she said and decided just to blurt it out and deal with the consequences.

"I am not in love with you, Denzel," she said looking straight out at the garden. "I know one time we discussed marriage, and you have been so helpful to our family. I love you, but more like a brother than a husband. I am so sorry if I have hurt you, but I needed to tell you before…" she trailed off, not wanting to bring Caleb into the conversation just yet.

"Before you and Caleb actually walk down the aisle together?" Denzel said.

Grace's head shot around to see Denzel smiling. "Everyone knows how in love you two are!" His smile was genuine, and he nudged her shoulder with his. "Mama told us the day of the picnic that the two of you would be married before the snow flies!"

Grace did not know what was more shocking. The fact that Denzel was not upset, or that other people knew they were in love long before they did. "Denzel Benson! I do not believe you are saying these things to me!"

"Tell me I am wrong. Are you not in love with Caleb Rogers?" He raised his eyebrows and waited for a response.

"I guess I am, but I am very upset that your family knew it before I did."

"Oh, the entire community knows it! Everyone on the ridge knows it! Even Hulse and some of the others in town know it. It is THE talk of the summer!" Denzel's laughter went a long way to soothing Grace's embarrassment, but not far enough. She covered her face with her hands and mumbled something he could not understand.

After a few minutes, she stood and walked around in front of him, and finally asked, "Why have you been hanging around the house all year? You have been at our house more than you have been at your own since we moved here! Why? If not to see me, then why?" Grace did not even think about how egotistical that sounded. She just wanted answers, and was relieved enough that Denzel was not upset with her that she just blurted out the question.

Denzel hesitated to answer, then finally took a deep breath and said, "Because, I am in love with Elizabeth."

Grace plopped down on the bench beside Denzel and said, "Elizabeth? You are in love with Elizabeth? She is older than you are, Denzel! Elizabeth? Really?"

Denzel looked beaten. Grace realized that it had taken a lot for him to confide in her, and she had not at all been a good friend to him. She thought about how supportive he had been of her love for Caleb and quickly amended her response. "I guess she just seems older because she is older than I am, but I had not thought about the fact that you are older than I am as well, so maybe the age difference isn't as great as I thought."

Denzel said, "I do not think about that much anyway, because the point is that I can have a part of Pa's farm, and we can start our lives off already set up to have a family and all. It isn't like we would be starting out completely on our own."

Grace thought about this for a minute, but then saw the look of hope on his face and decided to shed a positive light on the subject. "Have you told her yet?" Grace flashed a glittering smile at him to let him know she was behind him all the way.

"No, I was hoping to earn a little money first. I could make a better case for asking her to marry me if I had a little money set by. Pa talked to me and Elias about splitting up the farm, so I know which part would be mine and which part would be his. We are going to share the pond with Pa for watering animals, but the rest of it is all separated out."

"Well, before you make many more plans, I would speak with Elizabeth about it. I don't know of any beaus she might have, but someone might come calling before you speak your mind, and you do not want that to happen do you?"

Denzel stood up with a sense of urgency and said, "You are right, is she home? Could you ask her to come up here and talk to me? It sure would be good to get this out in the open."

Grace agreed to go get Elizabeth, and on the way down began thinking about the fact that there could be two weddings in the Waters' household before the snow flies, as Denzel put it. What would Mama and Papa do with just the two of them, Kevin, Little Ben and Rebecca in the house. Then she realized after listing all those people that they might actually be relieved! She was smiling as she entered the house.

"Well, you look happy," Sarah said as she enjoyed her daughter as only a Mama can.

"I am happy, Mama! And I am going to tell you all about it just as soon as I fetch Elizabeth."

"Elizabeth? What on earth for?" Sarah asked.

"Denzel wants to talk to her," she said, trying not to make it too special so as to give away the secret.

Elizabeth agreed to walk up to talk to Denzel and left without anyone guessing what the conversation was about. So, Grace said, "Mama, could I talk to you about something?"

"Of course, you can talk to me about anything, Grace. You know that." Sarah said as she packed up her sewing and set it aside.

Grace began with the story of what happened in Parkersburg, and her fear that Ben and Sarah would be angry with her for leading the authorities to them. She explained that Kevin had left no trace of where he was going, and that Officer Morris had released her to come home and now she felt safe again.

Sarah wanted to discuss why she had not felt she could tell them sooner, but they had limited time so Grace asked her just to listen. The words tumbled out as she told what had transpired with Caleb the day he saved her from the would be attacker. "Mama, I told Caleb I had been raped," she said without of hint of being upset. "I told him, Mama, and I thought he had told everyone, but he hadn't."

"I wish you would have shared all this with me, Grace. I could have helped you through it." Grace saw the hurt in her Mama's eyes, and wished she could fix it for her.

"Mama, I am growing up. There are things that are between me, and… the man I want to marry."

It took a moment for Sarah to process what she was hearing. First she realized that life was changing right before her eyes. Although she had enjoyed being the Mama, the comfort, and guide for this little girl, Grace was now moving toward a life she would share with her husband. Sarah realized that Caleb would now be Grace's comfort, her confidante, and her dearest friend. He would be the one who could cheer her, make her feel safe, and help solve her problems.

But second, she realized that Grace had found the man she wanted to share her life with! *"The man I want to marry."* Was that what she had said? "Are you sure, Grace?"

"Yes, Mama. Caleb said that when he asked his Mama how she knew she wanted to spend the rest of her life with his Papa, she said that it wasn't so much that she knew she wanted to spend the rest of her life with him, it was just that she did not want to spend the rest of her life without him. And that is exactly what I want, Mama. I cannot imagine spending the rest of my life without Caleb."

Sarah only had seconds to process all the changes that had happened in that moment, and discovered it was not enough time. Instead, tears welled up in her eyes and she embraced Grace, not only to congratulate the woman who was to be married, but to say goodbye to the child she had loved so much.

The two of them were looking at each other, smiling with tears running down their faces, when Benjamin walked into the room. "What on earth?" he said puzzled by the smiles and the tears.

"Papa, I have a lot to tell you, could we talk for a while?" Grace asked. She and her Papa did what they did best. They took a walk and talked in the cool of the evening, and eventually Sarah saw from the porch, the two of them embracing under the ramada.

When did she get to be so tall? Sarah asked herself as she noticed that Grace stood as tall as her Papa's shoulder. She looked at the field in front of her and remembered the little girl who had joined her in 'the girls against the boys,' snowball fight, and the memory nearly brought her to her knees. She turned away from the window and saw the cabin floor where Benjamin had dumped water over Grace's head and then put her into her room!

Sarah hugged her arms around herself and sat down in the rocking chair and remembered the first Christmas morning when Midgie had brought them a basket of food. How tiny Grace had looked sitting in the corner of that room, wishing she could walk by a house and see a tree in the window, hear the laughing, and know she was welcomed in that home.

She almost hoped that Ben would forbid the marriage, or at least suggest they wait a year or so. Sarah, who had not been ready to be a parent, now was not prepared to have a child move out of her house. She was sitting in the chair, weeping, when Ben and Grace entered the house.

"Mama?" Grace questioned.

"Oh, Grace," Sarah replied in tears, "I'm just not ready for you to not be my little girl anymore!"

"I will always be your little girl, Mama!" Grace said as she embraced Sarah in tears again.

Benjamin said dryly, "Well, while you women have a good cry, I am going to get back to work." He smiled teasingly at his girls, put his hat on his head and exited the house to the porch. He stopped on the porch and looking up into the field, remembered the walk he took with Grace on Christmas Day, before Granny had died. He remembered turning Grace toward the cabin so she could see the tree in the window, then reminding her of the time when she had made that wish to see a house with a tree, and know she was welcome there. He was fulfilling that wish to that skinny, little, girl who had known nothing but heartache, and now suddenly she was a beautiful woman on the brink of marriage.

He walked on into his workshop and attempted to get started on new orders he had received, but instead he retrieved his handkerchief from his pocket, blew his nose, and wept like a child.

Chapter Twenty-Nine

As the evening wore on, Sarah and Grace talked about Grace's future. It was difficult for Sarah to imagine only seeing Grace once a week, or less in bad weather, but she tried to keep her feelings of sadness trapped beneath the joy she was feeling for Grace. Caleb was a fine man, who was good to his mother, and apparently understood the importance of love and loyalty. Sarah was pleased with the way Caleb had handled the news of Grace's past, and was beginning to feel comfortable with the thought of Grace being married to him.

But as Sarah's thoughts turned to supper, the door opened and Elizabeth entered the room. Grace had completely forgotten about the conversation between Elizabeth and Denzel, and ran to Elizabeth's side to hear the news.

Grace knew immediately it was not what Denzel had hoped for. Elizabeth's face showed it all. "What happened, Elizabeth? Where is Denzel?"

Elizabeth said she needed a few minutes to herself, so she went to her room leaving Grace to explain what was going on to Sarah.

Little Ben came in with a bang, laughing and talking about the fish Ira had caught. He stunk of mud, worms, and fish, and Sarah insisted he go outside and shuck off his clothes, then take a bath.

"Mama!" Little Ben began, but as usual he got nowhere with his protests.

They had a rain barrel behind the house for watering flowers, the horse, and any other needs, so Little Ben stripped down to his skivvies and began washing, then dumping water over his head from the barrel.

Inside, Grace was explaining the conversation she had with Denzel, and his professing of his love for Elizabeth.

Sarah said, "Do you mean that Denzel was hanging around this house so he could see Elizabeth? How did you feel about that, Grace? I mean we all thought he was completely in love with you!"

"Oh, Mama, I must say it was quite a shock, but after all was said and done, it was a relief to me. Finally, the women could not wait to find out what had happened, and knocked on the bedroom door to talk to Elizabeth.

"Come in," Elizabeth said.

"Are you alright?" Grace asked, sitting on the bed with Ben's sister.

"No, I broke the heart of a fine young man, and had no idea I had any role in it until today. I do not feel I encouraged him in any way, and yet…"

"You did nothing at all to encourage him, Elizabeth. Why, we were all shocked that he was in love with you!" Sarah said innocently.

The look on Elizabeth's face made Sarah realize how terrible that sounded, and the three women laughed at the awkwardness of the situation.

"You have to laugh," Elizabeth said, "Or else you would just cry! It was a terrible thing to have to say to someone who is so kind and sweet. His heart was broken to find that I was in love with Elias!"

Both Sarah and Grace were dumbfounded. They sat there in complete silence, both staring at Elizabeth. "When did this happen, Elizabeth?" Sarah asked.

"Well, Elias purchased my luncheon at the Boxed Lunch Dinner, and while we were eating, he proposed that we get to know each other better. He said that he had been interested in me for quite a while, and I had to admit I had been eyeing him at church. Some afternoons, we meet and wade in the creek, or he has taken me out in his boat onto the lake a couple of times. It is like we have known each other for, well, always!"

Grace's heart went out to Denzel. It would have been better had she just said she was not interested, but to go home and have to face Elias may just be too much for Denzel. She decided to give him a day, then she would go to him as a friend tomorrow and offer support.

The three women were chattering away when Benjamin and Kevin arrived for dinner. "What is all this?" Kevin asked as the women continued their discussion energetically.

A hush fell on the room as the focus instantly fell on Grace. "Well, I have been asked to marry Mr. Caleb Rogers!" Grace's entire body vibrated with joy at the news!

Then Elizabeth smiled and said, "And," Elizabeth looked around at the faces of Grace and Sarah before continuing, "I may be marrying Elias Benson this fall!" The three women beamed at the news, but Benjamin nearly upset his chair.

"What?" he demanded. "I do not recall any Elias Benson talking to me about such goings on!" Everyone thought he was joking, but Ben's face told how shocked he was that his baby sister had been involved in a romance to the point of discussing marriage, and he had not one clue!

The atmosphere in the room took on a more subdued tone as Elizabeth realized she should have told her brother before announcing it to the entire family. "I'm sorry, Brother," she said. "It just came up in conversation this afternoon with Grace and Sarah, and I blurted it out without thinking.

"Don't you think you should have discussed it with me first?" Ben said, genuinely hurt. Or at least, Elias should have come to me! Caleb came to me!"

Elizabeth's first instinct was to put her brother in his place and tell him she did not need his permission, but then saw him as a husband and father, and knew instinctively that she needed to treat him with the respect he deserved. "I am truly sorry, Brother. Might we take a walk after supper and discuss it? I do so want you to be a part of it, and I truly want your blessings."

This went a long way toward reinstating Benjamin's position in the household, so he smiled and said, "After supper then." But his heart was broken to think that both his beloved daughter and his sister might be moving on with homes of their own. He could not help but feel that he had been cheated. Most men had their daughters for 15 or 16 years before having to give them to another man. And he had only been with his sister for a few months and she was talking about leaving as well. He needed time to think about the situation, time to pout, and time to go to the outhouse. *Why does everything affect my stomach?* he thought to himself as he wiped his mouth and said, "Excuse me, it seems I am not very hungry tonight." He stood, put on his hat and left the cabin with a stunned room full of people staring at his back.

That night was a full moon, and as Sarah rested her head on Ben's shoulder, the moonlight came through the window in their bedroom and lit their faces. Both sighed with their own thoughts, but Sarah was the first to speak. "You have been awfully quiet this evening," she said.

"I guess I just don't have much to say," Ben said, with one arm behind his head and the other around Sarah.

"It is a lot to take in, isn't it?" She asked in the hopes that he might talk to her about the many changes that were occurring in their household.

"Yea," was all he said.

They lay there in silence for a while, then Ben heard the telltale sniff that indicated Sarah was crying. He turned toward her and wiped the tears from her eyes and said, "Hey! What is this?"

"I feel like I won't be Grace's mother anymore. She won't need me for anything after she is married! Oh, I don't know. I just wasn't ready for all this yet."

Ben could not speak because he was feeling exactly the same thing, so he just pulled Sarah to him and hugged her tightly, unable to voice his fears for Grace on her wedding night, and his anger at his sister for not telling him before announcing it to the entire family!

Although the moon did not shine directly into Grace's room, her room was much lighter than usual as she lay their daydreaming about keeping her own home, having a husband to love and to love her, and someday having children of her own. The last thought left her feeling guilty about Rebecca, and wondering if she should tell Caleb about her. Or should she offer to take her to raise? She fell into a pit of despair at that thought and was tossing and turning when the door opened a little and Little Ben said, "Sissy? Can I come in?"

Grace threw back the covers and scooted closer to Elizabeth to make room of him to join her. He quickly jumped in with his back to Grace, and when she threw the covers across him, he felt the comfort that he had always known, even when they were homeless. His tears came easily as he said, "I don't want you to move away." He cried as if his heart were broken and Grace rocked him back and forth, whispering, "Shhhhh, shhhhh. It's ok, Benji," just as she had done hundreds of times before.

"I never thought about us being separated before," he said so sadly that it broke Grace's heart. "What am I going to do without you here? I have never been without you, Sissy!" He began sobbing in her arms, and she realized that she was all he had ever know of family, and that this was going to be traumatic for him.

"You are tired, Benji," she said knowing that when he was tired there was no consoling him. "Stay right here with me tonight and go to sleep, and then we are going to have a long talk about it tomorrow, just the two of us."

Little Ben *was* exhausted. He knew that he was too tired to talk about it tonight, but he just couldn't stop his brain from imagining life without his sister. Grace understood that about him, and said, "How on earth did you get so stinky today, Ben? What were you doing?"

She smiled as the distracted boy became very animated as he told all about the day of fishing with his friends, and the promise he had gotten from one of the bigger boys, Jason Cooper, to go giggin', or "frog huntin'" as Little Ben said, repeating Jason verbatim. Before long, her little brother was fast asleep in her arms. His legs were longer than hers now, she thought, and now that he was bigger, there was no room for her to move with him in there. Eventually, she had to wake him up and say, "Go on, go to bed now, Ben. You are too big to sleep here with us." And Ben staggered out of the room closing the door behind him. Grace managed to stay awake long enough to hear him use the chamber pot, and then climb the ladder to his loft, then she fell into a deep sleep.

Kevin lay in his room struggling with his own thoughts, tossing and turning, too hot one minute, then cold the next. He walked over to the window in his room and looked out at the moon in the distance. He had always been the one people came to for advice, and now it seemed he had no one with whom to speak about his own troubles.

It seemed he wanted to marry; to be a husband. As a matter of fact, he wanted to marry Eileen Rogers. But he had taken the vow of chastity and knew he could never marry. Even as a child he knew that marriage was something he would never experience, so why was he now so tormented by the thought. Had he not promised his God and King never to marry? So why was it now so difficult to be as satisfied with his life as he always had been? Was Satan nipping at his heels? Was this the evil temptation he had always spoken of as instructed at the Monastery he was reared in? Did he have any choice in becoming a Priest? Was he really called by God or was it his only option, and did that matter?

And yet love was such a wonderful thing. After a lifetime of service, why should he deny himself the one thing he wanted the most, the love of a wonderful wife? His thoughts tormented him more and more as the long night wore on. He was happy for Grace and Caleb, happy for Elizabeth and Elias as well, and yet, he was being eaten alive by jealousy of their freedom to fall in love and marry whomever they liked. He chastised himself for those feelings and wished again he had someone to talk to who could give him some answers.

As he returned to his bed, he sat down and remembered his brother in England. Both of them had decided as children to enter the Monastery rather than to go to an orphanage, and although his brother was far, far away, they had remained close. He was feeling the effects of not sleeping, so he determined that he would write to his brother first thing in the morning and ask his advice. If anyone on earth would see his point of view, and, without judging him, help him to see all sides to the issue, it would be his brother. Satisfied that he had finally thought of a perfect solution, he lay down in his bed and went sound asleep.

The booming on the door startled the entire Waters family awake. Ben pulled on his pants, picked up his shotgun, and went to open the door. It was barely daylight as he stared out onto the porch at the dark form standing there. The man lifted the light so Ben could see that it was Abram, then Ben stepped back to allow him to enter the house. By then the rest of the family had awakened and assembled to hear what had happened.

"It's Denzel. He has run off to join the war. He left a note tellin' us so. We are getting a group together to go find him before he does something stupid."

Without having to be asked, Ben shoved his feet into his boots as Sarah, who had followed him into the room, handed him his shirt. He grabbed his coat and hat off the hook and went out to saddle Patsy. Kevin followed with Little Ben right behind him.

Abram said, "Little Ben, you are going to have to stay here with your Ma. I don't have enough horses, and besides, there'll be fightin' where we are going." He aimed his last words at Sarah, knowing she would know what to do. She stepped up and put her hands on Little Ben's shoulders to stop any argument he might give, and the women stepped out of the house to watch them go.

Elias looked down from his horse at Elizabeth, and the sorrow in his eyes was heartbreaking. She wanted to go to him and tell him it wasn't his fault, that she wished she had not told Denzel about the two of them, that she was wracked with guilt. But as Abram handed the reins of a horse to Kevin they all headed out to find Denzel.

They had been gone four days. Midgie was inconsolable, and Elizabeth riddled with guilt. How could this happen? And why had no one seen it coming? Sarah, Elizabeth, and Grace cooked and kept the children fed and the household running. Little Ben helped Jason Cooper and some of the other boys with the chores, and they all prayed. They prayed for the safe return of Denzel, the men who were looking for them, and especially Abram and Elias, who must have felt the burden of the entire world on their shoulders.

The day they left, Abram asked for volunteers to go to Parkersburg to see if he might have gone there to enlist. Although Kevin and Benjamin knew they would get home sooner if they volunteered for that trip, they sat quietly, not wanting to have to go any place where they might be recognized. Abram chose Hulse and Jeremy Wilson to head up the group and several men veered off toward the west.

Abram turned to the men remaining, and said, "He can't have more than a few hours on us, so if we ride pretty hard, we can catch up with him." Kevin wondered if he said that to encourage his men, or himself. He looked defeated, but continued on with the energy of a man who had set out to correct a wrong, and was willing to do whatever it took to bring his son home.

The remaining men divided up into three groups and decided which would go north and south, with Abram heading east into the worst of the fighting. Before they left, Abram said, "I appreciate you all for coming out to help me bring my son home." The words stuck in his throat and he had to take a moment to compose himself. Then he continued, "Now I know you men are farmers, and business owners, and I know you can't stay long some of you. So when you feel you need to go back, you just go. And know that I appreciate it my friends, I truly do."

The men searched until long after dark, in the hopes of seeing a campfire that would give away Denzel's location. However, unlike the men who were looking for him, Denzel had packed food and had no need for a campfire. After a good night's sleep and a belly full of beans, the men set out again to look for the boy they knew as well as their own sons and brothers.

Ben and Kevin had long given up hope of finding the boy to the north, when the leader of their group announced that he was heading home. After a discussion by all involved, followed by a vote, they decided to give up the search and go home. They agreed that a boy like that would have headed south or south east in order to join the fighting, and it was unlikely he would be found any farther north. "Besides," Ivy Yoak said, "He could be home by now, safe and sound with his father." His brother, Paul, agreed, so they headed home.

The first group to return was those who had gone West to Parkersburg, Elizabeth, Burning Springs and beyond. They found no sign of the boy, and no one who had seen him.

Some of the men who had jobs in town were in the next group to return. It was a second blow to Midgie, and one that almost was her undoing. She needed Abram. She needed Abram to return with both her sons in tow, and she needed them right now. She was so distraught that her milk was drying up, and the twins needed it desperately, especially Roy Paul.

Sarah confided in Grace that she feared Roy Paul might die if Midgie didn't come to her senses and relax, so Grace decided to try a different approach. "Mama, do you think we could find some beer?" Grace looked left and right to see if anyone could overhear her.

"Whatever for?" Sarah asked.

"Well, I have heard that if a woman's milk is drying up, a glass of beer will help her make more." She looked very much like a healer when she said that, until she continued with, "Plus it would make her relax, and if she doesn't she is going to have a heart attack!" The smile on her face made Sarah laugh. Then they set out to locate some brew for their dear friend and fellow church goer.

Sarah decided that Pastor McCauley just might have shared the Gospel to some of those who drank at some time and have an idea as to where he might get some beer to help Midgie. "Jason," she shouted out the door. "Could you please hitch up the buckboard and take me out to Preachers?"

"Yes, Ma'am," Jason answered, and Sarah was happy he did not ask why. Out the road they went to visit the Preacher to ask for beer, and Sarah could not help but grin the entire time she was riding along beside Jason.

With Jason still sitting on the buckboard, Sarah asked Preacher if she might step inside to speak to him about a private matter. Jason waited patiently as the door closed, preventing him from being privy to the conversation.

The Preachers laugh was priceless! Jason grinned as he heard the mighty and powerful laugh continue, in spite of intermittent protestations from Sarah. She came out onto the porch, clearly with her feathers ruffled, then the door opened again, and Preacher, who was still laughing, attempted to apologize and asked her to step back in.

Apparently, they reached an agreement, and a very unsettled Sarah returned to the wagon, jerked her hat down over her eyes and said, "Alright, let's go." Jason clucked to the horses and he began turning the buggy around.

Preachers' wife, Dee, entered the room with a puzzled look on her face, and Preacher said, "That was Sarah Waters. She needs my help to get Mrs. Benson drunk!" His laugh was delightful and joyous, and could be heard by Sarah as the wagon pulled away. She could not bring herself to look Jason Cooper in the eye, and only hoped he did not ask any questions.

By that evening, Preacher and Dee entered the Benson's residence with a far more subdued attitude. Preacher had a burlap bag with two jars inside it and he presented it to Sarah with a humble attitude. "I am really happy to help you, Mrs. Waters," he said, and then began to smile. Dee was not amused at his behavior and turned and looked up at him with a look that immediately changed his attitude to one of great empathy.

"Thank you, Reverend," Sarah said with an attempt at dignity. But the silliness of it hit her, too, and she said with a grin, "I will let you know how it goes!"

Midgie was not of a mind to take a drink of Satan's Brew, as she called it, but she did know she needed rest, so when Grace appealed to her motherly instincts and pointed out again how much the twins needed her milk, Midgie agreed, and said a prayer asking God to forgive her for what she was about to do.

The drink was hideous, if you could believe the look on Midgie's face. Yet it did not prevent her from wanting more after she had downed the first gulp. No one in the room knew how much was the right amount, but they guessed it was not the entire quart, however, Midgie would have nothing to do with their warnings. They had given it to her to drink, and drink it she would do. She fell deeply asleep just before finishing the entire first jar of beer, and just after an enormous, rumbling burp.

The next morning when she could not be awakened, Grace feared they had poisoned her and set to fretting about what they had done. "Mama, I promised God that if Mrs. Benson lives through this, I am done with doctoring! I will never try something so ridiculous again as long as I live."

Sarah sent for Little Ben and asked him to go back to their cabin, and leave a note for Benjamin and Kevin, telling them where they were, and that they were going to be there for several days, just in case they came home and found them gone. Ben and Ira were thrilled to have an excuse to get out of the house for a while, and joyfully left to do as told.

"I didn't know you could read and write, Ben!" Ira said as they walked through the woods swinging sticks at the tall weeds.

Ben could tell Ira was impressed, and he said, "Mama taught us. She could teach you, too, if you want!" Ira was not impressed with the idea of actually having to sit still and learn how to read, so he took off running as a challenge to Ben to race back up the hill to the Waters' home. Neither would give in to let the other one win, although they were both breathless.

Just as they crested the hill, Little Ben stopped and stared at the top of the hill in front of their cabin. He could see his Papa up on the hill, just starting to lead Patsy down to their home. "Papa!" Little Ben shouted. It was obvious to Benjamin that Little Ben could not run the distance to him, so he set Pasty off in a trot toward his son.

Little Ben was so happy to see him he held onto his Papa's foot until Ben said, "Come on," and offered his hand to the boy so he could join him on Patsy's back.

"What about Ira, Papa?"

"Well, I guess there is room," Ben said as he turned Pasty toward Ira and kicked her sides to approach him. This time when he scooped up Ira, who was much smaller than Little Ben, and seated him in front of himself before turning to walk the horse home.

There were tales to tell about the war, what they had seen, what the world was like outside of their little community... but all the boys wanted to do was tell Kevin and Ben the story of Grace and Sarah's getting Midgie drunk! And... with the help of the Preacher!

Kevin and Ben laughed all the way back to the cabin, where they sent the boys to care for the horses while they went out back and washed up. They assumed that Denzel had not returned home since the boys didn't mention it and were saddened by that. Although they were

255

happy to be home, they dreaded telling Midgie they had returned without Denzel. Maybe getting her drunk was not such a bad idea.

Chapter Thirty

It was nearly a month before all the men returned. Abram and Elias were the last to come home, and were extremely disappointed to find Denzel still gone. There was little to no hope of hearing from him before the end of the war, if he even survived that long, since mail service in Calhoun County was discontinued in the early 1860's, and it cast a pall over the entire community.

Midgie mourned the loss of her son almost with every breath, and a darkness covered Abram in everything he did and said. Benjamin felt the loss of Denzel, as well as the loss of his close friend, Abram, because although Abram was there, physically, his mind was with his son. Ben wondered if things would ever be the same again.

It was a sad day when a Benson boy came to the Waters' home, and it was not Denzel. They were so used to having Denzel around that it was more like mourning a son than a neighbor. When the boy got close to the cabin, they realized it was Elias, and tried to muster up the greeting he had always given Denzel.

"Hello, Mr. Waters, is Elizabeth home?" Elias said almost regretfully as he dismounted from his horse. There was no spring in his step, no sign of a young man courting a young woman with all the joy that should have been present in him. Ben wished he could comfort the boy, but he himself was feeling the betrayal of Denzel, and although he knew Elias did not mean to break his brother's heart, he had, and that was difficult thing to wrap his mind around. He wanted to ask Elias if he had known his brother was in love with Elizabeth when he bought her Boxed Luncheon that Sunday, but it was none of his business, so he kept it to himself. A good thing, he thought to himself, if only he could be happier for the couple.

Mr. Waters, could I have a word with you?" He hesitated and then said, "Please, Sir, I have something to say, and I would appreciate it if you would give me audience for just a minute."

Benjamin appreciated a boy stepping up like a man to face things head on, so he said, "Sure, what's on your mind, Son?"

Elias took off his hat and looked down at it, picking of little pieces of grass until he got up his courage. "Well, Sir, I just want you to know that none of us knew Denzel was in love with Elizabeth. All he had ever talked about was Grace, and we all thought he was spending time up here because of her. I would *never* have..."

Ben started to speak when Elias' words caught in his throat, but Elias recovered and said, "I would never, in this lifetime, have hurt my brother like that if I had known."

Ben looked at Elias, waiting for him to finish, or at least say more. Elias became aware of that, and said, "That's all I got to say. Just that not one of us, in our entire family, knew Denzel had feelings for Elizabeth." There was another pause, then he said, "I just needed for you to know that." He put his hat back on, looked at the ground and headed for the house.

"Elias," Benjamin said to the boy's back. Without saying a word, Elias slowly turned and looked at Benjamin. "I appreciate your telling me that, Son. You are a good man."

Elias visibly stood a little taller. He inhaled slowly, straightened his back, and said, "Thank you, Sir." Then he turned and walked up to the door and knocked.

Ben watched as Sarah opened the door, then went back inside to get Elizabeth. Elizabeth's face lit up at the sight of Elias, and Ben knew she loved him, and although he could not fully admit that Elias was the man for her, he knew he would come to believe it in time. Meanwhile, he would have to get used to Elias' coming to the house, instead of Denzel.

"Brother, we are going to walk up to the garden." Sarah beamed at Elias as she took his arm as they began walking up the hill. Ben watched them go, and wondered if he would ever adjust to all the changes that were happening around him. How he longed for the days when the children were small, and there was nobody in the cabin but the five of them, learning how to have snowball fights, reading the Bible and Sarah's books by the candle light, while learning how to love and respect each other. Those were much simpler days, and yet, he loved every one of those people who had come into his life. Granny, Kevin, the Bensons, his sister, Elizabeth, Grace, Rebecca, Little Ben, and Sarah. Oh, his beloved Sarah. How he loved that woman with all his heart. And now that she was going to have his baby, he felt his heart would burst with joy.

As if his longing for her somehow summoned her, she opened the door and smiled at him. A quick glance around told her there was no one near, so she scurried out to him, took his hand, and pulled him toward the ramada. There were benches there that were covered from the sun, and there was a lovely breeze that kept the air cooler than it felt inside the cabin, or outside in the direct sun. Surprisingly, neither of them felt a need to speak. They sat beside each other looking around the farm they had worked so hard on, and now owned, and felt the exact same feelings. Without speaking, they looked around at the house with the flowers growing in the flower bed Granny had made, the new sawmill beyond the cabin, the portion of the garden they could see from where they were, and down below the garden where the clothes hanging on the clothesline flapped joyfully in the wind.

They both thought about Elias and Elizabeth sitting on the bench under the old Oak tree, and watched Little Ben as he came out of the cabin to check the horse and the cow. "He has grown so much," Sarah said absently.

Ben said, "My guess is that he was a lot older when we found him than we thought."

"I was thinking about that, Ben. Do you think he could be closer to thirteen or fourteen than we thought? Look at him, he looks and acts like a grown man!" Sarah said, keeping her eyes on Little Ben as he walked around.

Ben said, "The problem is that we will never know for sure how old he really is. What if he wants to get married in a year or so? We certainly cannot say he is too young, because we really have no idea how old he is."

They fell into a comfortable silence again, then Ben said, "Do you think they will be ok?"

Without having to ask, she instinctively knew he was talking about Elias and Elizabeth, "I don't know, Ben. It is a horrible thing to have hanging over your head. Denzel could already be dead for all they know." Ben looked at her feigning shock, and she said, "Seriously! No one found a trace of him, Ben. Wouldn't you think someone would have found something if everything were alright?"

"I hadn't thought of it quite like that, but, yes, the thought has crossed my mind that he might be gone. What is Elias to do? Wait until the war is over before he continues his life? He just told me that not one member of his family knew of Denzel's feelings for Elizabeth, and I believe him. But there will always be a cloud of suspicion over his head. From himself if not from others."

Sarah sighed because she knew that was the truth. "Elizabeth is head over heels in love with him, Ben. I just hope they can find a way to get past this."

"Well, if God could bring us together, I am sure God will work it out for them as well," he said as he put his arm around her and hugged her gently. He kissed the top of her head, then lingered there to inhale the scent of her hair. "Lavender, isn't it?" he said with a quizzical look on his face.

"Why, yes, it is! It is the next to the last bar I have that Mama helped me make." She smiled at him, then her face became shrouded in sorrow, "I miss her so." She inhaled sharply in an attempt not to cry, then Ben hugged her again and buried his nose in her hair.

"I love you, Sarah Waters," he said sincerely. "More than you can imagine."

"I would say I love you, too, but that just doesn't seem to say what I am feeling. I want to really tell you how I feel, and to restate that I love you really doesn't do it justice."

"I agree," Ben said. "But on this side of the grave, I think that is the best we can do. Because *you* know what *I* mean by that, and *I* know what *you* mean by that. And nobody else in the world can possibly know what we mean to each other. So, just know that when we say it, we are together, in the same place, where nobody else exists."

She was overwhelmed by that thought as she turned her head to look up at him. Her lips looked so kissable that Ben bent his head to cover her lips with his, when they heard, "Mama! Rebecca's awake!"

They stopped what they were doing, and looked up at Little Ben who was standing holding the cabin door open. Both of them laughed as they stood and headed back to the cabin.

"Ben," Sarah said, "You and I need to find some time to talk privately about something."

"How 'bout in bed tonight?" Ben said as he bumped shoulders with Sarah and began grinning from ear to ear. She gave him her best, "behave yourself" look and said, "No, I am serious. Could we figure out a way to be alone for an hour or so?" She looked at him and saw the same twinkle in his eye, and said, "TO TALK! WE NEED TO TALK!"

Her look was priceless. How Ben loved teasing her when she could not respond appropriately, but he realized this was important, and said, "I can send everybody on some errands tomorrow. Or better yet, why don't you and I go somewhere tomorrow. Grace and Elizabeth can run things around here. Why don't we go to town tomorrow, just the two of us? I hear the town is growing! They have new shops, and a couple of places to get cloth, gardening supplies, and even tobacco!"

"What do you want with tobacco?" Sarah asked as they entered the cabin.

"I would like to trying chawing, Papa. If you are going to get tobacco, can I have some?" Little Ben was thrilled with the idea, but one look from Sarah left both of them knowing there would never be any tobacco in or around their home.

"I have never whipped you, Little Ben, but if I ever hear that you have had even one leaf of tobacco in your mouth, I just might rethink that," Sarah said as she held up her chin in an attempt to look a little taller. "It is a filthy, smelly, and disgusting, habit, and I will have none of it in my home. Is that understood?"

"Yes, Ma'am," came simultaneously from both Bens at the same time. Sarah shot a look at Benjamin that made everybody laugh, until she turned and said, "I mean it." Her left eyebrow lifted into a high curve which left no doubt in anyone's mind that she could, and would, whip anyone who dared defy her.

As she turned around, the two Bens gave each other a knowing look, then went on about their business.

"What are you whittling on now, Ben?" Benjamin asked.

Little Ben had become so good at creating animal figurines out of wood, thanks to Elizabeth's fine tutelage, that they had caught Kevin's eye. "I say, Little Man. How would you feel about my taking those to Parkersburg with me and selling them for you? I believe they would sell for a great deal of money, and I happen to be friends with just the fellow to ask about it. He has a shop right on Market Street where they sell these kinds of things."

"Is it alright, Papa? Mama?" The excitement on Little Ben's face was contagious, and before long everyone was excited at the idea.

While Little Ben was sorting out his works of art, deciding which ones he would live without, and which ones he would keep, Ben picked up a bucket and headed out the door.

"Where are you going?" Sarah asked.

"Uh… up to check out the garden," he said as he tried to hurry out the door.

"Benjamin Waters, do not bother those kids. They are fine up there!" Sarah said accusingly.

"I know. I am just going to make sure of that," he said as he took his hat off the nail, and headed out the door.

Chapter Thirty-One

The next day was gloriously beautiful. There was a hefty breeze that kept threatening to snatch Sarah's hat off her head and send it tumbling about the meadow, and the sky was unbelievably blue, with snowy white clouds floating overhead.

When she had awakened that morning, she had decided *not* to go to town with Ben this day, because the children might need her, there was food to prepare, and...

But Ben would have none of it. Although she protested, he continued to prepare for the day. As she was telling him there was no need to pack food, he continued to put thick sandwiches in a basket. She soon decided she should fix her hair and change her dress or else she would be thrown onto the wagon in her night clothes.

Now she was filled with joy that Benjamin had insisted. As she rode along in the wagon, she noticed the beauty of the golden hay against the blue, blue sky. Never had she felt so free, so unencumbered, and so safe.

Benjamin was watching her as she looked at the world in total awe, and felt such glee to see her face as she took in the scenery.

"It just occurred to me, that you have not been off this ridge since the day we got here!" Ben said, feeling a little ashamed of himself for not thinking of this sooner.

"Oh, but I had the opportunity to go back to the cave when I taught that little boy and his father how to read!" Sarah said with such enthusiasm that it was like a knife in Ben's heart.

He vowed, in his heart, to take her to town more often from now on. "Have you even been to Jimmie's?" he asked.

"No," she said in all innocence, "but whatever I have needed, I just ordered it and it was brought right to me!" Her smile was killing him.

"Sarah, I feel just horrible that I have not made more of an effort to get you to town. From now on, I am going to be a better husband."

She did not protest what he had said, because both of them were remembering Mama's saying, "I'm not worth much today, but tomorrow I am going to be a better woman!"

Then Sarah heard the full weight of his statement and said, "What do you mean you will be a better husband? You are the best husband any woman could want! Why would you say that?"

"Well, I am not going to try to explain it. But, just know that the fun we have today, is going to happen far more often from now on."

Sarah smiled and said, "Well, you cannot beat that proposition. I am already having and incredible day, thanks to you."

They stopped at Jimmie's store at the top of town hill, and bought some sewing things, like needles, white thread, and a new pocket knife for Little Ben's whittling. A penny's worth of rock candy was plenty for all those in the cabin to have a taste, and by the time they were ready to leave Jimmie's, Sarah was feeling as though she had already had all the fun one person should have in a day.

But again, Benjamin took the lead, and headed down town hill to show her the new community that was growing up in the bend of the river. By the time they got there, Sarah's eyes were wide with wonder. New buildings were going up everywhere, and often as not, she could see folks she knew from church.

"It has changed a lot hasn't it?" Benjamin said while looking at the wonder in her face.

"I have never been here before, Ben. We came right from the boat landing, up Leaf Bank, and to our cabin!"

Ben inhaled slowly, closed his eyes, and dropped his head in shame. "I cannot believe you have never been here! I am such a horrible person!"

"Stop!" she said laughing! "I had no need to come down here or you would have brought me! Now stop this right now! You are not going to ruin my day!"

He continued down the dirt road between the buildings until he found a place he could pull his buggy out of the way, then wrapped the horse's reins around the post provided for that. As he circled around the buggy to lift Sarah down from the seat, he was overwhelmed with her beauty, and began to notice the other men around him who were staring at her as well.

Sarah was lifted away by the busyness of the day. After being in the cabin for nearly two years, having only brief bouts of visiting at church, the number of people in the town was overwhelming! Her heart sailed as each new sight met her eyes! And Ben was the proudest man in Calhoun County as he walked with this beautiful woman on his arm. To be loved by her was the greatest thing a man could ask for, and he whispered a prayer of gratitude as he walked by her down the streets.

They determined to walk all through the town before they sat down to have their picnic. When they got to the other side, they discovered the town was almost built to the edge of the bank of the Little Kanawha River. "What will they do when they get to the river bank?" Sarah asked.

"I guess they will have to start building up town hill, or up the sides of these mountains, either one!" he said with a smile that nearly knocked Sarah over. They held hands and walked to the northern part of town, and sat down for their picnic. She wanted so badly to kiss him right there under the shade of the old Gingko tree, but her upbringing would not allow that. She sighed heavily, and Ben said, "I agree!" Which brought chuckles from the two of them.

It had been a glorious day, and now that Sarah knew there was a proper fabric store there, she decided to take Ben up on his offer to come down more often.

On the way home, Ben asked, "What is it that you needed to talk to me about, Sarah?"

Sarah was surprised that she had almost forgotten the important matter she needed to discuss, and said hastily, "Oh! It is about Grace."

Ben immediately became the protective father and his worst fears got the better of him, "What about Grace? Is there a problem?" He stopped the horse and turned toward Sarah, saying, "Tell me the truth, right now!" he said. "I can handle it if you tell me right now!"

Sarah had to chuckle at the change in him, but quickly decided she needed to tell him her thoughts before his head blew off. "Nothing that shocking, Ben. Nothing is wrong with her at all."

"Are you sure?" he said, "because I don't want to be the last to know if something is wrong!"

"Benjamin Waters! You aren't thinking that she is… that she is…!"

"Well, she and Caleb spend a lot of time together, and, well, she is a beautiful girl, Sarah, and…"

"Wait. Stop. Calm down." She waited for a second then said, "Take a deep breath. Grace is not with child, if that is what you are asking."

Relief flooded over Benjamin's entire body, and when he relaxed, he looked as if someone had dumped a bucket of water over him. "You scared me to death, Sarah!" he said as he turned and slapped the reins over the horse's back to get her going again.

Sarah sat and stared at him for a minute, a smile on her face at the new insight she had in her husband. "Well, what I do have to talk to you about it not nearly that exciting. In fact, it is sad, really."

"Did Caleb break her heart! I swear, I will go get that boy, and…"

"Benjamin Waters! Will you please shut up and listen to me?"

Since Ben had never heard her say the words, "shut up," before, he was rather taken aback. "Ok. Easy now! Go ahead, I will just listen."

"Thank you," she said smugly. "Now, do you remember the first week we were all together in that cabin, and you boys took a walk so Grace, Rebecca and I could bathe?"

"Sure," Ben said.

"Well, when Grace was bathing, she took off her clothes so I could wash them and I saw her naked. She had her back to me, and I noticed scars across her back, as if she had been beaten."

Ben gritted his teeth and Sarah could see his jaw working back and forth, as the vein in his temple began to stand out. "That son of a b…"

"I know. I know, Ben." Sarah said as she gave him a minute to process the news.

He spit off the side of the wagon, and stared forward with an anger seething in his soul that made him want to find the man who had done it, and beat him summarily.

"I know you are angry, Ben, but I need to speak with you about what that means for Grace, now that she is getting married."

Ben thought of her wedding night, and Caleb's discovery of the scars. What could Grace say? Caleb already knew she had been assaulted, so he would not expect her to be a virgin, but what could she say about the scars? He would wonder if Benjamin had done that to her, and if not him, then who?

When Ben turned to look at Sarah, they both knew the problems that would arise. "You have to talk to her, Sarah."

"I have thought about that, but I am not even sure she knows they are there! I mean, how many of us have ever seen our backs?"

"She will be mortified," Ben said sadly. "What lovely young lady wants to have wicked scars on her back on her wedding night?"

"Hence, my dilemma," Sarah said hopelessly.

They both rode along in silence, lost in their own thoughts. Then Ben said, "We need to have a talk. You, me, Grace, and Little Ben, without Kevin and Elizabeth anywhere within earshot."

"That is a brilliant idea, Ben. But how?"

They both thought about that for a while, then Ben said, "Kevin has been talking about going to Parkersburg for some time now. Before, he did not feel well enough to travel, but he is stronger now."

Sarah said, "We talked about someone going with him, why not Elizabeth? They would be gone for several days at the least, and we could have time to talk things through."

"I really like that idea, but don't you think you should talk to Grace first? She needs to know what is going on. She needs time to get used to the idea."

"I agree, but I never have time with just Grace. There are so many people living there now, that..."

"I know," Ben said. "Well, as soon as the two of you are alone, you need to talk to her."

Sarah sighed, not looking forward to having to break Grace's heart. Then she said, "I know. You and Little Ben can take Kevin and Elizabeth to the boat. Grace and I will have some time alone, and we can talk then."

"That is a great idea. I will bring the subject up at breakfast tomorrow morning. Encouraging Kevin to sell Ben's whittling will be a good start."

"I feel so much better now," Sarah said, as she finally saw the lights in the cabin. Her misgivings about leaving the cabin this morning crept back up as she resumed worrying about the children. But when they entered the cabin and saw their supper on the table covered with cloths, Grace sitting in the rocking chair with Rebecca on her shoulder fast asleep, Kevin reading in the corner by candlelight, and Elizabeth finishing the dishes, she knew they had survived the day without her, but she didn't know whether she was happy or sad about that.

Chapter Thirty-Two

Benjamin was up first that morning, had the coffee on the stove and the fire lit for cooking before anyone else got up. Kevin had tossed and turned the night before and was the last to get up, which put him into a rush to get his things together and out in the buggy before it was time to leave.

Sarah packed an extra sandwich in case he got hungry prior to the lunch stop, since he had no time for breakfast. She shoved it into his pocket and tiptoes to kiss him on the cheek as she said, "There you go!"

Kevin felt there was some kind of rush to get them out of the house, and it was working. Before they knew it, Kevin and Elizabeth, along with their luggage, were being taken to town by Benjamin, and Little Ben.

Little Ben was uncharacteristically quiet as they rode along, but only he knew his mind was filled with thoughts of the horrible scene that occurred in Parkersburg the last time he was there. It had again occurred to him that his life could change in an instant, and even getting near the boat dock brought him great concern.

Back home, Sarah had thought so much about what she was going to say, and how she was going to say it, that Grace finally said, "Mama? Is something wrong? You have been awfully quite this morning."

Sarah said, "Could I be brutally honest with you, Grace?" She smiled to ease Grace's fears and pulled out a chair beside her at the table for Grace to sit down in.

Grace immediately thought about the baby, looked at Sarah's belly and asked, "Is everything ok, Mama? I mean with the baby?"

"Oh, yes, Grace, I am just fine. I just have something to discuss with you."

"Ok, Mama," Grace said as she steeled herself.

"I am not sure how to go about this, but…"

"Mama, just say it. This family has never been one to hover around an issue! We haven't had time to in the past! We just blurt things out, and then we all deal with whatever it is. Just say it, Mama."

"Alright. I am so pleased that you and Caleb are talking about getting married. And I want you to be just as happy as any two people can possibly be."

"Thank you, Mama, but now you are just making me nervous. Please, just say what you have to say before my imagination fills in the blanks!"

Sarah sat up straight and tall and said, "Do you remember when your Papa and Little Ben took a long walk in the winter snow so we could bathe?"

Grace grinned and said, "I remember that well. It was when I first began feeling safe with Papa."

"Well, at one point during that day, I saw your bare back, and something caught my eye."

Grace was thoroughly confused and imagined a huge birth mark, or a mole that covered half her back and nearly became undone.

"Mama! What?" She stood and began to feel her back to see if she could feel whatever it was.

"Sit down, Grace." When Grace had returned to her seat, Sarah continued. "It looks as though someone had beaten you, Grace. You have long thin scares on your back, in lines, so that it appears you have been beaten."

Grace's eyes teared up, and she immediately shrunk back into the pitiful little girl she had once been. She cried silently while Sarah held her hand. "Will I ever been free of him?" Grace said sadly. "I thought after what happened in Parkersburg that I was done with him; that he couldn't hurt me anymore. And now, here he is, right in the middle of my wedding night. Now, I have to answer questions. I have to explain to my new husband why I am ruined! And scarred! And ugly!" She sobbed in self-pity and anger, while Sarah waited patiently for her to process all the information.

After the sobbing subsided, Grace blew her nose and said, "Honestly, Mama! Right now I do not even want to get married." Her shoulders slumped and she fell back into her seat completely defeated.

Sarah knew she didn't mean that. All Grace needed was a minute or two that she didn't have to deal with the bad news. Just a moment of grace where that horrible man had not intruded on her good fortune, and just one more moment where she could actually enjoy being a young girl looking forward to her wedding.

They both sat there in silence: Grace feeling defeated, and Sarah saddened by the fact that she was the only one who could deliver the news.

"Are you alright?" Sarah finally said to Grace.

"I suppose," Grace said hopelessly. "What can I do about it? I feel like there are going to be three of us in my marriage. Me, Caleb, and Mr. Dunge!" The tears began to flow, and as she blew her nose again, she said, "Always, Mr. Dunge!"

Sarah became a bit agitated at Grace's self-indulgence, and said, "Grace, you are marrying a fine man who took your past in his stride. Before you even knew him, you blurted out your innermost private secret, and he did not judge you, he did not shame you, and he kept your secret in his confidence. If you are going to marry someone, you need to trust them."

"Mama! Enough is enough! This is too much to tell him about. And what am I going to say to him?"

"Well, that is why Papa and I worked it out so you, Papa, Little Ben, Rebecca and I can be alone tonight. So we can discuss what to say to him."

"Why? I do not need the entire family to make decisions for me! I may be the damaged one, but I can still think!"

Sarah stood and said calmly, but lethally, "I beg your pardon! I am aware that you are feeling sorry for yourself right now because you do not know how to approach your wonderful husband-to-be about a simple problem that will NOT affect your entire marriage! But that certainly does not give you the right to be rude and disrespectful to me."

It was the first time Sarah had really scolded Grace, and Grace was shocked. Before she could gather her thoughts well enough to speak, Sarah continued, "We have never thought of you as damaged, and you know that." Sarah's left eyebrow was raised as she gingerly wiped the crumbs off the table and snapped the rag loudly before folding it and putting it on the sink.

Grace became aware of how wicked her words had been, but again she was too stunned to speak. She had never seen her Mama angry before, and the fact that that anger was directed at her was overwhelming.

Sarah continued, "For your information, this does not affect only you, Grace. You might think of how it will affect your Papa, because who else would have beaten you? What is Caleb to think when he sees those marks, other than *Benjamin* had beaten you?"

Sarah picked up her chair and set it down so loudly that it startled Grace, then shoved the chair noisily under the table. "When you decide to act like a grown woman again, instead of a spoiled child, you need to approach me again to discuss what we can say to your betrothed. And I strongly suggest you find a way to approach me with *great* respect."

With a flip of her skirts, Sarah turned and left the cabin, quickly lifting her bonnet from the nail beside the door.

Grace sat and stared at the closed door with nothing but regret for treating her Mama so badly. She had forgotten about Caleb, about the scars, about Mr. Dunge, and everything else she had been pouting about, except the hurt look on her Mama's face. She suspected that Sarah was upset to the point of tears, and knowing she had caused that pain in her heart was hurting so deeply she could scarcely breath. But she did not have the words just yet to fix what she had done, so she went about her morning chores, deep in thought.

An hour later Sarah returned with a basket of tiny, little, new potatoes, that were half the size of a hen egg, and full of juice. The skin was soft and tender which made them great for cooking. She was planning on creaming them with the new peas, and sat at the table to shell the bunch of peas she had picked as well.

"Mama, I am so sorry," Grace began. She was looking at her Mama's back and expected her to turn and greet her with a smile, but she didn't.

Grace went to the kitchen, retrieved a bowl, then sat at the opposite side of the table. She reached over and collected a handful of peas to shell, and said to her Mama, "I *am* ready to discuss our problem like a normal human being, Mama."

Sarah looked up at her with both eyebrows up and said, "I just don't know what to say to you, Grace. In the first place, I have never heard you speak to anyone with such disrespect, let alone, me!" Sarah had more to say, but she had been close to losing her tempter again and decided instead to concentrate on shelling the peas.

"Mama, I do not want to contradict you at this obviously bad time, but, even you must admit, I was *far* more disrespectful to Papa when he had to dump water over my head to calm me down!" Grace smiled a tiny bit and looked up at her Mama through her eyebrows while continuing to shell peas.

Sarah sighed. She knew her anger had gone out the window with Grace's comment, and as she looked up at Grace, the laughter escaped her lips and the two of them laughed at themselves. They began their conversation again, but this time it was far more productive.

"I spoke with your Papa about this, Grace, and we decided we need to talk about this without Kevin and Elizabeth. So... we encouraged them to go on this trip so we, as a family, can have some time alone."

"So Papa knows?" Grace asked accusingly.

"Yes, and it was all I could do to keep him from tracking down Dunge and beating him to death with his bare hands!" Both women laughed at that, then Sarah said, "Grace, I think that we need to work through this one problem, and then you will be truly free. It won't have anything to do with your having children, or your standing in the community. Once we get through this one hurdle, you should be free of Dunge forever."

"Mama, I feel like I will never be free of him," Grace said as she sniffed and wiped away new tears. "I am not trying to be overly dramatic. I just feel like... like he has won."

Sarah thought about her words, and said, cautiously, "So, you feel this one thing will ruin your entire marriage?"

Grace thought about that for a time, then said, "It will ruin my wedding night, and that is the beginning of my new life with Caleb. That inserts him into my life with Caleb, right from the very start."

They both tried to think of a way around what they were facing, when Sarah asked, "And you aren't serious about not marrying Caleb are you?"

Grace smiled a deep, shy smile, and said, "Not really, Mama. I want to spend my life with him, but..." The tears welled up in her eyes and her shoulders slumped in defeat again. "I just wish..." Sarah touched

Grace's hand compassionately, then patted it and went back to shelling peas.

"Ok, you and I are smart enough to figure this out. We are not going to let this ruin your wedding, or your marriage. We *are* going to work this out," Sarah said confidently, just as they heard the men coming back.

Sarah greeted Benjamin at the door and noticed that Little Ben was nearly as tall as his father. When Benjamin entered the door he put his arm around Sarah and kissed her lightly. Little Ben came in next, and the sudden realization that they were all alone in the house together gave them a festive feeling!

Suddenly, they did not have to watch their words, and the fun of being together again was exhilarating. They giggled and visited with each other, happy to have the house to themselves again. Through fixing and eating lunch, they laughed and celebrated just being a family.

"The only thing that would make this better would be if Granny were here," Little Ben said sadly.

There was a moment where they all thought of the feisty little woman who had colored their lives forever, then Grace said, "Oh, she is here alright. Every time I enter the cabin, I hear her scolding me for tracking in snow, or mud!"

Everyone took their turn at telling 'Granny stories' that brought laughter to everyone in the room. Little did they know, the stories they told would be repeated down through the years and in to the next century as a part of their family history. But for now, they all sat together, lost in their own memories of their beloved. Memories so vivid, and fresh, they expected her to walk into the room at any moment.

Their thoughts were interrupted when Grace said, "Tell me if I am wrong, but I suspect Uncle Kevin knew Granny before we introduced her to him.

"Why do you think that, Grace?" Sarah said, mortified at the thought that Kevin had known she had been lying about her Mama all along!

"Well, when we were cleaning out Granny's room, I knocked her bird house on the floor when I was stripping the bed. Uncle Kevin picked it up and looked at it with tears in his eyes, and said that she had had that bird house for years!" Grace looked at the shock on everyone's face, and continued, "There was a very awkward moment, then we went back to work, but I really do think he had known her before."

Sarah fell back into her chair, completely exasperated, and said, "Of course he did. She was living right behind his church! He had to have known her. I am so embarrassed!"

"Why, Mama? Why would you be embarrassed that Uncle Kevin knew Granny?" Little Ben said innocently. "They seem to like each other."

Sarah and Grace had forgotten they had agreed to let Little Ben believe Granny was really Sarah's Mama. They sat there staring out into the room until Benjamin, aware of the awkwardness of the moment, said, "Alright, it is time to cut that delicious cinnamon cake and sit down for a family meeting!"

Sarah leapt to her feet to get two cups of coffee, Little Ben got the milk, and Grace took the cake from the kitchen to the little table. Before long they were complimenting Grace on her first attempt to make Granny's Cinnamon Cake, and laughing about the funny wedding cake she had made for Mama and Papa on their wedding day.

Within moments, the conversation died down as they began eating their treat, and Grace decided to take the lead. "Mama has shared with me the fact that I have scars on my back that might take some explaining if I were ever to be married." Little Ben hung his head and began using his fork to play with the crumbs from the cake.

Grace realized he had probably known all along, but had never said anything about it to her, so as to not hurt her feelings.

"I would never want anyone to even think for one moment that Papa, or Mama had ever hurt me, so I was thinking that I should tell Caleb that Little Ben and I are adopted," Grace said without looking up at anyone.

"Not me!" Little Ben yelled. "I have always wanted to be a Junior and now I am. I don't want anyone to think I am not a real Junior!"

"Well, if I tell him that I am adopted, that would mean that you are not my real brother! I don't want that either!"

Benjamin spoke next, "Now wait a minute here. We pledged not to tell anything about our pasts. I am not sure I am comfortable with leaking out bits of information now that we are settled. We still could be found out, you know."

Sarah became concerned at that point and said, "Well, we cannot let Caleb see those scars and not have an answer for him. What do you want her to say, Ben? That you did it?"

Grace felt like saying she just would never get married, but knew that was a promise she would never keep. So, she said, "Mama pointed out to me that Caleb is an honorable man. He has kept my secrets so far, and I feel he would keep this one if I asked him to."

The room fell silent as they all became lost in their own thoughts.

"If we did agree to say that," Benjamin began reluctantly, "what is to stop him from wondering what other secrets we have and checking into things?"

Silence followed again.

Little Ben said, "Just don't tell him I was adopted. I want to be a regular boy."

Grace was hurt and her face showed it when she looked at her brother.

Little Ben started to defend himself, but then knew that what he had said was a betrayal of his sister, and simply dropped his head again.

Sarah and Benjamin had watched the scene unfold and exchanged glances over the tops of the children's heads. Everyone simply looked at the table as they sat in silence once again.

"Grace," Sarah said, "I was thinking about our conversation before, about *when* to tell Caleb." Sarah's eyes met Grace's in a silent acknowledgement of the conversation about Grace's wedding night.

Sarah continued, "I was thinking… the sooner you tell him, the better. Don't wait until your wedding night, give him time to think about what you have said, and get his reaction beforehand so the two of you could have time to discuss it."

Grace liked that idea. The thought of discussing it with him long before the date was ever set for the wedding, had a safe feel to it. She would tell him the next time she saw him. If he was not going to accept what she said, it would be better to know before she had lost her heart completely.

"What would we say?" Grace's shoulders slumped and she looked discouraged. "If we say I got off the Orphan Train, then he will want to know where I came from and that would open a book on my life, that I do not want him to read."

"No! No!" Benjamin stood and walked around the room, using his coffee cup to punctuate each sentence. "We cannot say anything that might trigger a connection in his mind to any posters he might see in Parkersburg. We do not want him even thinking about the Orphan Train."

Little Ben, who was usually quiet in this kind of conversation, said shyly, "Well, we could…" Then he stopped because he was afraid, first of all, that they would think the idea silly. But second, he was tired of lying. He did not want to make up any more lies, or tell any more lies, or have to remember and live any more lies. However, he knew that this one more lie was a necessary evil, so he gave it his best shot.

"What, Ben?" Benjamin asked.

When Little Ben hesitated, Sarah said, "Ben, if you have an idea, I would really like to hear it."

Little Ben stood a little taller, and said, "Well, I was thinking about what Grace said. I don't want people to think we are not related by blood either, so I was thinking, maybe we could tell him that Grace was the child of a family member. Maybe Mama's sister. And her husband was so hard on the child, that you two agreed to adopt her. That way, Grace and I would still be related by blood," he turned and looked sheepishly at Grace, then continued, "a little, anyway. And there would be no Orphan Train in the story."

"Well, I would not feel comfortable saying that my sister gave away her child. But we could say that she died in childbirth, and raising a daughter was just too much for her Papa. That when we expressed a desire to adopt her, he was relieved."

Ben filled his coffee cup and turned, anger in his eyes. "Sounds too sweet and polite to me! I would prefer that we said he and I came to an agreement and we brought her with us. That is what I *would* have done, anyway. I would not offer to take her, I would announce that she was coming with us, and then dare him to argue."

"Calm down, Benjamin," Sarah smiled up at him. "It is just a story, after all. But it has the ring of truth to it. I like it."

They all agreed, sadly, upon the new lie they had created. Grace would ask that he not tell anyone, that she preferred everyone think she was their child. Their lives depended on whether or not Caleb was an honorable man, but it was the best they could do.

"Oh," Grace said, "I told Mrs. Benson that I was there when Benjamin and Rebecca were born, so you took me in before that, I guess."

All of them were weary of the lies. They lived every day in a community that was filled with upstanding people and the lies they had invented seemed so far removed from their new life, that they actually forgot from time to time, that they were not a real family.

This was a painful reminder that their lives were built on many, many lies, and they found themselves uncomfortable with being deceitful.

"Maybe you could tell him that Little Ben doesn't know, and neither will Rebecca," Benjamin said after a time. "And that is why we do not discuss it."

Grace said, "That certainly would be an added incentive to keep it to himself."

The falsehood cleverly crafted, they all sat quietly wishing life were different. Their pasts they had tried so hard to leave behind, seemed to insist on rearing their ugly heads upon occasion as if to remind them that they had lives they did not deserve.

The silence was broken when Little Ben said gently, "Remember who we are. We are precious children of God, adopted by the blood of Jesus into the family of the Creator of the Universe. He loves us, and wants us to be His. To trust Him in all we do, say, think, and believe. You cannot be a finer human being than that."

The family looked at Little Ben as if they had never seen him before. And perhaps they never had. Here he was, nearly a grown man, speaking about the Bible with the great authority and emotion. As a tear slid down his freckled face, he looked up at his father and said, "Papa. Jesus and I have a lot in common."

"You do?" Ben said trying to encourage him to continue because he had no idea where he was headed with this statement.

"Yes, Sir. We do." Little Ben was crying now, and wiping his eyes on the shirt he was wearing. He stood up and walked around the room in the hopes that he might get control of his emotions, but it wasn't working.

"What is it, Son?" Benjamin asked.

Little Ben looked at his father from across the room and said, "Well, we both had fathers who were carpenters."

"That's right!" Ben said as he looked around the room at the smiling faces.

"But, like Jesus," he paused to drum up his courage and then blurted out, "I want to go into the ministry, Papa. I have thought about it a lot since you and I talked, and I want to become a Preacher like Rev. Morrison and Rev. McCauley. In fact, Rev. McCauley and I have been talking…" His voice drifted off, then he continued, "Papa, I know you are building this business with the promise of passing it down to me, but…"

"Whoa! Whoa! Wait a minute, Ben!" Little Ben braced himself for the disappointment in his father's eyes, then Benjamin continued. "You want to be a Preacher?"

Little Ben just nodded his head and looked up at his Papa sadly.

"Well, Benjamin Waters, Jr. I can't say that I am not disappointed that you won't be working the mill with me. I am." Little Ben's shoulders slumped. "But, more than anything in this life, I want my children to be free. Free to do what they want to do. Free to be happy, and healthy! Free to love whoever they want to love, and be whatever they want to be. And I have to say, I am proud of you, Son. I will get over my disappointment, then I will just get happier and happier that you are doing what you want to do with your life."

Sarah stood and walked toward her son, embracing him as he stood to meet her. "When did all this happen, Ben? How long have you been thinking about it?"

"The thought first crossed my mind when Granny made me go carry water to the plants the day after we first planted the garden. She said I had to put feet on my faith, and carry water up and water the plants I couldn't see. Just trust that God would produce what we needed, and act like I was grateful before the blessings came, because even a heathen can thank him once the blessings were there."

They all smiled in remembrance of Granny and the funny way she had of saying things.

"I remember thinking that all the time before you came into our lives, I trusted Grace to look after me. The thought that Grace wouldn't find enough food, or somewhere to sleep, never crossed my mind. Because I knew she loved me, and I thought she could do anything."

Grace was in tears at his mention of her care. He had never spoken of his feelings for her and she was overcome with relief and joy at his faith in her, knowing clearly that there were many, many, times when she had not found enough food, or a good place for them to sleep.

Little Ben continued, while Sarah, Grace, and Benjamin stared in awe at him, "Then one day I realized that Grace was just a human being, like me. And that as much as she loved me, she was not the one who had actually put us all together. I somehow realized when we were learning the 23rd Psalm, that there was a God who helped *her* protect *us*. A God that wanted a protected life for Grace, too." Tears came again as he looked at his sister, his mother, and his friend – Grace.

"I guess it has always been in me to trust, although I did not know who it was that was protecting and guiding us, I knew there was a mighty presence all around me. And I want to help others see what I saw. Because sometimes, I do not believe people see Him, or are aware of Him, or need Him enough to know He is there for them." They sat in silence for a minute, processing the huge amount of information they had just received. Then Little Ben said, "Are you sure you are alright with this, Papa?"

Benjamin wiped the tears from his eyes, stood, gave his son a bear hug, and said, "Of course I am, Ben. I am proud of you, Son! You could not have made me prouder!"

"But what about the mill, Papa?"

That mill will be just fine with Kevin and me working it! It will be there for you when and if you ever want to retire! And between appointments, you can work here for extra spending money. It is all going to be fine, Ben. I don't want that to ever cross your mind again!"

"Thanks, Papa," Little Ben said. This time, his father shook hands with him in recognition of the man he was becoming, and Little Ben stood a little taller from that day on.

Chapter Thirty-Three

The Waters' family was shocked when it was time to go back to town to pick up Kevin and Elizabeth. It had felt like only minutes since they had left. They stood in the front room of the cabin and held hands, heads bowed in prayer, as each one took their turn speaking words of gratitude to the God who had loved them so perfectly, before they even knew Him. As they said the final, "Amen," Little Ben nearly jumped out of his shoes with excitement, since this was the first time he was allowed to take the wagon to town on his own.

"Now be careful not to get going too fast down town hill, Ben," Benjamin warned for the sixteenth time. "Those brakes won't hold you if you let that wagon run away with you."

"I know, Papa!" Ben tried to say politely, but the truth of the matter was that he just wanted to scream that he had already driven it to town, under his father's watchful eye, several times, and had never let the wagon get away with him.

Just a little *before* the family was finished with their warnings and shouts of good luck, Ben clicked his tongue, and with a slap of the reins on the horse's back began his journey.

Benjamin was not pleased at his behavior, but Sarah slid her arm around his waist and said, "Let him go, he is just excited. This is a big step for him."

Benjamin was irritated that she was smiling up at him, as if to say he was being a doting mother hen about his son's first adventure as a man. The thought made him chuckle as he looked down on her face, so he reluctantly gave in. Suddenly, something caught his ear and he turned to look toward the cabin.

"Hey!" Benjamin shouted, "Hey, you! What are you doing with my cow?"

The soldiers tried to run with the cow, but Bessie was having none of it. Ben wished he had his gun, but knew if he went in to retrieve it, the men would be long gone when he got back.

Ben had caught up with them, with Sarah, Elizabeth, Grace and Rebecca running behind, just as they pulled the cow into the center of the group, in a stand of ownership. Ben grabbed the closest one by the shirt and said, "I need that cow! I have children who need the milk. Let go of her right now!"

In an instant, the men gathered 'round their leader and began pushing Benjamin from man to man. Rebecca's scream filled the air at the sight of her Papa being shoved around by the men, but before Sarah could get to her, another soldier bent down to her and said kindly, "Now, don't you cry," he said, to Sarah's shock. He carefully used the back of a filthy knuckle to gently wipe away the little girl's tears, then said, "We ain't gonna hurt your Pappy."

As Sarah approached Rebecca, she saw love in the man's eyes. She wondered if he had left a little girl behind, and if he would ever see her again. The soldier looked up at Sarah, stood, tipped his hat, and for a brief minute, looked at her with such sadness she thought her heart would break. As soon as he turned his back, she lifted Rebecca into her arms and ran back to Elizabeth and Grace.

By that time, the men were long gone with the cow. Sarah wanted Ben to leave well enough alone, but he insisted on following the men. As he grabbed his gun, he said, "Make me up a sandwich or two," as he threw everything he would need into a small saddle bag.

As he tossed the saddle bag over the mare, he glanced up at Sarah and nodded his head slightly to indicate that he wanted to speak to her privately. Grace and Elizabeth took Rebecca back into the house, as Ben removed his hat and looked down at Sarah. "I won't be gone long, Sarah. I am nervous about leaving you all alone here. Lock the doors and keep the gun beside you at all time. If someone gets in, don't hesitate to shoot."

Sarah set her jaw resolutely, nodded in agreement with her husband, then turned and went into the house without watching him ride away. When she opened the door, she announced that no one was to leave the house for any reason until Benjamin got home. She placed the chamber pot in the front corner and pulled the curtain closed on it, then brought the gun into the front room and asked Grace to keep Rebecca close to the kitchen, so if anyone tried to come in through any of the windows, she would not have to worry about shooting her children.

It was dark before Ben returned home. Little Ben ran out the door to meet him with Kevin right behind. "What happened to the cow, Papa?" Little Ben really didn't care about the cow, he was so happy to see his Papa alive and well he just asked as an excuse to run and be near him.

"Take care of the horse, Ben," Benjamin said tiredly. Ben didn't have the cow with him, so it was clear to his son that it wasn't coming back.

As Benjamin walked in the door, Sarah ran to hug him. "I am so happy to see you," she said smiling up at him sweetly. She realized he could not retrieve the cow, but wanted him to be clear on what her priorities were, and in this case, it was his safe return.

He washed his hands and greeted his sister and Kevin before discussing what happened to the cow, and as it happened, Little Ben was there for the telling of the story. "By the time I caught up with them, they had butchered Bessie and were cooking up a fine meal over the fire."

Sarah's shoulders slumped, and then she remembered the man who had been so kind and loving to Rebecca. How would she have felt had Benjamin been out there, far from home and family, and, of course, hungry. Her heart softened and she said, "They were hungry. They were just hungry and they did what they had to do." No one argued, and although the idea of Bessie becoming someone's meal saddened them all, they did understand the need to eat.

Ben sat down at the table with a hot cup of coffee and begrudgingly realized how lucky he was to have a home to come to, with people who loved him after this day of traveling through the woods. There was no telling how long those men had been away from home, or when they might get home again. Still yet, he would breathe easier after a few days when he was sure they were gone.

"Ben, would you say grace, please?" Benjamin said as he sat up and shrugged off the negative things he had been feeling.

"Yes, Sir," Little Ben said as he bowed his head and prepared to speak. As his parents watched, he took a moment to breathe, then listened for the Holy Spirit to speak to his heart. "Holy Father, we are blessed to have you in our midst. We are aware of your presence, our Father, our Protector and Guide... always aware of your presence. We are eager to follow your will, but as human beings, we rarely see the opportunities you place before us, until it is too late. And often, our own wills create an anger, a resentment, and a sorrow that does not come from you. We thank you for the grace to understand, to see your will, and to respond appropriately. Help us, Lord, to learn to respond to what you want, quicker, and with more enthusiasm, and in celebration of all that you provide for us, sometimes at the cost of others. Amen"

Sarah, Ben, and Grace looked around the table in recognition and remembrance of when they arrived in this community with nothing, and the community provided all their needs, without question or hesitance. Benjamin dropped his head and continued his son's prayer. "Thank you Father, for this opportunity to give food to hungry men. I am humbled to have so much, and yet I begrudged hungry men a meal. Forgive me, Lord. Amen"

"Amen," Grace said, followed by Sarah's, Amen. Elizabeth and Kevin were aware there was far more behind what they said than they knew, but politely kept it to themselves. The meal continued as

Elizabeth and Kevin filled them in on what had happened in Parkersburg while there. Kevin had not thought about what the other Priests would think about his traveling with a beautiful young woman, and took a bit of ribbing about it. Elizabeth was pleased with the shops she had seen there, and wanted to go again as soon as possible.

"Well, Little Man," Kevin said, "My friend was very impressed with your carvings! He says he will look around and decide what is a fair price, and then sell them for you for quite a profit."

"Does he want more?" Little Ben asked.

"Oh, yes! He said by the time you have carved more of them, he should have sold the ones we left there!"

Everyone agreed that that was good indeed. Little Ben's carvings were going to sell, and he had the blessing of his family to become a Preacher.

As the evening wore on, they all discovered they were exhausted and decided to go to bed early, each lost in their own thoughts, but the next morning Grace was ready to take her life back. She had decided that Dunge was going to be a part of her life no more. She had prayed about it the night before, fallen asleep with no clarity as to what she would do, then awakened with a new spirit; a spirit to fight for her life with the man she loved. Dunge was not going to leave her life until she threw him out, and that was what she was about to do. She knew her family would be coming along for the Sunday service, but she wanted to go early in order to speak with Caleb. Alone she could travel faster and hopefully have a moment in which she could share with Caleb that she needed to speak with him. She knew he would eventually come to see her at her house, but she needed to take the initiative in order to feel she was striking a blow to Dunge and his memory.

When she got to the church, there was no one there except Rev. McCauley, so she entered the church to greet him.

"Good morning," Preacher said as she entered the church.

"Good morning, Preacher!" She smiled at him; a smile that made him stop and look at her.

"Well, Miss Grace, you have the look of a young woman who found the flow of God's will, and jumped in, clothes and all!"

Unbelievably, her grin broadened. "I did, Preacher! I certainly did!" He had summed it up perfectly, and the realization thrilled her.

"Well, young lady," Preacher said with that ever present smile on his face, "I hope you always walk in His path. And if you are ever tempted to go astray, remember how good you feel right now. That'll turn you right around!" His belly laugh filled the church and rumbled in the rafters!

Grace realized she loved that Preacher as her own family. He had such a loving heart for God, and she wanted him to be part of her wedding. She had toyed with the idea of having her Uncle Kevin marry them, but that would have taken a lot of explaining, and to be honest, a lot of lying, and hopefully she was finished with the lies. Without hesitation, she asked, "Preacher, how would you feel about performing a wedding?"

Preacher's face lit up, and he said, "Oh, my! I understand now why all the smiles! And would the lucky groom be Mr. Caleb Rogers?"

Grace was shocked! Being a young woman, she had no idea that the entire community knew they were in love, long before she and Caleb did. Why, there was even talk back at the Boxed Luncheon when they were fighting so much, and the old men had placed bets on when the wedding would be.

Her cheeks reddened as she looked at the floor for a moment to gain her composure, then she shyly looked up at the smiling face of Preacher, and said, "Why, yes, it is." She was tempted to ask how he knew, but then she really did not want to hear the answer.

"I was hoping to speak with him for moment before the service," she said as she turned and walked to the door, watching for him to arrive, "but I don't see them coming yet."

Slowly, the church filled to capacity. Even the Waters and the Bensons had arrived, but no Caleb. Grace's shoulders slumped in disappointment as she turned to take her seat with her family when Preacher began the service.

After the scripture was read, the door opened in the back and everyone turned to see who was entering. Caleb removed his hat, and said, "Sorry, Preacher. My Ma isn't feeling well this morning, and asks that you remember her in your prayers."

As he began to take his seat in the back, Grace and Caleb locked eyes, and in an instant he knew Grace was upset.

"Well, we certainly will keep her in our prayers," Preacher said. "But I am wondering if, perhaps, you should take Miss Grace out to check on her. I wouldn't want her to suffer needlessly, and I hear that our Grace has quite a healing hand."

Grace turned quickly and looked straight into the smiling face of Rev. McCauley. Try as she may, she could not keep herself from smiling as she said, "Certainly," and stood to go.

Caleb stood, and said, "That is mighty nice of you to think of her, Preacher. Ma will be grateful for your thoughtfulness."

Caleb held the door open for Grace, but as soon as it closed, Grace turned and smiled at Caleb and said, "I must admit, I am quite grateful for this opportunity to have time with you, Caleb."

Caleb said, "Well, I gotta admit, Mama just ate so much yesterday at our family reunion that she had the belly ache this morning. But I wasn't about to tell Preacher that. Especially since he seemed to think you and I needed to go see her right now!"

He was disappointed that she had ridden her own horse to church because he was looking forward to having her seated in front of him, with his arms around her for the entire trip out and back. And after deciding she would not like his assistance onto her horse, although it was in his upbringing to do so, he simply held the horses head as she mounted, then mounted his own horse.

Scott, Caleb's stallion was acting up, side stepping and throwing his head high in the air and then drawing it down, but Caleb skillfully mounted him anyway. Instead of going forward, the stallion lowered his head and walked backward a few steps, until Caleb gave him a kick, and laid the reins low on the back of his neck, then tugged powerfully to make Scott lift his head and turn in the direction of his Ma's house.

"What is wrong with him?" Grace asked. "I have never seen a horse behave that way!"

As Caleb turned Scott and made it clear to the animal that he *was* going home again and *not* turning around, Scott lurched and kicked in protest. Caleb said, "Whoa, now, boy!"

Grace was a little frightened of Scott's behavior so she hung back at a safe distance. Her little mare was no match for the massive stallion, and Grace was more than a little frightened of the situation. "Do horses get rabies?" Grace asked innocently.

"No," Caleb said, "That is not what is wrong with him." He didn't volunteer any more information, but as Grace brought her horse up beside his, she could see that Caleb was grinning.

"Caleb Rogers, what are you smiling about?" Grace was no fan of being made to look like a fool, so she was adamant.

"Well," Caleb said with a smile, "You are riding a mare, My Grace. And Scott is a stallion." He looked sideways at her with that smile that drove her crazy, and it only made her angrier because she had no idea what he meant.

Her temper flared so she stubbornly pulled Patsy to a halt. She did not have to say anything to Caleb to convey she was not moving from that spot until he explained completely.

He turned his horse to look at her, and with that ridiculous grin, he said, "I believe your mare is in heat," he paused to let that sink in, then continued pointedly, "and my stallion stands ready to answer the call."

His grin was teasing her now, but still she did not fully understand, until the horse turned sideways in a magnificent display of maleness.

Her jaw dropped as she looked underneath the horse in wide-eyed innocence. She was shocked, disgusted, embarrassed, and mesmerized all at the same time, but try as she might, she could not take her eyes off the scene before her. It suddenly occurred to her that Caleb's huge stallion wanted to mount her little mare, *while Grace was riding her*! Fear filled her eyes as she looked up to see Caleb's face. His eyes were gleaming with laughter that he could no longer contain. He turned his horse toward home, once again, in order to give Grace the time she needed to recoup her dignity, but she could hear him chuckling as he rode away, and that wounded her pride even more.

She rode the rest of the way far behind him. *How will I ever look him in the eye again*, she thought to herself. She rode with her head down for the best part of the trip, but after a while she began to be amused at herself, and settled into traveling closer behind her husband-to-be, and actually enjoyed the beautiful day as they traveled together. She watched him as they rode, his left fist on his left hip, his muscular arm sticking out to the side. She listened as he hummed a song while riding along as if he could conquer the world if he needed to. His reins were held in his right hand. He had taught himself to ride like that because he was left handed. His legs were long and straight, his boots fit comfortably in the stirrups. What a magnificent sight he was riding that powerful horse, and, oh, how she loved him.

There are few things more sacred than the love of a young woman, riding horses with the handsome man she loved, on a beautiful summer day. The world was hers and she could feel it. She had indeed, "found the flow of God's will, and had jumped in, clothes and all," just as Preacher had said. The thought of Preacher's kindness made her smile again until she remembered she had to talk to Caleb about the scars on her back.

She was greatly subdued by the time they got to Eileen Roger's house, and Caleb noticed the difference. They visited with Caleb's Ma for a few minutes, then after Eileen's embarrassed explanations as to why their visit was not necessary, and her apologies that there was not a meal prepared, Grace broke the tension by saying, "Mrs. Rogers, I had confided in Preacher this morning that I had come to church early in the hopes that I might get some time alone with Caleb before church. I think what Preacher did was to give me that time."

Eileen's eyes twinkled with understanding, then she took her hanky out and swatted at both of them and said, "Go on then. Leave me in peace! This is a beautiful day for young love, go on now, and enjoy your time together."

The two of them were smiling as they each hugged Eileen and left, closing the door behind them quietly.

Grace was in the yard before she noticed Caleb had stopped on the porch. As she looked up at him, he said in a teasing way, "What is this about your telling Preacher you wanted time alone with me?"

He grinned that way that made her weak in the knees, and she said, "Not here, could we go somewhere and sit in the shade for a bit?"

Caleb did not respond other than to keep his eyes on her questionably while he mounted Scott. She could not bear his scrutiny any longer, and turned to get Patsy.

Finally, he left the road and lead her over to a massive Oak tree with limbs that went above their heads, then draped like graceful arms back to the ground again. They were sitting in plain view of the road, and yet shaded by the loving limbs of the Oak tree. Grace looked at the mammoth trunk of the tree and saw names carved, with hearts and arrows, and wondered how many young lovers had enjoyed the company of that gigantic tree down through the years. It seemed safe there on the edge of the Radabaugh property, in full view of the public, and yet private enough for dreamers to dream.

Caleb could stand it no longer, and finally asked Grace why she had wanted time with him. He instantly regretted it, because the change in her demeanor validated his worst fear, that she was ending their relationship.

She tried to muster her courage, lift her head and look at him, but fear held her back. Finally, Caleb stood and said, "Say what you came to say, Grace!"

His sudden departure from their safe little spot, seated together in the shade, frightened her. He was standing above her, angry, and it seemed as if her worst fears were playing out before her. "Stop!" Grace shouted. "I am afraid, and worried enough without your standing before me shouting like a man I don't even know!"

Caleb heard only the words, "I am afraid and worried," and that was enough to bring him gently back to her side. "What is it, Grace? Are you ending our relationship? If so, just tell me. I can't stand this."

Grace looked up with tears in her eyes and her bottom lip quivered. Regardless of the fact they were in full view of anyone who would travel by them, Caleb put his arm around her in comfort and in love. She may not love him anymore, but he loved her, and would not withhold his love under any circumstances.

As the tears subsided, she looked up at Caleb and said, "I have something I need to discuss with you before the wedding."

'before the wedding,' Caleb thought. *She isn't going to leave me!* And with that he prepared himself for anything. "Alright, go ahead, My Grace."

Another round of tears came then, "Oh, please don't call me that, Caleb. You may not want me after you hear what I have to say."

Caleb found that difficult to imagine, but he waited patiently for her to tell him what the problem was.

She straightened her dress, wiped her eyes and said, "What I am about to tell you must never be repeated, Caleb. I am serious. Even Little Ben and Rebecca must never, ever know. We do not talk about it at all in my family, but, well... My Mama and Papa, are not my real parents, Caleb." She paused to wait for a reaction from him, but got none.

Grace regretted having to lie to him as he sat there looking at her with such love and acceptance, but lie she must. She continued, "My real Mama was Mama's, I mean Sarah's sister. She died in childbirth, and my real Papa was not, well, capable of caring well for me." She looked at her hands to gather her courage and said, "He beat me, Caleb. I have scars."

Caleb's only reaction was to hold her tightly in his arms. He hugged her so tightly, and yet tenderly, she felt nothing could ever harm her in this lifetime.

When they broke their embrace Grace noticed tears in Caleb's eyes. He said simply, "I hate to think of your going through that, Grace. How could anybody do that to a child?"

His next reaction was anger, "I wish I would have been there!" Every cell in his body tensed until Grace placed her hand on his arm. When he came back to his senses, he turned toward her and said, "Ok, go on."

"What do you mean?" Grace asked.

"Go on. Tell me what the problem is you were talking about."

Grace looked at him, too stunned to speak. "That was it, Caleb. I am adopted," she said, nodding at him as if she expected a reaction. "And I have scars on my back." He didn't react so she added, "Ugly scars, Caleb!"

He was looking baffled, so she stood and shouted, "I am damaged goods, Caleb. I am not a virgin, I am not a true Waters, and I am scarred! Do you not hear me? I am not fit to be your wife, Caleb Rogers! I am simply not fit!"

She stared down at him, knowing that this was the moment that decided her future. She had lain all her ugly past out in front of him, and he alone had the power to stay or walk away.

Much to her horror, Caleb burst into joyous, boisterous, laughter! When he could get his breath, he said, "You are one little, feisty, Banty rooster aren't you?"

She was unable to speak. Had Granny been there she would have said that Grace was mad enough to go bear huntin' with a switch!

He stood up and looked down at her, trying his best to get control of his joy and relief that she wasn't leaving him, and wound up smiling that stupid smile that just melted her heart. "Stop it." Grace said as she hit his chest with her hand. "Stop smiling at me like that when I have just made myself more vulnerable with another person than I have ever been."

Caleb recognized how fragile she was at that moment, worn out by fear and imagination of how things might turn out. But he continued to laugh anyway, in spite of himself.

She said not one word. She just walked toward her horse, confused, humiliated, and exhausted emotionally, while Caleb ran back to get his hat so he could catch up with her.

"Wait," he said grabbing her arm to turn her around. "Wait, Grace. I am so sorry I hurt your feelings." She faced him with utter heartbreak on her face. "I was not laughing at you, Grace." She started to turn so he continued, "*I* thought you were going to leave *me*."

Grace turned back and looked at him, puzzled at his comment. "I guess I let my imagination run away with me, as did you," he said accusingly, "and when I heard that you weren't leaving me, I could not imagine what could be so dastardly that it warranted the long face and the need to talk. I was laughing from relief, my darling. *And* at what a feisty, little, Banty rooster you can be!"

She looked up at him with one eyebrow raised, and Caleb said, "Ok. I *was* laughing at you, too." There was that grin again! She turned away, sincerely not amused, so he tried to make her also see the humor in it. Not a good tactic.

"So, I looked up at you and you had your fists to your sides, stomping your foot, reading off all the reasons I would not want to marry you, and you just looked so adorable!" He thought he had made an excellent case, and stared at her as if he thought she, too, would burst into laughter. But that was clearly not the situation, he quickly realized.

To his alarm, without any change in her facial expressions at all, fat tears began streaming down her face. One after another, they slipped down her cheeks unbidden.

He embraced her, and although she did not fight him, she wept against his chest in pure exhaustion and resignation. It was only then he realized how torturous it must have been for her to have to admit all that to him.

"I am truly sorry, my precious Grace. It's only now that I see how worried you were, and how much that admission cost you. I am so sorry."

The weeping became audible and Caleb decided just to let her cry. He rocked her gently back and forth as she wailed the most pitiful sounds he had ever heard in his life. He reminded himself that this was his love, his life, and to never be that careless again with her feelings. What he did would have been fine with his brothers, but she was different. He had to remember how closely her heart was tied to her emotions, and care for them both tenderly.

When she had cried until there were no more tears, she felt completely drained and defeated. She had nothing more to say. She knew this needed fixing, but had no clue as to how to begin, and no strength to do it. She had put all her thought into just telling him. She was now completely depleted of emotional energy to carry this conversation any further.

Caleb instinctively realized that it was his job to move forward. So he found another small shade tree and led her over to it. He seated himself in front of Grace so he could see her face. He hooked his fingers under her chin and lifted her gaze so she could see his sincerity.

"Grace, I need to be really clear here." She sat motionless, so he continued, "I do not care that you are adopted. I do not care that you are not a virgin." She looked down in shame, but he once again lifted her face to him. "I don't care." Tears rolled down her face as he said, "And although I hate knowing what that monster did to you, and I will be upset for you the first time I see the scars, it will be because you were hurt so. Not because you are damaged goods. It kills me that those words even came into your mind, Grace. It breaks my heart that you even thought of yourself in those terms."

This time she leaned in to him for comfort. As she pressed her head against his chest, and felt his embrace, she knew she did not have to pick herself up and move forward. For the first time in her life, she had someone she could trust to care for her. She felt all her burdens unload onto him, and knew he was big enough to handle them.

Even with her Mama and Papa, she had felt it necessary to do her part caring for the children, and in the keeping of the house. She thought tiredly, of the morning she decided her Mama could not help bathe and dress Granny for her funeral, so she had stepped up and taken over.

It seemed her whole life had been comprised of coping with one crisis after another, and now, she had Caleb to lean on. Caleb, who took all her worries and burdens in his stride, was hers to love for the rest of her life. She felt safe as she lay against him, listening to his heart beat, and smelling his masculine scent, and she never wanted to leave his embrace.

The whole world seemed to disappear as her senses filled with the nearness of him. She lifted her head to look at his handsome face and their lips touched. Suddenly, she desired to be much closer to him, and her need fueled a passion she had never experienced. Her arms surrounded his warm chest and back, and her hand went to the back of his head to draw him nearer to her. When she felt his grip tighten, she knew he wanted her, too. Slowly, his hands slid to her sides, and it became questionable as to whether or not he was touching the sides of her breasts. Grace felt the thrill of his touch, when suddenly, he jumped to his feet, dumping her unceremoniously onto the ground, and said, "We need to be getting back."

Grace ran along behind him, trying to catch up with his long strides, when she heard him mumble something she did not understand about being no better than his horse.

Grace asked him what was wrong, and he said, "Nothing, I just want to talk to Preacher about setting a date. How is tomorrow?"

Chapter Thirty-Four

The next week flew by. Sarah's protestations succeeded in getting the young couple to wait until the following Sunday at least, but there was still a great deal to be done in little time.

Word spread throughout the community quickly, and an impromptu covered dish dinner was planned to the dish. The older women scurried about, cleaning the church and decorating with brightly colored flowers, and the older men gathered to speak of A.I. Ward's great luck in winning the bet as to when the wedding would be.

There was an air of celebration within the entire community and Grace was enjoying being the center of it. But on this day, she noticed something different about Little Ben. "Hey, Benji," she said familiarly, come talk to me while I pack."

Little Ben stood in the doorway to Grace's room and stared at the floor. "I have been so busy with my own life recently, that I have completely lost track of what is going on in your life." She turned to look at him and realized he was upset. "Come here. Sit on the bed with me and talk."

Little Ben walked over and sat down by his sister, turned and hugged her like he had so many times as a child, and cried. "Hey, Little Man," she said, using the phrase Kevin had called him, "What is wrong?"

He sat back up and wiped his nose on the arm of his shirt, and said, "I have never lived without you. I mean, I feel like you are my sister, but I feel a little like you are my Mama, too. And I feel scared about losing both of you. I just can't imagine life without you."

Grace's heart broke for him, but she knew there was nothing to be done about it, so she said, "I have a great idea. Why don't I leave Pasty here with you, so you can come see me any time you want?"

"You mean it, Grace?" Ben jumped to his feet, all worries forgotten.

Grace smiled in her heart to see him so tall, and healthy. His whole life flashed before her eyes and she could see him as a newborn, then a toddler, the night their Mama left them alone, living in Parkersburg, sitting in the cabin that first Christmas day, and now… here he stood, much taller than she, safe, and on his way to manhood. It pleased her so much to say, "Yes, I mean it. She is yours to keep forever and ever, if it is ok with Mama and Papa. After all, they gave Patsy to me."

Little Ben respected that, and he tried to maintain his joy at having his own horse, but found his sorrow drowned out any remaining pleasure he could find. He did not want to burst into tears again, so he puffed several breaths out noisily, and sat back down beside his sister.

Grace took his hand and held it like she had done so many times before, "Is that all that is bothering you?"

Ben chewed on his lower lip, and shook his head, no. Grace could hear him breathing heavily and recognized it as his way of gaining control over his tears. Finally, he said, "What if he hurts you?"

Grace didn't quite hear what he said, so she bent to look him in the face and said, "What? I didn't understand you."

Ben looked up and said, "What if he hurts you, and I am too far away to help you?" His face did not change, but the tears puddling up in his eyes finally rolled down his cheeks, and his chin quivered a little.

"Oh, my Benji!" Grace put her arms around him and pulled his head down to her shoulder. "You have been my protector for so long. It was a burden that never should have been on the shoulders of such a wee boy. But you did it well, and I can't thank you enough for it." She paused and realized that he was releasing all the tears that had been pent up inside for most of his little life, so she let him cry, and continued speaking, "But you do not have to worry about Caleb, Ben.

He is a good man, like Papa, and like you are going to be. He would never hurt me, Benji, I am certain of that. What can I do, my Benji, to make you feel better? I do not want to have to worry about you when I leave. How can we fix this?"

Little Ben quickly stood up, shoved his hand into his pants' pocket and brought out his favorite, and sharpest, whittling knife. "I want you to take this with you. It is small, and you can hide it beside your bed. If you don't need it, you can give it back, but if you do, you will have it."

Ben looked so sincere that Grace decided to take his offer very seriously. "Yes, I will take that, Ben," she said with all sincerity. "It will be a comfort to me to know that my brother is right there with me if I need him." She smiled at him and said, "Thank you, Ben. You are such a good, good, man."

Ben nodded at her in appreciation, then said, "There is one more thing. I feel really bad because I chose being a Jr. over being your brother. I, literally, owe my life to you, and what I said was…"

"Oh, my goodness!" Grace said as she stood up. "Do not think one thing about that ever again! I do not blame you one bit! Caleb understands that in my heart you are my brother and he is the only person in the whole world who will know that little lie anyway!"

"Really? You aren't mad or disappointed in me?" Ben asked.

"No! I am fine with how everything turned out. And I could never be disappointed in you. You are my brother and nothing can ever change that!" She hugged him until he squirmed to get out of her embrace, then said, "Ok, help me get all these boxes out to the wagon."

Since it was quite improper for Grace to go to Caleb's home alone, Sarah volunteered to go with her, to help her get moved in. Along the way, Sarah said, "I am having trouble wrapping my mind around the fact that you are a grown woman, with a home of your own, Grace."

"I know, Mama," Grace said with a smile. "I think about the time I was planning to run off and marry Denzel, and live in one of the hunter's shacks on Mr. Benson's property!" The two women laughed at the memory, and the ridiculousness of the idea. "I thought I was so grown up, and in charge of my own life!"

A pall of sadness fell over them as they thought of Denzil and of what might have become of him, but determined not to bring the day down, Sarah asked, "Have you ever been inside Caleb's house, Grace?"

"No," Grace said. "And I feel odd going into it without him even being home. But, he said I was welcome to come in and move anything I wanted to. I think I am just going to leave all the boxes inside the door, however. I think it will be more fun moving into the house with him helping me decide where things will go."

"I agree," Sarah said. "If you want, I will take them inside so you can wait until you are married to actually see the house."

"I really like that idea, Mama. If you wouldn't mind," Grace said.

"Certainly," Sarah said.

For a while they just rode side by side in the wagon, filled with mixed emotions of joy and sadness. They passed their little church and began climbing the hill on yon side of it, when Grace said, "Mama?" Grace looked over at Sarah and continued, "I…" She started again, "Do you think…"

Sarah said, "What is it, Grace?"

Grace smiled from ear to ear and said, "May I be brutally honest?"

Sarah smiled at her, so she continued, "I am not quite sure how to say this, Mama, so I will just say what I have to say, and trust you with my inadequate words."

"I think that is the best way," Sarah said smiling at her lovely daughter.

"Do you think I am wicked because I have no desire to take Rebecca with me?"

Sarah was shocked to her toes. Her heart skipped several beats, her mouth went dry, and try as she may, she could not recover in time to say something clever.

"I mean, I know it is not possible without telling the entire community my history, and that she is my daughter and not yours, and… well, I am aware that it is not possible. But, that being said, I cannot help but feel that there is something wrong with me that I have no desire to take her with me. I feel nothing but relief that she is staying with you, Mama. In fact, I truly think of her as my sister, and not even my own daughter."

Sarah finally recovered enough to say, "Was it ever a question that you might take her, Grace?" Sarah had to hear from Grace's lips that she was in no way considering it before she could relax and converse about the situation without panic rising in her throat.

"No, Mama," Grace said with such conviction that Sarah had no doubts she was telling the truth. "And that is what bothers me about it all." After a moment of silence, she blurted out the entire truth to the one person she trusted more than anyone else in the world, to handle this kind of conversation. "Am I cold hearted? Has this world left me so jaded that I am not capable of loving my own children?"

"Oh," Sarah said, "So this really isn't about Rebecca at all, is it. Are you concerned that you might not be able to love any children you might have with Caleb?"

Grace felt as if a weight was set upon her chest and she could no longer breath, because that was exactly what it was.

Sarah laughed a little and said, "Oh, believe me, Grace Waters, you are so going to love Caleb's babies. Don't you worry about that one bit. When that tiny, wee, baby is born, and has Caleb's eyes, and your fingers and toes… a baby that was wanted and created in love, you are going to discover what love really is. There is something about having a child in your life that just brings out the best in you. Knowing that you, Little Ben, and Rebecca needed me to love you, feed you, guide you, and care for you made me a better woman than I ever knew possible."

"But, I did not, and do not, feel that for Rebecca, Mama. All those things are true for you. We aren't even your real children, and I can literally feel the love you have for us. But I had a child that has my blood in her veins, and…"

"Grace, something happened to you that should never happen to any child, and Rebecca was the result of that. She was not a child made from the love of a Mama and Papa, and you were far too young to be engaged in such an activity with a man. It was unfortunate at best. But you did the best you could with the horrific hand life dealt you, and now it is time for you to move on. Rebecca is *my* daughter, and God gave me such a powerful love for that child, Grace. You gave me a wonderful gift, and now I am giving you the gift of a guilt free life." Sarah patted Grace on the knee, and said, "I promise you are going to love Caleb's children more than you can imagine. There is nothing wrong with you, nothing at all."

Grace was not totally convinced, but she had to trust her Mama who had never lied to her. She was trying to reconcile that in her mind when Sarah said, "For now, just worry about loving your husband. Enjoy every minute with him because soon enough, the babies will start coming and your time will be split with him and the children."

Grace rode along in silence thinking about living with Caleb, cooking his meals, watching him in the evening candle light, and smiled at the thought of being married to him. Then the things Benji had said to her began to ricochet inside her head, and she said, "Mama," Grace said, "I am afraid… Well, what if I can't… I am afraid I will…"

"Stop," Sarah said. "I want you to take a deep breath, and boldly say whatever it is you want to say. There is unconditional love between us, and I am not going to think badly of whatever it is you want to say. So, take a deep breath," Sarah watched as Grace inhaled slowly, then continued, "Now, just say it."

Grace blew out her breath and with it, all the tension and nervousness that had built up inside her. "What if I feel all the disgust and panic I felt with Mr. Dunge, when I am with Caleb. What if I don't want him to touch me. What if I am fine in the beginning, and then… I just want to run, or scream, or…" A sob caught in her throat. "What if I can't, Mama? What if I never can!"

"Ok," Sarah said, "Grace, I want you to stop this wagon and look at me." Sarah waited until the horse had drawn to a halt, then continued, "First of all, I want to say to you, what I have said before, but I am going to try it in different words. You are no longer alone in this world." Grace looked at her in a way that made Sarah say, "I know. You have Papa, and Uncle Kevin, and Little Ben, but I am talking about you. When you stand there at the church, in front of God and your loved ones, and take your vows to be Caleb's wife, the two of you are going to become as one person. And I believe your other half has proven himself worthy of your secrets, and your pain. Honey, talk to him about it. Then if he does something you do not like, or you become frightened, stop and tell him about it."

"Mama! In the middle of…"

"Yes," Sarah said. "No one has to do anything they do not want to do, or like to do, especially in bed."

"Mama!" Grace was shocked and embarrassed by her Mama's boldness.

"Grace," Sarah said, "I am your Mama, and there is nothing we cannot discuss." She smiled so sweetly that Grace felt more at ease, and although she still dreaded the discussion, she felt it at least possible now.

"Ok," Grace said looking away from her Mama. "Maybe I should talk to him about it before the wedding, like I did before."

"Yes," Sarah said, "The best time to solve a problem is before it even comes up. Just tell him of your fears, and see what he has to say. Caleb is a good man, Grace. He will be alright with whatever happens."

Grace thought about that for a minute, then picked up the reins and began the journey again. Her mind drifted to the images of actually living with the man she loved, and she was smiling at that thought when they pulled up to the house where she would be living the rest of her life. "Oh, Mama. This is just so exciting!"

Sarah remembered sitting on the boat that took them to Pine Bottom, with her arm around the tiny, underfed little girl, and the prayers she said on that trip. All of them had come true. And her beautiful, healthy, full grown daughter was looking at the home she would run, and be safe in forever. "God is so good, Grace," Sarah said in awe at the wonders God's hands had wrought.

"Yes, He is, Mama," Grace responded. "Every day of my life I will thank Him for His guidance, His faithfulness, and His never ending love."

"And you make sure you raise your children knowing all that about God," Sarah said in a very motherly voice. One eye brow was raised, so Grace knew she meant business.

"Yes, Ma'am, Mama, I surely will."

Chapter Thirty-Five

August 29, 1863

The day had finally arrived for Grace and Caleb to be wed. It was a cool day for August, although the church hand held fans with pictures of Jesus knocking on the latch-less door, or praying in the Garden of Gethsemane, were waving back and forth, sending hair flying up in big intermittent poofs as the welcomed air hit the faces of the ladies.

The men stood in the back of the church so they could step out when the air in the crowded room became stale.

The Waters family had not attended church that day in order to prepare for the wedding, so when Abram, who was standing in the back of the church watching for them, saw Benjamin pull his wagon up to the hitches, he closed the door so Caleb would not see the bride.

Rev. McCauley preached on the sacredness of covenants in preparation for the wedding. He had prepared the congregation for the ceremony that was about to begin by reminding them of God's love for us, and His willingness to send His one and only son to die for us. "That is what a covenant is," Preacher said. "It is an agreement, made with great love, that ties people together in a way that a contract on paper, or made with a handshake, cannot possibly do. Just as Jesus willing went to the cross to save our souls, and give us eternal life, we must be willing to give our lives for each other."

Heads nodded in the church as Rev. McCauley continued, "And I am not calling for everyone to fall on their swords to prove their love! If we all did that, there would be no one to cook marvelous meals like the one we have waiting for us." People chuckled as Preacher continued, "I am saying that sometimes it is difficult to live your life in a way that reveals Christ to others. But that is what God asks of us.

To keep our covenant with Him, as He has kept His with us. And to live your life in a way that extends God's grace to everyone you meet."

A twinkle in Abram's eye alerted Preacher to the fact that the lovely bride had arrived at the church. Preacher held the Bible in his hand, lifted it into the air and said, "And now may the grace of God bless this wedding, and the families that are brought together in love as these two young children are joined in Holy Matrimony. May those who are here to witness this event, be brought to remembrance of the vows they have taken to their spouses, to their community, and to their God, and may those vows be renewed today as we walk together through this wedding ceremony. In Jesus' name we pray. Amen and Amen!"

The doors opened as Caleb stepped forward to the alter in anticipation of seeing his bride as she entered. The first person to enter was Little Ben and the disappointment showed on Caleb's face, bringing a stir of laughter and mumbling from the congregation.

"Be patient, Boy! You are going to have her for a lifetime!" one of the older men shouted bringing guffaws of laughter from the other men present. The women of course, thought it a rude and inappropriate remark, so they turned to chastise their husbands, and quickly brought order back to the onlookers.

Sarah stopped in the aisle to gather Eileen Rogers up to move to the front of the church where she would be able to see her son get married a little better. As the women settled in the front row, with Rebecca playing on Elizabeth's lap, the door opened again revealing what appeared to be an angel, accompanied by her very proud, yet sad, father.

The light glowed behind her adding to the image of a lovely angel, and Caleb felt his knees buckle. How could he have been so lucky? This woman, this beautiful, feisty, independent woman, chose him, and he would forever try to live up to the vows he would take today.

As they came down the aisle, Bernie and Dorothy played a beautiful rendition of, Blessed Be the Tie that Binds, and Eileen began to cry softly.

Benjamin gently placed Grace's hand in Caleb's and seemed to be caught in time. He could not turn, and walk back to his seat beside Sarah as he was supposed to. He simply looked at his daughter, mesmerized by her beauty. The gown she wore had been Eileen's when she married Caleb's father, and it fit her tiny frame like it had been made for her. He thought his heart would explode at the joy he felt over how far she had come, and what a splendid future she was to have. He became aware that those behind him were laughing softly at his hesitancy, and knew he had to leave her there. He stepped forward and kissed his little girl on the cheek, then with tears in his eyes, he turned and sat down beside Sarah. They sat beside each other, holding hands, and watched their beloved daughter walk out of their lives, and into the arms of a wonderful man.

Chapter Thirty-Six

September 1, 1863

No one had seen or heard from the newlyweds since that Sunday afternoon when they were wed. August had ended and it was the first day of September when a scream filled the air.

Little Ben looked down from his loft to see a light come on in Ben and Sarah's bedroom. He hurried down the ladder to meet Elizabeth and Kevin in the front room.

Suddenly the bedroom door opened and Benjamin said, "I need someone to go get Midgie, the baby is coming."

Little Ben said, "But it isn't due yet, Papa! Is Mama going to be ok?"

Benjamin heard another gut wrenching scream and saw panic on Little Ben's face; panic Benjamin did not have time to deal with. Ben quickly thought of Grace and said, "Ben, saddle up Pasty and go get Grace. Hurry!"

Ben didn't even know why he wanted Grace there, but for some reason, he could not bear not to have her present when… when what? Was he afraid for Sarah's life? No. He could not allow himself to think such thing. He had to remain calm.

He turned to Kevin and said, "Kevin, would you go get Midgie?"

Kevin nodded his head and returned to his room to quickly pull on some clothes. Since Little Ben had taken Patsy, Kevin was left to manage the hills by foot. Instead of going by the road, which would have taken twice as long, he opted instead to head straight down over the bank so as to get there as quickly as possible.

Ben and Elizabeth instantly went in to check on Sarah and discovered a large pool of blood on the sheets. Sarah had stopped screaming and was perfectly still, and eerily calm. She was as pale as a ghost, and Ben had to grab her and shout into her face to prove to himself that she was not dead. When he did, she rolled her head toward him and said, "Is the baby alright? It isn't crying."

Elizabeth tore away the bedclothes Sarah was wearing, and there was the most pitiful sight. The tiniest little baby anyone had ever seen, lay motionless on the bed, and no one had an idea in the world what to do next.

Sarah lay somewhere between consciousness and a deep sleep, and had to fight to stay awake. "Where is my baby?" she asked over and over. "Give me my baby!" she shouted with such force that a new flow of blood spread out slowly on the bed.

Benjamin, thinking only of calming Sarah whispered to Elizabeth, "Get me a blanket for the baby!" He then picked the tiny infant up and held it in his left arm, curled up, completely in the palm of his right hand. He began to pray for the child and giving God the glory for the life he was holding. He begged God to save his wife and this child they loved so much, as he took the blanket from Elizabeth and wrapped the pitiful child in it.

"Where is Midgie?" Ben shouted in frustration. "What is taking them so long?"

Sarah tried to lift her head, and spoke so softly that Ben had to place his ear right over her lips to hear her, "You have to cut the cord."

Ben said, "What? What cord?"

Chapter Thirty-Seven

Little Ben had finally reached the Rogers' home. Before the horse had stopped, he jumped down and ran to the porch, knocking hysterically and shouting, "Sissy! Sissy! Come quick! It's Mama!"

Grace appeared at the door and looked on in horror as her brother explained that their Mama was having the baby. "But it isn't time!" shouted Grace. "She is months away from having that baby!"

Ben could stand it no longer. He grabbed his sister by the arm and shouted, "Come on! Mama needs you!"

Grace thought for a moment, about going back into the house to dress, then thought against it. If her Mama hemorrhaged, one minute might make the difference in life and death. Instead she grabbed her winter coat from the peg beside the door, and threw it on as she ran for the horse. "I'll take Patsy, Ben, you can come with Caleb."

At that she turned and kicked Patsy into a full gallop. The sun was up a little more than when Ben had ridden to get her, so she ran Patsy as fast as she could through the gardens and fields of her neighbors, jumping fences as she rode. She took the shortest route possible and within minutes was back at her home, beside her Mama.

Sarah was trying her best to repeat what Grace had told her about giving birth, but had spent all her energy the first time. As her head fell back onto the pillow, Ben heard the door slam open and bang against the wall as Grace entered.

Grace's stomach lurched as she entered her the bedroom and saw her Papa covered with blood up to his elbows from the blood pouring out on the bed. She looked for the baby, but it was so tiny she could not see it, even when they tried to pull the blanket back and find it.

Grace expertly tied off the cord in two places, then quickly cut the cord between the two strings. "Take him, Papa. Rub him and try to get him to cry."

Ben looked stunned as he looked back and forth between his wife and his newborn son, so Grace grabbed Elizabeth by the wrist and said, "Here, you do it. Take the baby and hold it upside down, try to get it to cry!" Grace shouted at Elizabeth. This was no time to be dainty and Grace was ready to slap Elizabeth when she finally snapped out of her stupor and took the baby from the room. "Clean out his mouth, Elizabeth! Make a clear airway. Do it NOW!"

Elizabeth was determined not to lose that baby, so she stuck her little finger into the baby's mouth to scoop out anything that might keep the baby from breathing. Then she held him up and realized that he was turning blue. "Live, baby, live!" She gritted her teeth and said, "You are going to breathe, and live, and grow up here in this house! LIVE!" Tears flowed down her face as she massaged the baby briskly, pushed on his tummy in an attempt to force him to breathe, and lifted him upside down as she was told.

Suddenly, his arm grasped the air and a pitiful little mewing escaped his lips. His chin quivered as he attempted to open one eye. He trembled as his weak cry subsided, and Elizabeth thought he might be cold, so she wrapped him gently and took him back to the room, pulling on his arms in order to keep him awake and crying.

Ben was afraid Sarah was going to fall asleep and never wake up again, so when he saw Elizabeth with the baby, he said, "Sarah, wake up, the baby needs you. Here, do you want to hold him? Sarah! Sarah!"

A smile formed on Sarah's tired lips, and without opening her eyes, she said, "Him? We have a son?"

Ben laughed through his tears and said, "Yes, we have a son. Now he is going to need his Mama, Sarah, you have to fight."

While Grace was working to stop the flow of blood, Sarah was seeing her son for the very first time. His tiny head fell forward as Elizabeth handed him to Sarah, but Sarah just turned him around and laid him on her chest. She kissed the top of his head, and looked down at his tiny fingers as they wrapped and unwrapped from around her little finger.

"He is so tiny," Grace said. "He is going to live, isn't he?" But her question was met with silence. "Is there something wrong with him?" Sarah asked in a panic.

Grace simply said, "He came awfully early, Mama. He is living now, but only God knows the future. We will do all we can."

Suddenly, Sarah could not get close enough to the tiny son she and Ben had created. She opened her bed jacket and placed his naked body against her bare chest, and held him close to her. Ben covered the two of them with the warmest blankets, and Grace said to let her rest.

Ben sat in the rocking chair and watched the two of them sleep. It was a peaceful sight, although he was painfully aware that everything could change in a heartbeat. His eyes went from Sarah to the baby, watching for any signs that either had stopped breathing.

Grace had gone to the kitchen to wash up, and came back into the room with a clean shirt for Benjamin. "Papa, I want you to go wash up, change your shirt, and have a cup of coffee. You need a break if you are going to see Mama through all this." Ben hesitated, but Grace insisted, promising to sit by them and never take her eyes off them.

Ben did as he was told, and as he washed up, the cold water awakened him completely from the nightmare that began from Sarah's first scream. He was drying his arms and chest with the clean towel Grace had left him, when Little Ben and Caleb entered the cabin. In the interest of time, they had not taken an extra moment to hitch up the wagon. Little Ben had just ridden in front of Caleb on his stallion, Scott.

As Ben put on his new shirt, Caleb poured himself a cup of coffee and asked Ben if he could get him one. Ben said, yes, and then said, "I sent Kevin to get Midgie, and they haven't gotten here yet. I wonder what is keeping them?"

A shudder went through Little Ben. Without a word, he turned and ran out the door, jumped onto Caleb's stallion and headed off for the Benson house. "Mrs. Benson!" he shouted as he banged on their door.

"Well, I never!" Midgie said as she opened the door. "Benjamin Waters, what are you making such an infernal ruckus about?"

"It's Mama. She had her baby and he wasn't due for months. She is weak, and the baby is tiny, but he is breathing." Ben said.

Midgie calculated how early the babe was, and grabbed her shawl to leave. "Elias, get a horse saddled for me right now! Bessie, watch the youngin's 'til I get back, and Ira, go find your Papa and tell him where I have gone!" Ira looked at his friend with unspoken compassion, then ran to do as he was told.

"Mrs. Benson," Ben continued. "My Papa sent Uncle Kevin down here to tell you hours ago. Did you not see him?"

Midgie said, "Why no, boy! Had he come, I would have been there already!" She tugged her shawl tighter around her shoulders, walked passed Ben and shouted, "Elias, get a move on! I need that horse!"

"I'll catch up with you later, I'm going to look for Uncle Kevin!" Ben said as he again mounted Scott and headed off at a gallop.

Fear gripped his gut as he thought about the cave. *Had anyone ever explained to Uncle Kevin the dangers of the cave?* Ben wondered. The large horse had a difficult time navigating the narrow and tree lined path to the cave, so Ben jumped off and ran as fast as he could.

Thankfully, he saw no sign of his Uncle Kevin, so he carefully walked along the upper edge of the cave and looked over. There, crumpled and broken, lay his Uncle Kevin.

Ben turned and ran down the side of the cave and over to get to where his Uncle Kevin lay. There was blood coming from his head, and one of his legs twisted at a series of unusual angles. He laid his ear to Kevin's chest to see if he could hear a heartbeat, but heard none.

He did not want to leave his Uncle behind, but knew of nothing else to do. He caught the horse by the reins and drug it behind him through the thickest of the trees until he hit a clearing. He then mounted Scott and pounded the ground between him and the Bensons.

Chapter Thirty-Eight

September 2nd, 1863 dawned upon three members of Benjamin Waters' family who were fighting for their lives. Ben was cautiously happy about the son Sarah had borne, but the fear that he would not survive loomed over his head like a cloud.

Sarah had slept deeply through the night, and even with Grace's promises that she would not take her eyes off them, Ben could get no sleep.

Kevin clung to life under the watchful eye of the Benson family. Abram and Elias had fetched him from the creek bed where he had fallen and hit his head on a rock. Kevin did not respond to any pain or movement, and had not stirred from where he was placed since they put him in that bed.

Caleb had gone to tend to the animals at his farm, and stopped to tell him Mama all the news. For reasons Caleb could not explain, Eileen was extremely upset at the news of Kevin's fall. After being assured that Sarah and the baby boy were still stable, she turned her concerns to Kevin and what would become of him.

Caleb realized that she was not only fretting over the situation and moving about quickly as she spoke, she was packing! "Mama, what on earth are you doing?"

"Well," Eileen said she went to the kitchen to gather old rags and aprons, "The Bensons cannot possibly look after Kevin for much longer. Why, they have a house full of children! And Sarah and Ben can't look after him! They have their hands full just setting things right!"

Although Caleb agreed, he still had no idea why his Ma would be packing. As if she read his mind, Eileen said, "I am going to take care of him, Caleb. It is the right thing to do." Then as if that was not convincing enough she added, "It is the Christian thing to do."

Caleb grinned at that, and said, "Well, I am sure there are good Christian folk who live nearer to them, that could do their Christian duty and care for him with less trouble."

Eileen shot around and said, "It is no trouble, Caleb. And besides, what is life worth if you have no one you care enough about to trouble yourself now and again?"

Caleb leaned against the door frame and said, "Do you, Mama?"

Eileen looked overly annoyed and said, "Do I what?"

"Do you care for him? Kevin, I mean." Caleb tried not to grin, but his face would not cooperate.

"What? Caleb, don't you have something to do? Get out of my way, now. I have things to get in order." Eileen was so flustered her face was red. And a kind hearted daughter would have left it at that. But not a son. Son's just had a way of finding their Mama's last nerve and dancing on it, and Caleb was no different.

Finally, Eileen turned and looked Caleb in the eye and said, "I DO care for him Caleb. I care a great deal. And I am worried that the first man I have had any feelings for since your Pa died, may die before I get to tell him that. I am frightened, and I cannot just stay here and wait for the news!"

Caleb had not seen his Ma that upset since she found out that his brother Seth had been killed in the war. He took a step forward and pulled his Mama to him in a warm embrace. Standing there with her sobbing on his chest, he saw his Ma for the first time as a woman, not just a Mama. He thought of Grace standing in his arms, crying from a thoroughly broken heart, and realized that his Mama had better things to do on this earth than just be his Mama.

When she stood up and blew her nose, Caleb said, "Ok, what are you going to need? We had better get going if you want to be there tonight!"

Eileen, who was expecting teasing from the young man standing there, was relieved to find a grown man instead, who was accepting of her fears and longings and was prouder of him than she had ever been.

The smile on her face was a lift to Caleb. After all the sorrow, the thought of a budding romance pleased Caleb. He kept looking away from his Mama as they traveled, to allow his constant grin to erupt from his face.

Once when he turned around, Eileen saw the amusement on her son's face and said, "I bet you think I am an old fool."

"Mama, I don't." Caleb tried his best to keep a straight face, and as long as he did, his Mama believed him. But when that grin came back, she said, "Go ahead. Laugh at me. I may be an old fool, but I am certainly due a little happiness, and I am going to take it where I can get it."

Caleb pulled the wagon to a stop, then turned and looked at his Mama. "Ma, I am not smiling because I think you are an old fool." He noticed his Ma trying to hold her chin up and be brave, so he placed his big hand on her tiny, fragile one, and said, "I am smiling because I am so happy for you. I want you to be happy, Mama. And you are right, you do have some happiness comin' to you. I'd be as pleased as pie if you could find what Grace and I have."

Ma placed her wrinkled old hand on top of her son's and said, "Do you mean that, Son?"

"Yes, I do. And to prove it to you, I am going to get you right down to the Bensons as quick as I can." At that he slapped the horses' backs with the reins and bounced along so fast that Eileen had to hold on to her hat as she giggled lightheartedly and shouted for him to slow down!

Chapter Thirty-Nine

Week by week, the family healed. The biggest problem with the baby was that his mouth was too small to latch on to his Mama's breast. But after ten children, Midgie had a trick for everything so the boy got fed, just like a baby bird. If he got too hungry, he would cry until the milk ran out of his mouth and into his ears, so Elizabeth and Benjamin took turns feeding the baby every hour.

Sarah was able to sit up now for a few minutes at a time, and kept the feedings up during the day, except for when she was napping. By the time the child was five weeks old, he had gained enough weight to look like a newborn, and by mid-November, he was breast feeding like a champ.

"He is not very big," Ben said, "But he is getting fat, for sure! Look at those rolls of fat on his legs and arms!"

Sarah looked at him with so much love in her eyes and said, "You know, we cannot keep calling him, "the baby." Now that we know he is going to live, I think it is high time we name him, don't you?"

Ben hadn't wanted to discuss the name for fear of worrying Sarah, but now that she brought it up, he was delighted. "Have you thought of any names, yet?" he asked.

"Well, I did think of Benjamin, but I think we have enough of those in our family, don't you?"

"Yes, I do agree with that. But…"

"What?" she said curiously.

"Well, I was thinking of naming him Kevin, Kevin Lloyd Waters, after my father and your brother." Ben said as he winked at Sarah. "Kevin is never going to have a son, in fact, he may not…'

Sarah touched his arm and said, "Don't. Do not do that to yourself. We have no idea whether Kevin is going to wake up from this nightmare or not. But he has excellent care at Eileen's house, and if anyone can help him, it will be her."

"I saw Caleb yesterday, and he said Kevin has spells where he opens his eyes and is alert. But he still hasn't spoken. He smiles at Eileen when he sees her, but he is not communicating in any way," Ben said.

"Well, if he brightens up when he sees Eileen, he certainly is communicating!" Sarah said with a smile.

Both Elizabeth and Sarah giggled and Ben shrugged as if he didn't get the joke.

"It is a female thing, Brother," Elizabeth said.

"You would not understand," Sarah said. He still did not get what they meant, but he loved that two of his three favorite females in the world got along so well.

Little Ben said, "Papa, maybe Uncle Kevin would like to have his Rosary Beads. After all, he…"

Ben cut him off short in case he was going to mention that Kevin had been a priest, and said, "Thank you, Ben. If you would fetch them out of his room for me, I will take them with me tomorrow."

Little Ben reentered the front room with the Rosary in his hand just as his Papa said that, and said, "Where are you going tomorrow, Papa? Can I go?"

"Benjamin Waters, Jr." Sarah said, "May I go! MAY I go!"

Little Ben knew his Mama was going to say that, and he did it to get a rise out of her. So just to egg her on more, he said, "You have to ask Papa, if you want to go, Mama! Not me!"

His Mama swatted at him with a cloth she was using to burp the baby, and Little Ben ran from her playfully. "May I, Papa?"

"No, Ben, not this time. I need you to stay here with your Mama in case someone comes by, or if she would need something. Plus, you are going to have to do your chores tomorrow, and mine as well! So you are going to be a busy man."

"Ok, Pa," Ben said reluctantly. He knew he was too old to whine about it, but he really wanted to. Instead he asked, "Where are you going, though?"

"Well, if your Mama feels like it, I am going with Abram early in the morning, to Eileen's. We are going to try to build a chair with wheels on it so we can get Kevin out of the house some. And hopefully, we will be able to put two tracks over the steps to run the chair down so he doesn't have to sit on the porch all day."

Sarah said, "Would there be a way to get him to the boat? Maybe if he could see a doctor in Parkersburg, they could help him."

"That is a great idea, Sarah, I will mention it to Eileen tomorrow. Thanks for the Rosary, Ben. That was mighty thoughtful." Ben said as he tucked the beads and cross into his pants pocket.

Benjamin knew his son was disappointed, and that he was taking it like a man, so before he headed off for bed, he said, "Ben?"

"Yes, Sir," Ben said.

Benjamin said, "I am not going to worry one bit about our family when I am gone tomorrow, because I know I have a good man watching over them. I hope you know how much I count on you as another man in this house."

Benjamin could see his son straighten taller than he was before, and Little Ben said, "Thank you, Papa. That means a lot to me!"

Benjamin drank a lot of coffee before he went to bed that night, and sure enough, his bladder woke him up in time to be ready when Abram got there. Abram refused the coffee offered to him, and said they were burning daylight as it was. Benjamin laughed at that, because it was still pitch black outside, but he gathered his tools and headed out anyway.

Abram had brought lamps with him, so the ride to Eileen's was slow going, but safe. As they neared the church, Abram caught the smell of wood smoke and expressed a hope that no one's house was on fire. But the mystery was solved as they neared the church and saw smoke puffing out the chimney.

Benjamin was grinning as he approached the church while remembering the night he and Sarah had a fight and he found shelter in the church.

The door opened and the figure of a man stood up quickly from the pew where he had been sleeping. Both Abram and Benjamin held up their lanterns to see who was there.

"Well," Benjamin drew out slowly. "Mr. Caleb Rogers, I believe! Now, what on earth are you doing here?"

Both men smiled as Caleb stumbled around for words. Then Ben said, "Never mind. We have all done our share of time on that pew, Son. You may as well come work with us for the day. We could use another hand, couldn't we, Abram?"

Abram said, "We sure could! Isn't it just like our Heavenly Father to use young love to provide us another man who knows his way around a hammer?"

Caleb tried to protest, but Ben just said, "Then, by the time you get home this evening, she will be more likely to listen to your side of it."

Caleb wanted to protest, or at least explain himself, but one more look at their grinning faces and he said, "Oh, what the heck. I wasn't too eager about going back there this early anyway."

The men pounded him on his back as they all headed out to Eileen's to build the chair with wheels, and the ramps over the stairs.

At the end of the day, the two men shook hands with Caleb and thanked him for his help. Caleb said, "You think she is going to be in a better mood since I stayed away all day?"

Ben said, "No, I think she is going to be mad as a wet hen, now! Good luck to you!" He pounded Caleb on the back and grinned at his worried face.

Abram shook hands with Caleb and said, "Better you than me, Son!" He also pounded Caleb on his back and said, "Good luck!"

The two men were exhausted, but happy with their work as they headed home. They were too tired to talk for the most part, but at some point, Benjamin said, "Do you ever think about how lucky we are to have homes to go to after a hard day's work? And wives that love us? And beautiful, God-given children?"

"Every day, Ben. Every, single, day."

Chapter Forty

The snows had hit and the world was beautiful. Little Ben stood looking out the front window at the snow, and remembering that first Christmas when they had the snowball fight. Then he had been the baby of the family, other than Rebecca. But she was so small that all she did was sleep. Now he was the oldest, and had a younger sister and brother around his feet.

Anything he didn't want Rebecca to have, he simply put up in his loft, which infuriated Rebecca. She would stand at the bottom of the ladder, try to reach all the way up the stairs, and scream as she stomped her foot.

Little Ben had to admit, that seeing her that upset about his winning in the end, was a little bit pleasing, but it drove his Mama crazy. "Benjamin Waters, Jr! Must you antagonize her?"

"I'm sorry, Mama. But she wanted one of my pocket knives, and she wouldn't leave it alone. So I put it out of her reach."

He knew she couldn't argue with that, and *she* knew she couldn't argue with that, so she said, "Well, then. It seems to me that you have enough spare time on your hands to take her outside to play!"

"Ah, Ma! I was just going to whittle," Ben said, hearing himself come so close to whining, that if frightened him.

"Well, you take her out for about an hour, then she will be ready for a nap. Then you can whittle without her bothering you."

That made too much sense for Ben to argue with, so he put on his boots and jacket, and prepared to take her out while his Mama dressed her up in her winter clothes.

The Power of Grace

He then grabbed the sled his Papa had made with a rope that crossed her waste so she wouldn't fall out, put her in it and began to pull her across the snow. He had to admit, he loved her tinkling little laugh, and he decided he was going to be kinder to her; just as Grace had been kind to him. When they had made the same circle several times, Ben's arm began to hurt, so he turned to face Rebecca and began pulling her as he walked backwards.

Bump! He backed into something that was softer than a tree, but did not budge at all. When he turned around, he saw an Indian standing there, with dark red skin, and ornamented clothes that he could not take his eyes off of.

"Sell," said the Indian. "Want?" he asked.

Ben didn't know what to say, and he was afraid he couldn't get Rebecca out of the sled and back to the house safely. Nor could he pull the sled fast enough to get her back without the Indian catching them. So he stood there, speechless, until he heard his Papa asking, "What can I do for you?"

The Indian looked down at Benjamin's weapon and waved his hand in a dismissive way so as to say, 'You are not going to need that.'

Ben stepped in front of Little Ben and his sister, and without looking back at them, he said, "Go in the house, Son."

Ben pulled the sled back to the house as fast as he could, then stared out the window at his Papa and the Indian. They were close to the same size, but had different clothing. Other than the clothes, they could be the same man. Ben didn't know what he was expecting the first time he saw a real Indian, but it sure wasn't that he would be an ordinary man. Why, Ben could see him having children of his own!

Ben jumped away from the window as the two men turned and headed toward the house. When they got close, Benjamin offered to let the Indian come in, but he refused.

"Sarah," Ben said calmly, "gather up some extra food, if you can. I think his family is hungry. We are going make a trade."

Sarah immediately placed Lloyd in his bed, and with the help of Elizabeth, filled a gunny sack with the kinds of things Indians would be familiar with; ham, potatoes, and dried vegetables. She opted not to give anything in a glass jar, or the pickled beans and corn that they may think had gone bad. She gave everything she could think of that they might eat, and even threw in some candy.

The native was happy with the amount of food, and even tried to throw in his tomahawk, but Ben said no. The food for the handmade trinket, or no deal. The Indian gave a quick head nod, grabbed the bag and thrust the leather trinket into Ben's hand, all in one motion, then trotted off into the woods.

Ben looked up into the snow sky, and wondered how the Indians would stay warm tonight when the snows came and the winds blew. He wished he had offered to put them up, and began thinking of just how many people he could squeeze into that small cabin.

Later, inside, Sarah walked up behind him, put her tiny fist into his massive hand, and said, "That was a good thing you did, Ben."

"I wish I could have done more," he said watching out the window and the snow dashing to the ground.

"We did what God asked of us. That is all we can do. God will take care of the rest."

"I guess you are right, Sarah," Ben said as he turned and enveloped her in his arms.

"Now," she said as she stepped back and looked at him. "Day after tomorrow is Christmas, we need to plan out our dinner meal! Let's see, this year there will be Grace *and* Caleb, Kevin *and* Eileen, you, me, Elizabeth, that is seven…"

"Oh," Elizabeth said sheepishly. "Is there room for Elias? I think he is coming this year."

Sarah looked at Ben and smiled at the wonderful changes that had happened to them over the years. Their house was going to be bulging with family and guests, there would be an abundance of children around, and best of all, they were going to be together. No matter what the new year would bring, they had each other now, for this Christmas.

Chapter Forty-One

Christmas Eve, 1863

Eileen Rogers' Home

Eileen hummed as she happily kneaded her famous light bread. She knew she had made too much food for tomorrow, but she was pleased at how it had all turned out. Her life changed dramatically when Kevin had moved into her house after his fall. She had someone to care for, and work to do every day, so feeling sorry for herself was a thing of the past.

"Kevin," she shouted. Do you feel like walking to the table tonight? Or do you want me to bring your dinner to you?"

"None of that!" Kevin's brother, Dale shouted in a British accent. "He is not allowed to baby himself now that I am here. Come on, Kevin, up and at it!"

Kevin had written to his brother, who had also been a priest, in England, and asked if they could retire together, at his new home. His brother had happily accepted the invitation and had arrived in Grantsville four days before Christmas, to live with Kevin for their remaining years.

It was as if they had never been apart. Dale and Kevin spoke the first night, into the wee hours of morning, about the family Kevin was now a part of, and how completely Dale would be accepted and loved. Dale was also instructed as to what to say, and what not to say, and was made privy to the secrets they all shared. The two men decided that Dale would be introduced to the community as a priest, since there was no need to say otherwise. Kevin expressed the hope that Dale might become a part of the furniture/sawmill business.

"I am sure Benjamin will be happy for the help," Kevin said. "His son, Ben, wants to be a Preacher, and will not be helping after all."

The two men sat at the table, laughing at the prank they were going to play on the Waters' family the next day, when Dale walked in with Kevin, and would be introduced as Kevin's brother.

Eileen sat down at the table, stared at the two men, and said, "Would you please pass the gravy…" she hesitated, then said, "Dale?"

Kevin's identical twin brother laughed and said, "Yes, I am Dale, and I would be happy to!"

"I do not think I will ever be able to tell the two of you apart! I cannot wait to see the reaction on the faces of the Waters' family when you walk in. Did your family have any trouble telling the difference in the two of you?"

"Well, Mama never did," Kevin said.

"But Pa wasn't around us as much as Mama was," Dale said.

"So he had trouble," they both said simultaneously.

"Then Dale grew a couple of inches taller than I, and from then on, it wasn't difficult at all."

"Well, I am certainly looking forward to Christmas dinner with the Waters' tomorrow," Eileen said with a twinkle in her eye.

Christmas Eve, 1863

Caleb and Grace Rogers' Home

"I do not think it is possible to be any happier than I am right now," Grace said as she lay in Caleb's arms.

"It is after midnight," Caleb said, "do you want to open your presents?"

"Caleb Rogers! You are worse than a child!" Grace said hitting him on the chest.

"I can't wait to see their faces when Uncle Kevin and Uncle Dale walk in tomorrow."

"You are going to call them both Uncle?" Caleb asked.

"Why not? One can never have too much family!" Grace was glad it was dark so Caleb could not see the look of alarm on her face when she said that. Adding on to one's family by dragging a homeless woman off the street, or just calling someone Uncle, was in no way the socially accepted method of increasing one's family, and she would do well to remember that.

"Did you know," Caleb began, that their actual names are Kevin Duane, and Kevin Dale?"

Grace looked up at him with that dry look that told him she did not believe him. So he continued, "I am not teasing! They told me their father's name was Kevin, and he wanted both boys to have his name. When they were growing up, their family called them Dale and Duane, but when they were older, Kevin started using his father's name in memory of him, after he and their mother were killed in a tragic accident."

Grace found that interesting, but her mind soon wandered to her growing list of things she needed to remember the next morning. She counted all the foods she had made, recounted each and every gift, including something for Dusty, and then remembered with a smile,

Little Ben's knife. He had given it to her for protection from Caleb if things didn't go well. When she returned it to her brother the next day, she would whisper her thanks into his ear, then tell him she no longer needed it. She fell asleep wondering how much he and Rebecca had grown since last she saw them. It had been months, due to the heavy snow, and the fragility of her new baby brother.

Christmas Eve

The Waters' Home

As they lay in bed on Christmas Eve, Ben said, "Do you know what my favorite thing about tomorrow is going to be?" He waited until Sarah shook her head, no, to continue. "Tomorrow, when Grace and Caleb pull up in their wagon, Grace is going to see a house, with a Christmas tree is in the window, and know that she is welcomed here. I always want her to have that."

Sarah smiled and said, "Do you know what my favorite thing about tomorrow is going to be?"

"No, what?"

Seeing Kevin meet his namesake. I can't wait to place him in Kevin's arms and introduce him as, "his nephew, Kevin Lloyd Waters."

Ben turned until he was facing her, propped his head up on his hand and said, "Are you making Granny's cinnamon buns for the morning?"

"They are already made and raising!" Sarah said, and was rewarded with a kiss.

"Are you having a huge meal with lots and lots of good things to eat, tomorrow?" he asked again.

"Oh, yes! I am!" she said with a smile. Another kiss was offered as a small reward.

Sarah raised turned until she was facing him, supported her head with her hand, and said, "And are you going to get up a little early and run out and make us a bigger dining room table in the morning?" Sarah asked.

Ben moaned as if being mortally wounded, threw himself back on the bed and said, "I knew you were going to ask me for a bigger table!"

She laughed at his theatrics, and said, "A bigger table, for our many blessings."

"Well, I can throw some boards together and manage a set of legs that will support it, but, you are going to have to wait for the finished, polished, product."

"That is fine," Sarah said. "As long as I am with you, I don't mind waiting. I am so grateful to God for our blessings, Ben. Who could have imagined this life for us back on the first Christmas we were here."

Ben laughed and looked in awe at his beautiful wife in the moonlight. How blessed he was. How God had found him, blessed him, and loved him even him. The words to Amazing Grace came to his mind, and he sang, "Amazing Grace, how sweet the sound, that saved a wretch like me."

Sarah joined in for the rest of that verse. "I once was lost, and now am found. Was blind but now I see."

They kissed, put their heads down on their pillows, and fell asleep, holding hands, facing each other, but closer than they had ever been.

CONTACT INFORMATION

BOOK ONE, Strangers to Grace, is the first part of the Living Waters Series and is available on Amazon as a paperback, and Kindle edition.

BOOK TWO, The Gift of Grace, is the second book in the Living Waters Series, and is also available on Amazon as a paperback, and Kindle edition.

If you would be interested in further publications by Sharon Turner, please leave your email at:

https://businessoflife.infusionsoft.com/app/form/livingwaters

(Your email will never be given out, and will be used ONLY for alerts about my books.)

Thank you so much for reading my books!

And please, if you would like to chat with me,

please join me on:

Facebook

Sharon Turner, Author

Blessings!

And my you walk in

God's Grace,

forever more!

ABOUT THE AUTHOR

Sharon Turner is a native West Virginian who has a deep love for the beauty and history of the state, a deep respect for the wisdom of the mountain people, and a profound love for God that colors her world, and everything she writes.

She was raised singing shaped notes at her church and at home, and only converted to the round note system used today, when she went to what was then Fairmont State College, where she received a degree in Music Education. She also has a Masters in Communications from West Virginia University.

She and her husband now live in the Eastern Panhandle of West Virginia and have two children, four Grandchildren, and rescue small dogs, mostly, but actually, anything that needs rescued.

Story telling is a large part of West Virginia culture, and Sharon is a direct descendant of several winners of local Liars Contests, where many men, women, and children compete by telling the tallest tale they can manage. But story telling is not only used as entertainment, it also provides a living history of their past. Many of the stories she will be using in this series, are ones told by people living in her county, who remember the accounts handed down from generation to generation, about actual events that occurred during the Civil War.

Many descendants of those who fought in Calhoun County, are involved in the annual reenactment of those events, and represent their ancestors who fought there.

It is her hope that she can give the world a better view of the rich cultures that exist in West Virginia, as well as insight into God's deep and non-judgmental love He has for us, His children.

Made in the USA
Middletown, DE
11 October 2016